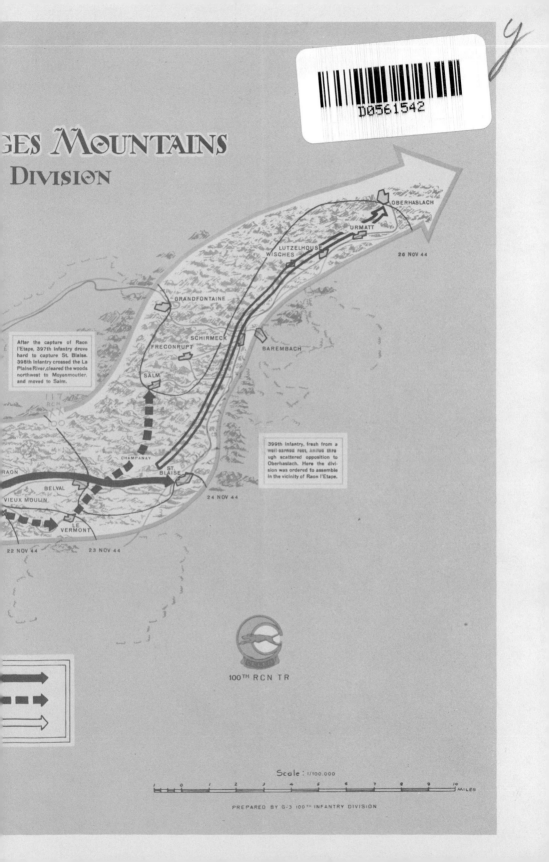

ɢES MOUNTAINS
DIVISION

OBERHASLACH

URMATT

26 NOV 44

LUTZELHOUSE
WISCHES

GRANDFONTAINE

After the capture of Raon l'Etape, 397th Infantry drove hard to capture St. Blaise. 398th Infantry crossed the La Plaine River, cleared the woods northwest to Moyenmoutier, and moved to Salm.

SCHIRMECK

FRECONRUPT

BAREMBACH

SALM

117
RCN
XX
100

399th Infantry, fresh from a well earned rest, drove through scattered opposition to Oberhaslach. Here the division was ordered to assemble in the vicinity of Raon l'Etape.

CHAMPANAY
ST. BLAISE

RAON

BELVAL

24 NOV 44

VIEUX MOULIN

LE VERMONT

22 NOV 44   23 NOV 44

100ᵀᴴ RCN TR

Scale : 1/100.000

0   1   2   3   4   5   6   7   8   9   10
                                        MILES

PREPARED BY G-3 100ᵀᴴ INFANTRY DIVISION

V-MAIL

Keith Winston, March 1945, just after
the move into Germany.

Pfc. Keith Winston

V···-MAIL

Letters of a World War II Combat Medic

Edited with a preface by Sarah Winston

Introduction by John S. D. Eisenhower

Algonquin Books of Chapel Hill   1985

WITHDRAWN
LVC BISHOP LIBRARY

Algonquin Books of Chapel Hill
Post Office Box 2225
Chapel Hill, North Carolina 27515-2225

© 1985 by Sarah Winston. All rights reserved.

Library of Congress Cataloging-in-Publication Data

Winston, Keith, 1912-1970.
  V-mail.
  Includes index.
  1. Winston, Keith, 1912-1970—Correspondence.
2. World War, 1939-1945—Personal narratives,
American. 3. United States. Army. Infantry
Regiment, 398th. Battalion, 2d—Biography.
4. United States. Army—Medical personnel—Biography.
5. World War, 1939-1945—Regimental histories—
United States. I. Winston, Sarah. II. Title.
D811.W496 1985 940.54'81'73 85-15031
ISBN 0-912697-28-8

Printed in the United States of America

321377

D
811
.W496
1985

to the loving memory
of my husband Keith,

and to our two sons,
Neil and David

S.W.

Contents

List of Maps and Illustrations   ix

Preface by Sarah Winston   xi

Acknowledgments   xv

Introduction by John S. D. Eisenhower   xix

Chronology of the Military Career
   of Pfc. Keith Winston   xxiii

1. Infantry Basic   1
2. 100th Infantry Division   69
3. En Route   95
4. Into Combat   105
5. Counterattack, Defensive   145
6. Attack, Pursuit   187
7. Victory over Germany   235
8. Victory, Peace   279

Appendix A: A Memory of Keith Winston
   by Samuel G. Cahoon   303

Appendix B: Roster of Second Battalion,
   398th Infantry Regiment Medics   305

Index   307

Maps and Illustrations

Maps

Summary of Tactical Operations, Vosges Campaign   117
Battle of Bitche   138
New Year's Counterattack, 1945   152
Battle of Heilbronn   207
Operations of the 100th Division, April 1945   213
"Pushing Jerry Around"   232

Illustrations

Basic training, Camp Blanding   20
Time out   32
Guard duty, Camp Blanding   61
Change of address notice   73
On board ship   99
GI reading letter   112
V-letter   124
V-letter   128
V-letter   134
Front page of *Beachhead News*, 10 December 1944   136
Wreckage of Freudenberg   142
GI, 398th Infantry   143
At the Battalion Aid Station   170
Germany, March 1945   191
Two soldiers   203
Officer and three POWs   209
Front page of the *Century Sentinel*   227
Front page of *Stars and Stripes*, 6 May 1945   239
Keith Winston's discharge notice   301

FOLLOWING PAGE 144

Basic training, summer 1944
925th Field Artillery, Raon-l'Etape

398th Medics evacuating wounded
Forward command post, Maginot Line
German soldier surrendering to 398th infantryman
Stringing barbed wire past body of dead soldier
Two 100th Division soldiers who killed more than 100 Germans
    during counterattack
Keith Winston: three photographs
Infantryman watches front line during counterattack
100th Division troops move through Bitche
All-soldier show, "Sons of Bitche"
398th Infantry patrol under artillery fire
View from citadel at Bitche
Refugees move through lines near Aachen

FOLLOWING PAGE 234
American flag being secured over Bitche
Captain Garahan being evacuated by medics
Co E, 398th Infantry, at Hohenstadt
Civilians clear a roadblock at Ludwigshafen
Shellfire sends 398th troops diving for shelter
Off-hours for the medics: three photographs of Winston
    and friends
Devastation: Heilbronn, 1945
100th Division troops advance through ruins, Heilbronn
Soldier looks out at Heilbronn from observation post
After V-E Day: three photographs of Winston and friends
Winston and fellow soldiers: three photographs

Preface

These diary-letters are a personal account of one soldier's involvement in war. They could well have been written by hundreds of thousands of servicemen who shared the same fears, the same hopes, the same frustrations—the same prayers for survival. There is a universal element running through them all, and highly identifiable.

It happened to be World War II. It could have been the Korean War, or the war in Viet Nam, or every war since man first conceived the savage barbarism they call war.

He was my husband, the father of our two sons.

I remember that bleak chill March day when we said our goodbyes, each of us holding back the tears that tore at us. I remember holding David in my arms, tightening my grip about him, with Neil close by, waving a last goodbye as a neighbor drove him off to the induction center—neither of us knowing what the future would hold, or when again we'd be together.

It happened quickly, suddenly, like a darkening squall; it was hard to believe it was happening at all. The "greetings" from the President, the grim order to report to the induction center in two weeks. Two weeks . . .

The details are now shadowed in haze; the only clear thing, my husband, my children's father, almost without warning was torn from our family and drawn into a conflict that could at any time alter the course of our existence.

When the order arrived we spent the two short weeks of grace racing feverishly about, putting things in order, settling pending affairs, Keith training a new man to replace him at the office, snatching moments to teach me to drive, and then accompanying me down to the barracks for my driving test and license.

We tried to wrest moments to comfort each other, to assure each other that heads of families would certainly be spared; they would not be shipped overseas into the thick of battle. There would be meaningful jobs to fill—important jobs—here in the States. Yes, that's where they'd assign him—here in the States. I grasped at any straw; it helped to relieve the misery of his leave-taking.

Then the interminable waiting; waiting for some word, waiting for the mailman. The endless wondering. To which camp would he be assigned? Would he be within reasonable traveling distance? Perhaps Fort Dix? The parting more bearable if we could be together each weekend, the break somewhat eased. Perhaps then it would be a little easier giving answers to our 7-year-old son Neil's constant questioning. "Why did Daddy go away? Where did he go? When will he be back?"

Why? Where? When? Over and over again. Mercifully, 6-month-old David was too young to question.

And then that first letter—like manna from heaven. That first letter that arrived on a Saturday morning. I shall never forget it. I called to Neil as I tore it open. "A letter from Daddy! A letter from Daddy!"

A letter that deftly concealed the pain he was feeling. And Neil raced down as I held it in my trembling hands, reading it aloud.

Keith was born in Philadelphia, 28 October 1912. When he was four years old his father died, leaving a wife and four small children. Subsequently his mother enrolled him at Girard College, a privately endowed, free boarding school for "fatherless boys" founded by the philanthropist Stephen Girard in 1848. Admissions standards at Girard College were extremely high—and still are. Keith played the clarinet and saxophone in the school orchestra, and was manager of the baseball team.

Keith wanted so much to go on to college, and he worked to earn tuition money. In 1930 he enrolled at the University of North Carolina at Chapel Hill, but before the first term was completed his education came to an abrupt halt when his mother, in training as a chiropractor, required his tuition money to purchase equipment to set up her practice. The decision to return home was a rending one, but he felt that his duty to his mother came first.

Jobs were hard to come by at this time—it was the depth of the Depression—but in 1932 he found employment as an insurance underwriter with the Metropolitan Life Insurance Company. In 1932 we met, and three months later were married.

Our marriage was unusually close, and when our sons were born Keith was utterly devoted to them. He now had the family and the love that he must have missed so greatly in his own childhood. Reading back over the letters he wrote home when he was overseas, I can see that he must have been haunted by the fear that if he were to be killed he would be leaving his boys without a father and his wife without a husband and sufficient means of support, just as had happened in his family during his childhood. When the war in Europe was over at last, he was terribly anxious to come back to us as soon as possible.

Following his military service he returned to his insurance work, as an underwriter and later as a consultant. He was with Metropolitan Life for 31 years, receiving many citations for achievement. Keith also free-lanced as a photo-journalist, collaborating with me in writing, editing and illustrating feature articles for various publications, including the *Sunday Inquirer Magazine*, the *Philadelphia Bulletin*, and *American Home*.

In the early 1950s we went through a harrowing time when our elder son suffered a mental collapse. At age 55 Keith took an early retirement from his insurance work, so that we could collaborate on our writing on a full-time basis, and do some long-hoped-for traveling. But this was not destined to be, either. On 20 March 1970, after three months of a grossly misdiagnosed illness, he died at the age of 57.

The letters that follow were written home to me and to his family by an American citizen-soldier, a civilian called into military service because of his country's need. Like most of the more than twelve million Americans who served in our armed forces during the Second World War, he did not want to be a soldier. We are not a military people; fighting and killing come hard to us. Especially for older men like my husband, married and with children, the sudden transition from civilian life to being a member of a vast military machine was enormously difficult.

Seven months and eight days after reporting for induction at New Cumberland, Pennsylvania, Keith, in combat as a medic, was wounded by an exploding mine near Rambervillers in the Vosges Mountains of France. Then and during the six months following he served as clerk of a medical battalion aid station, frequently under fire, often called on to go out as a litter-bearer to rescue wounded infantrymen. From all accounts he was a good soldier. His commanding officer later said that every military outfit needed someone like him, for he was "the indispensable man." When the war was over, my husband came home to us. Many others were not so fortunate.

I have transcribed his letters, and they have been edited for publication, because I wanted to show what manner of man he was, and to let others know what he, and millions of other Americans like him, experienced when they were called upon to go to war. Four decades have gone by since the close of World War II. Thousands of books and articles have been written about it, and about the American war effort. I hope that these letters will help to show a little of what it was all about.

Havertown, Pennsylvania   Sarah Winston
15 March 1985

Acknowledgments

The annotations, chronology, and the historical interpolations throughout *V-Mail: Letters of a World War II Combat Medic*, by Pfc. Keith Winston, selected and edited by Sarah Winston, have been prepared by the publisher.

In this preparation there are many debts to be acknowledged. Members of the 100th Infantry Division were generous in answering questions, furnishing information, providing illustrative material and documents, and doing all that they could do to assist in the publication of the letters of one of their comrades. The Century Division Association, whose secretary is Lawrence J. Masi, 131 Fourth Avenue, Newark, New Jersey 07104, is an active veterans group, meeting each year in reunion, and publishing a newsletter three times each year.

Larry Masi provided names and addresses of a number of Keith Winston's fellow medics of the 2nd Battalion, 398th Infantry, and a number of photographs of the 100th Infantry Division in action overseas.

Samuel G. Cahoon, of Warren, New Jersey, contributed a statement about Winston which appears as an appendix to this book. Mr. Cahoon and Pascal Pironti, of Kenilworth, New Jersey, furnished wartime photographs of Winston and helped in identifying persons mentioned in the letters. Douglas S. Smyth, of Bridgewater, Connecticut, also furnished photographs.

Jack Herland, of Riverdale, New York, aided with identifications and was able to explain an important incident to which Winston alluded.

Roland Giduz, of Chapel Hill, North Carolina, furnished information that enabled us to begin to assemble much of the information needed to annotate the book, and made valuable suggestions about the manuscript.

Herbert C. Davis, Jr., of Raleigh, North Carolina, furnished the endpaper maps, provided additional information, and loaned a copy of the *History of the 398th Infantry Regiment in World War II*, edited by Bernard Boston (Washington: Infantry Journal Press, 1947), from which much of the historical information used in this book was drawn.

William S. Joyner, M.D., of Chapel Hill, loaned a scrapbook kept by his future wife, Jane Linville Joyner, about the doings of the 100th Infantry Division during the war, which contained valuable information.

Robert N. Stegmaier, of Sun City, Arizona, provided useful references.

Al Vidmar, of Mentor, Ohio, contributed the wartime sketches of 100th Division activity that appear in this book.

Robert M. Edwalds, M.D., of LaCrosse, Wisconsin, furnished useful historical material.

Alden K. Small, of Hendersonville, North Carolina, aided with identifications of persons mentioned in the letters.

Colonel Leonard S. Olliver, U.S. Army ret., of Greensboro, North Carolina, helped with identification of personnel.

Raymond Denman, Jr., of New Providence, New Jersey, furnished copies of wartime issues of the 100th Division newspaper, the *Century Sentinel*.

Brig. Gen. Robert M. Williams, U.S. Army ret., of Greenville, Texas, wartime commander of the 398th Infantry Regiment, sent this tribute to the medics who served under him: "The officers and men of the medical detachments were greatly admired by the combat troops, for they performed heroic deeds under fire in the recovery of wounded, endangering their own lives to support and protect their comrades. I wish that I did remember Pfc. Winston, Captain Rich, and First Lt. Scarpitta. I'm sure that I did meet them during the period of our service together, for they each were awarded the Bronze Star Medal, and I always tried to personally present awards when the military situation permitted."

Abraham H. Kaplan, of Brooklyn, N.Y., sent several photographs and gave his memories of Keith Winston during the war.

In addition to Keith Winston's fellow 100th Division soldiers, other persons made valuable contributions to the preparation of this book.

John S. D. Eisenhower, of Kimberton, Pennsylvania, distinguished military historian and an officer in the United States Army in France and Germany during the period covered in this book, quickly agreed to write the introduction. Thereafter he provided encouragement and comments on the manuscript.

Professor Robert H. Walker, American Studies Program, the George Washington University, located photographs in the Signal Corps archives.

Martin K. Gordon, of Columbia, Maryland, assisted in locating a source of photographs.

Much of the illustrative material in this book, including maps, cartoons by Bob Clarke, and drawings by Marius N. Trinque, originally appeared in the 100th Infantry Division's official history, *The Story of the Century*, ed. Michael A. Bass (New York: Century Association, 1946).

Introduction

by John S. D. Eisenhower

Forty years after Nazi generals Wilhelm Keitel and Alfred Jodl signed the instrument of German surrender in an unpretentious French schoolhouse, the subject of World War II still retains a fascination for the reading public that sometimes baffles those of us who participated in it. And with all the tons of words that have been written, it might seem strange to contend that anything more can be added. Nevertheless, this book, V-Mail: Letters of a World War II Combat Medic, very definitely does add a new perspective—it constitutes a real addition to our understanding of that terrible conflict.

Most of our literature on World War II has come from processed material—newspaper accounts, official histories, memoirs of famous generals, and novels. By and large it has been written with an eye to the commercial market, doctored to fit the attitudes of the moment. Here, however, is a collection of letters never intended for publication, meant only for the eyes of a lonely and bewildered wife, written largely to keep her assured of her husband's love and to give him, in turn, the release from repressing views and feelings he would otherwise be forced to keep to himself. The wife, Sarah Winston, has edited these letters, and background material has been provided, but the flavor of the original letters has been neither altered nor abridged. Nothing of importance has been left out.

Keith Winston, drafted in early 1944 at the age of thirty-two, old, married, the father of two boys, was uniquely qualified to write this unforgettable compendium. Although without literary training, he was both literate and keenly observing. His pages therefore run full of events and stories, but they tell of the man and his feelings also, feelings that evolved as he developed from a frightened, resentful, lonely recruit into a confident combat medic, decorated with the Bronze Star and Purple Heart, who (though he refused promotion above PFC) was once called by his medical detachment commander "the indispensable man."

Winston's advanced age for an infantry recruit—his detachment was part of an infantry battalion—both hindered and helped him. Thirty-two was approaching the maximum for a foot soldier; many men of that age could no longer stand the physical rigors. But Winston, apparently active in civilian life, made it through infantry training without breaking down. And his age contributed indirectly to the quality of his letters, for he wrote with a clear, sober mind, not victimized by the temptations of the flesh that sapped the energies of his younger counterparts. Winston experienced no more of the trials of war than did they, but he reported events with a sensitivity and attention to detail that few if any could match.

Winston's attitudes were far from unique among those drafted in early 1944. He was devastated at being wrenched from his close-knit family, stunned by the impersonality of the Army, irritated by the supercilious attitude of young, incompetent leaders, and obsessed with the hope of avoiding overseas duty and getting home. As time went on, however, the letters reflected a growing interest in what was going on and a certain pride in the fact that he could make the grade. Though shocked by certain cruelties such as mass punishment of a unit for the violations of a few, he increasingly viewed events around him with detached observation; concern for his own personal welfare began to fade into the background. He accepted his inevitable shipment overseas philosophically, concerned, then as always, primarily about the feelings of his wife. In Europe he made close friends in whom he took joy. He played down his personal dangers as a combat medic in order to spare his wife worry.

But his lot was never easy. Aboard ship en route to Marseille he was violently seasick. In battle he was wounded (though only slightly). And finally, the war over, he succumbed to a nearly immobilizing anxiety to get home, a condition far more the rule than the exception among men of his category at that time.

Even his prejudices were typical: fierce pride for being with the infantry; a bitter resentment of those "rear echelon" troops who make up the bulk of the Army; an equally bitter denunciation of the Red Cross because of its apparent neglect of the front-line troops; a wish that the Russians would take all of Germany—let them have it—and an increasing resentment of the privileges of officers, especially those from the rear echelons who had never tasted combat. Those attitudes were sometimes adopted by those who aspired to be associated with the front-line infantry; in Winston's case they were genuine.

Winston's unit, the 2nd Battalion, 398th Infantry, 100th Division, was a good one. Perhaps because of its round number, perhaps because of the popularity of its commander, Major General Withers ("Pinky") Burress, the 100th was noticed more than the average AUS division when it arrived at Marseille toward the war's end. But it was never a headliner, always relegated to tough fighting in the underplayed U.S. Seventh Army. This lack of glamor, actually, helps to make Keith Winston's story more significant for what it is. Had the 100th Division hit the Normandy beaches, held a shoulder of the Bulge, or seized a bridge over the Rhine, readers would be tempted to refer to Winston's eyewitness account to learn about a special event. As it is, we are attracted to it only as the saga of a single combat medic—an aid man who previously fainted at the sight of blood. His personal story is undiluted.

In recent years, especially in the light of American frustration in Viet Nam, a tendency has grown up to regard World War II as the "last good war." Those who served in it, especially in the infantry, do not share in that rosy view. These fresh, readable, literary letters of one who was truly "there" will serve as a reminder of what that war was really like. No "Ike and Monty" controversies; no "Blood and Guts" flamboyance—just reality.

Chronology of the Military Career
of Pfc. Keith Winston

25 Mar 44   Inducted into Army, Reception Center, New Cumberland, Pa.

1 Apr   Shipped to Camp Blanding, Fla., for infantry basic training

5 Apr   Assigned to Co. A, 229th Inf Training Bn, for training as infantry clerk

9 Aug   Completes training cycle

10–27 Aug   Transferred to Fort Meade, Md., for reassignment, with 10-day "delay on route" to visit home in Philadelphia

28 Aug   Transferred to 100th Inf Division, stationed at Fort Bragg, N.C.

23 Sept   Assigned to Battalion Hq, 398th Inf Regiment, medical detachment

27 Sept   100th Div arrives at Camp Kilmer, N.J.

5 Oct   100th Div boards troopships, New York City

6 Oct   Convoy of eleven ships, carrying 100th and 103rd Divisions and advance party for 14th Armored Div sails from New York for Mediterranean; fierce storm encountered five days out

20 Oct   100th Div lands at Marseille, France, encamps outside city to await unloading of equipment

29–31 Oct   Div motors to staging area near St. Gorgon, joins U.S. 7th Army for attack on Vosges Mountains area

1 Nov   First artillery shot fired against Germans by 100th Div, twelve days after disembarking at Marseille

2 Nov   Div moving into lines in relief of 45th Div near Raon-l'Etape, Winston in Hq Co, 2nd Bn, medical detachment

8 Nov	100th Div fully committed in replacement of 45th Div, assault on German positions in Vosges under way; Winston wounded while rescuing injured soldier in minefield near Rambervillers–Raon-l'Etape highway (later awarded Purple Heart Medal)
12 Nov	100th Div begins attack to outflank Raon-l'Etape
13 Nov	2nd Bn 398th Inf moves north to vicinity of Baccarat
13–18 Nov	398th attacks across Meurthe River, fights way to La Plaine River near La Trouche
14 Nov	Winston transferred to Hq Co, 3rd Bn med detachment
19–26 Nov	La Plaine River crossed under heavy fire, 398th combat team formed at Moyenmoutier; German defenses in Vosges break as 100th Div takes Senones, La Vermont, St. Blaise, Champanay; 398th halts at Salm
26 Nov	100th Div withdrawn from line, reassembled near Raon-l'Etape, to undergo assault training for attack on Maginot Line positions as part of 15th Corps
2 Dec	398th moves to neighborhood of La Petite Pierre
3–13 Dec	100th Div drives toward fortress city of Bitche through Wimmenau, Wingen, Soucht, Meisenthal, Goetzenbruck, Lemberg until under fire of Maginot Line guns
11 Dec	Winston transferred to 2nd Bn med det
14–22 Dec	Assault on Maginot Line; Fort Freudenberg and heavily fortified Fort Schiesseck captured in heavy fighting; 100th Div poised to attack Bitche
23 Dec	Div pulled back from its salient and spread northward to fill gap left when 44th Div moves northward to restore front following German breakthrough in Ardennes on 16 Dec
23 Dec–1 Jan 45	398th holding position between Guising and Rohrbach, considerable fighting all along line
1 Jan	German counterattack, 2nd Bn 398th placed on flank of 399th Inf Reg to protect exposed position
3 Jan	Germans deepen penetration at boundary of 100th and 44th Divisions
9 Jan	Local attack by 100th Div gains Hill 370 south of Rimling

12 Jan	2nd Bn rejoins 398th; aid station in which Winston is working hit by shell
20 Jan	Following restoration of American front after Ardennes breakthrough contained, 100th Div moves into line along Sarreinsberg-Goetzenbruck-Lemberg; constant shelling, local fighting for next few weeks
15 Feb	100th Div conducts strong diversionary raids
17 Feb	100th Div defends right flank of 15th Corps and also engages in diversionary raids
28 Feb	15th Corps holds defensive line with 100th and 44th Divisions, with 106th Cavalry Group in reserve
13 Mar	Relief of 398th begun by regiment of 71st Inf Div, but breakthrough at Remagen by U.S. First Army changes plans; 2nd Bn 398th, on way for ten days of rest at Sarre-Union, called back, 398th ordered to capture Bitche
15–16 Mar	Bitche liberated after heavy fighting at Camp La Bitche
20–22 Mar	100th Div drives 100 miles to Rhine River through Hardt Mountains
26–30 Mar	100th Div moves into position near Ludwigshafen, awaits construction of pontoon bridge across Rhine
31 Mar	398th Inf Reg, motorized, crosses from Ludwigshafen to Mannheim, division swings southward to drive for Bavaria
2 Apr	398th at Heidelberg
3–4 Apr	398th, in relief of 255th Inf Reg of 63rd Div, arrives at Bad Wimpfen preparatory to assault on strongly fortified Heilbronn area, crosses Neckar River
6 Apr	398th crosses Jagst River, attacks Jagstfeld
7–9 Apr	398th throws back counterattacks by SS, Hitler Jugend
11 Apr	398th overruns Jagstfeld and Hagenbach, reaches and crosses Kocher River against strong resistance
12–13 Apr	Heilbronn captured, 100th Div heads east and southeast to cut off Stuttgart, with 398th on left flank of motorized advance
14–18 Apr	Drive continues, 398th in vicinity of Hütten

20 Apr	2nd Bn 398th pulled from pursuit, sent to Öhringen as guard for VI Corps Hq
21 Apr	100th Div seizes bridges across Rems, drives to within two miles of Stuttgart
23 Apr	398th links up with French 3rd Algerian Infantry at Bad Cannstatt–Stuttgart bridge, 100th Div pulled out of front lines after 170 days
7 May	With war in Europe over, 2nd Bn of 398th now stationed near Schorndorf
6 June	398th moved to Waiblingen
21–25 June	Winston makes trip to Dijon
1–7 Sept	Winston makes trip to Switzerland
26 Sept	Transferred to 12th Armored Div, Gerstetten, for shipment home
15 Nov	To Marseille
22 Nov	Departs Marseille on ship bound for home
4 Dec	Arrives at New York City
10 Dec	Pfc. Winston separated from service, Philadelphia, Pa.

1. Infantry Basic

Camp Blanding, Florida

March-August 1944

25 March 1944

Here I am in New Cumberland, Pa. and so far they're taking good care of me. Very low when I left but it helped to run into two boys examined with me—and just what I needed. One was married eleven years, has two kids. With few exceptions all the men are fathers. Glad you stayed home with the children. It was pretty hard leaving, and it would have been harder on both if you drove down with me.

The first thing after we arrived was a "complete" physical—an examination of our penis. That was all, but they call it a physical. Then lunch. Chow mein, fruit salad, cruller, coffee—and quite good.

Next we were inducted and finger-printed, sworn in and given a number. We then received our duffle bag, canteen, razor, raincoat, helmet, etc. but no clothes, which we get next Tuesday.

Am now resting in my bunk in a dormitory of 48 bunk-type beds, waiting for supper bell. Everyone seems especially friendly, both inductees and officers (like we're in the same boat together, boys) and that makes things easier. After dinner I'm heading for the Post Theatre to see movie. Lights go out at 9:15 but we're permitted around post till 11. We get up at 6 A.M. However, remember all these are this Reception Camp's rules, and in five or six days we're due to be shipped to a permanent camp. If I'm lucky enough to be here till next Saturday I believe I can get a pass home for a day or two. But make no plans.

So much for me. From my experience today, being so blue and low, then mingling and feeling better, I'm suggesting that you get out of the house early, see people and do things—even if the house suffers. I know it will help considerably.

Just came from supper—hot dogs, salad, soup, peaches, coffee. Everything is clean and spotless—not like you'd expect in an Army camp. So far it feels like some sort of vacation and I kind of feel guilty because you're having the full responsibility. I say again, try to regulate yourself—get out in the evening, too, with the girls—see a picture. That's the only way you can begin to acclimate yourself. Also, Dear, don't hold back on any problems, for in that way we can share some responsibilities together even though we're apart. It will help us both.

Don't write more than once since I may not be here later than Thursday. Will write again Monday—even Sunday if I have anything to say.

Remember now what I say about getting out. And tell Jack Vautier how much his consideration in driving me down helped my morale, and how much I appreciate it.

Keep your chin up, kid. With all my love.

27 March

Here we are again after a busy day. First I'll tell you what happened Sunday—nothing—though I was up at 5 A.M. Lots of activity around in the morning. Though we don't have to get up till 6, I hardly slept at all. The boys say it's the same with everyone the first night. Breakfast is at 6:30 and I surprised myself by eating heartily, for the food is good and ample. After that we returned to our barracks but weren't permitted to leave till released—which was all day—so we hung around sleeping, talking, reading.

Today was a little more exciting. First thing in the morning we had our I.Q. testings. I scored 132—110 is necessary for eligibility for Officer's Training. Then lunch and back to get classified. Here I had a typing test and did 40 words per minute which is acceptable to be classified as a typist. After that I fixed up your allotment, which is OK now.

First, you'll receive a "gift" allotment from the government within the next 10 days—then the regular one around the 1st of each month. Then the insurance was also taken care of, and deductions from my pay for bonds, monthly. I get around $14. after insurance and bonds are deducted which should take care of me. As to classification, I haven't heard, nor will I hear until I'm ready to move—even to the point of not knowing my destination till I arrive at the new camp. So just let's hope it's close by.

Tuesday, our uniforms, and needles on Wednesday. After that anything can happen. Please call Mother and read this letter to her as I'm somewhat bushed but will write her in a day or two when I know more about my possibilities.

29 March

Just received your first letter and I, too, can say it was a morale builder. Enjoyed every word, including Neil's and for the first time in my life, read a letter over and over again. I hope you mean it when you say you're doing well. Please don't hesitate to tell me anything, or about any problems that come up.

Since you're interested in all the details—here's what's happening. Yesterday we received uniforms—complete outfits—summer and winter clothing of every sort, money bag and things too numerous to mention. In the afternoon we were shown Army movies from 1–4 P.M., revealing the hard, bare facts of syphilis in action and it was sickening. And various other Army pictures exclusively made for instructional purposes. After supper went to the Post Theatre and enjoyed a double feature.

Today I received needles for typhoid and tetanus. While the injection was hardly felt, the after effects are annoying but not painful. Chicken was served for supper last night and it was contaminated, as everyone in camp had diarrhea, including me. In fact, it was so bad that when circumstances did not permit use of toilet, there was a lot of changing of underwear. Get it? However, everyone was given instructions by a doctor and soon it was under decent control.

Tomorrow our unit is on KP all day—14 hours. That means serving food, helping prepare it, washing dishes, etc. Most of the boys don't mind, and before we leave, everyone gets a turn at it.

I'm expecting to be shipped out any day now and will not know when I leave, even to the extent of an hour's notice. If it happens before I get a pass, I'll try (don't depend on it) to phone you. I won't know *where*—just *that* I'm going.

So far things continue decently and the Army seems to be interested in the welfare of each individual soldier. In return they expect you to do as instructed by your officers.

I'll ask you not to write here as mail is discouraged because of continual transfers, and besides I doubt if I'll be around much longer. Will continue to write as soon as anything develops. Keep chin up, Darling. If any emergency develops call this camp 7 P.M. *person to person*. Explain to operator it's an emergency, but don't call unless it is, as it requires an OK by proper authorities—they might even call up FDR first! Who knows! Remember now to get out and see a show once in awhile. Does the car need gas? Watch it closely on small speedometer. The B coupon is good for 5 gallons. Neil, I'm looking forward to some of those school papers you promised to send, and thank you for wanting to send the dollar Aunt Bess gave you, and if Daddy ever needs it he'll write you. How's that? My love to you all.

1–2 April   *En route*

Here it is 10 P.M. Saturday night, and if my writing looks shaky and hard to decipher it's because I'm lying on an upper berth heading South toward Georgia or Florida (probably Ft. Benning) but these troop trains travel under strict secrecy and no one knows anything except the Capt. and Lt. We left 4 P.M. and 500 men are aboard. There's no question but what I'm headed for an Infantry camp, but don't let that discourage you since almost everyone gets Infantry basic and then transferred to specialized schools, etc. after the end of the training period.*

Wasn't allowed to call home as I'd hoped, and I guess you had half a hope that I'd be seeing you over the weekend. Well, Friday I applied for a pass with all the other eligibles, and everything was all set. Then Saturday morning we received our call. You can imagine how broken-hearted I was—since we may as well face it—we won't see each other again till the end of basic, a minimum of 13

---

* With the cross-Channel invasion of Europe imminent, the U.S. Fifth Army engaged in heavy fighting on the Italian peninsula, and General MacArthur's forces preparing to invade the Philippine Islands, there was a heavy demand for combat infantry replacements, and most new draftees were assigned to infantry training camps.

weeks. Remember, Dear, thousands are in the same boots. Try to be a good soldier and take it.

It is now Sunday night after being on the train all day in the same upper berth. We're entering Florida which can only mean that we're headed for Camp Blanding, outside Jacksonville.

Today was uneventful—just riding and riding—except for a nice chat with the porter who became friendly when he learned I knew his boss in Philly, a policy-holder of mine. He did a number of small favors and tried to make the trip more pleasant. I sure did welcome it. (Hope you can read this as it's pretty bumpy up here.) I plan to call you Monday if I get the chance, so perhaps you'll get the call before this letter. All my love.

4 April   *Camp Blanding, Fla.*

Well, Dearest, today we're feeling a little better and beginning to get the swing of things. Here I am at Camp Blanding, a far cry from New Cumberland where you were treated as an individual and not a number. This is Army. No question about that. And I must admit the abrupt change is pretty unsettling, plus the disappointment of not being closer to home. Though I'm beginning to feel a little better, I'll confess to some bad moments. Chiefly, as I said, because I'm so far from home with no chance of seeing you, not to mention that this camp has no semblance to New Cumberland which was closer to Euphoria by comparison. I find it hard to take the harsh, rigid discipline handed out. I know I'm here to stay so I try to make the best of it, rationalizing that there's a good reason for every bonehead order that comes through from some feather-brained young Lt. just beginning to feel the magic of his authority. And it does make things a little easier.

Our Sgt. is stern and grim but with it all he has a quality and ability that commands respect, and it's men like him who really make the Army.

This week and next is geared chiefly to drilling, and you can't imagine how tough it is. Yet there's some satisfaction at the end of the day when you've executed the commands properly, and usually feel good physically. Also we have an hour of calisthenics daily, such as you see in the movies. If you're not exhausted after all this, you're superhuman. Incidentally, I was appointed squad leader (15 men).

About how I live—we have a hut, similar to a lake cabin and five men share it. My bunkmates are fine fellows—all married with children, and contrary to 95% of Army men, rarely cuss. The hut (so-called) is screened in all around and protected by flaps. The Army requires they be open on two sides at all times, but generally they're open all around as the days down here are pretty warm. Already after two days, with half the day cloudy and rainy, I'm beginning to tan and will probably be dark when you see me. We wear suntans—our official summer uniform.

We're now being reclassified as to occupation—although out of 180 men in our Company, I doubt that more than 25 will be moved from the Infantry to another branch (in the same camp) of the service.

There's a possibility I'll be transferred to the Clerk's School. The men who interviewed me said they'd recommend the change and gave me a #1 rating. I'd still get 6 weeks of Infantry which includes drilling and rifle instruction.

So much for me—now to my main concern. You and the boys. Are you getting down to a system yet? Remember the importance of getting out of the house. I keep repeating this, otherwise your home life will turn into drudgery at this time. How is that big boy of mine? And my little fellow? I miss you all so much. Dear, lights are about to go out so I'll close with all my love to you all.

5 April   Co. "A"—229th I.T.B.   Camp Blanding, Fla.

Note the new address—which means I'm now a member of the Clerk School. I believe it may be easier than Infantry training since we receive only 6 weeks of basic instead of 17. After that we get 9 weeks of school which includes practise in Army offices throughout the camp. Then 2 weeks of maneuvers to finish—and then an assignment in this camp or elsewhere. Your letters will reach me now, Dear, and I'll be looking forward to them. I must admit I'm terribly homesick and praying this mess is over with soon.

Physically, I'm well. Haven't written to anyone—tell them I'm unsettled and will probably write later. All my love.

6 April

I've been painting tables all day. Can't wait for basic training to start (to get it over faster), then 6 tough weeks. Then school.

Last night we were permitted to leave the barracks for the first time and it really helped. Saw a double feature. Was going to call you but the lines were cluttered with at least a 2-hour wait. However, I'll call the first chance I get. Have paper and pencil handy in case I want you to jot anything down.

My roommate, Jim, is an awfully fine boy—from Philly.* We both like the same things and are quite compatible. He's a tall, thin quiet fellow, has 2 children, too, and we find we have much in common.

Tomorrow KP duty and I rise at 4:30 A.M.—but getting up in the Army doesn't seem to be too hard. The meals are pretty decent. During the day we wear fatigues. Have 3 sets. When they get dirty I send them to the laundry.

Honey, it looks like they mean business. They've given me a rifle, a bayonet and a gas mask.

This place is really tremendous—125,000 acres. Free busses take you any place you want to go, many movies, PX's, Service Clubs— and is a big city in itself—though no civilians live here. Most of the men come from N.Y., Pa., and W. Central States.

I think of you and the children most of the day, and assure you the toughest part of this grind is being away from home. It's not easy for a man who loves his home and family.

* James N. Johnston, Jr., of Philadelphia, who later served in Headquarters Detachment, 100th Infantry Division, and was promoted to Technician 4th Class. Johnston died of cancer not long after the war.

It won't mean much but I've learned that Jacksonville is 18 hours from Philly by Silver Meteor and $23.40 round trip for servicemen. We're 37 miles N.W. of Jax. My love to you all.

8 April

I've been wanting to write you a number of times about how I really feel. I wanted to write—and then I didn't want to write. But you'd be the only one who could understand what mental anguish I'm going through. I know you'd understand how it feels to have a paining and aching and gnawing heart inside a completely exhausted body. A condition which exists frequently. But that's all I'll say along these lines—and already I'm sorry I said it. Now I'll tell you what's going on.

In the first place, I got into the Infantry. I and a few hundred thousand more were immediately going to get a transfer out of this branch. But that was pure fantasy. The very first thing they told us was "You cannot transfer out of the Infantry—so don't try it— there are no exceptions." And we learned soon enough these were the hard facts. Well, after reclassification I was transferred to the Infantry Clerk School—and now I consider myself fortunate in getting here since the platoon is made up of 75% family men—mostly all business men or professionals, and I can truthfully say, as a unit, they're about the smartest bunch I have ever run into.

So, Darling, while things could be a lot better, they could be a lot worse.

9 April

Today is Easter Sunday. I took a walk around and ended up here in the Service Club—a beautiful place with a balcony where the boys can write letters. Downstairs is the lounging room, cafeteria, telephone exchange, etc.

Earlier today I visited the boys from my old Company—before my transfer. They're a great bunch and I could almost go through the regular infantry course without a yap just to be with them.

Downstairs are 2 pianos and I hear the boys playing—privates— as no officers are allowed here.

One distasteful thing at camp is the constant waiting in line for everything you want to do. As was the case last night when I tried to go to the movies and couldn't get in—and to bowl—where I had to wait at least an hour—and you know I wouldn't wait. There's a long wait even to buy a hot dog. And to make a telephone call, you have to give the operator the number and she calls you when she can complete it—usually from 2 to 6 hours. Here in the Service Club it works out much better; you leave your number with the operator, come into the Lounge or Balcony to write, and when the call comes through they page you by microphone.

I feel badly my mail hasn't been getting through. You have no idea how heavy the mail is in these camps. One Co. of 180 men has upwards of 8 to 10 bags of mail a day—and it's given out twice daily, including Sundays.

All my love.

11 April

Receiving mail is a big problem here, and a disappointment. It's all mixed-up. I'm not getting any, and one of my bunkmates hadn't received a letter since leaving home for the induction center—then this morning he got 13 at once!

Well, Honey, today the real training started and I want to tell you it's rugged. In one day I've exercised more than in any one month of my life. We're up at 5:45—breakfast at 6:15 and by 7:30 we've eaten, and barracks are in first-class condition. Then every hour is taken up with some sort of drill, exercises, rifle-practise, rifle-cleaning. This is to be our routine throughout six long weeks; we're told there will be back-crawling, hiking with packs on our backs, crawling on ground with live machine-gun bullets whizzing over our heads. Even when school starts Infantry will be supplemented. Tomorrow should be another toughy but with Monday under my belt, I'll be better prepared.

Today my teeth were examined and I'll be having them fixed for the next few weeks.

Thank God for the movies! Tonight I went—cost 15¢—10 tickets for $1.20. There are ten movie houses to choose from—if you want to walk. But after a day of training I prefer the one close by, regardless of what's playing. It tends to relax me.

The C.O. of our Battalion, a Captain, is a louse if ever I heard or saw one. He's absolutely merciless. He "welcomed" us into the Army saying he was going to work the pants off us 24 hours a day, and "now you're going to sweat out some of that war money you made while I was in the Army the last 3 years." Everyone hates his guts, for without a doubt he's a sadist of the worst sort, and takes it out on the men. Another example of stupid brass feeling their "power."

Now to something pleasanter—yesterday it was scorching, but today it was pretty nice. So far the evenings have been delightful—hope it continues. Many flowers are in bloom—petunias and lilacs in particular and many more. This Florida sun would certainly be good for you—and your presence would do a lot more good than the sun—but of course I'm only dreaming. How are my boys? I look forward to Neil's letters. And David? I guess he wouldn't know me now. God bless you all.

16 April

Started a letter last night but since the lights went off I'll begin all over again, using a soldier friend's typewriter.

Received letter #6 and while I devoured every word, it made me homesick. Sometimes I wonder if mail doesn't create an opposite effect on some people. Your letters bring me close to home, and after reading them I realize I'm so far away with so little chance of seeing you, I become very low. But by no means don't stop writing—and keep them coming every day if possible, even if only a few lines, because I'd probably feel worse if they didn't come.

Today I worked a detail—something like KP—but this time with a title, "Latrine Orderly." See how fast they promote you in the Army! My job? To see that the toilets, urinals and wash basins were cleaned; to take care of the hot water furnace and mop the floors. Nice job, eh? But that probably eliminates Sunday assignments for awhile. We all get hit with it, so no one should beef.

Enjoyed talking with you so much Friday. Your voice came through so clear, and when you told Neil to be quiet because Daddy was on the wire, it seemed like old times.

Had a tooth pulled at the dentist's today. They sure do things in a wholesale way in the Army. It took about 2 minutes and another soldier was in the chair. He did a nice, clean job however, and the after effects are trivial. Also received 2 more shots—smallpox and typhoid.

You ask how we're set up in Clerk's School. First, when we come to camp we're put in a rifle co. or heavy weapons, or an anti-tank company, and so on. I happened to be placed in a rifle company. Then we're classified. A couple of days later, if a change to another type of training is warranted, a switch is made. The few lucky guys are transferred to other companies which teach specialized training. Every month a platoon of 60 men, qualified for clerks, is selected throughout the camp. They live, eat and train together. Other specialized camps down here are cooks, auto mechanics, intelligence and messenger service.

As far as keeping me abreast of the news, don't worry about it. I'm amazed how little I'm interested in what's happening other than to see a swift climax to this war, and news of you and the family. Just write what's on your mind—what Neil says and does, and David's antics—and the garden, if any. With all my love.

17 April

Today 5 letters, including Neil's, and since I hadn't heard from you yesterday, I don't have to tell you what it does for me. Neil, I showed your paper to all my soldier friends and they thought I had a pretty smart son. Keep them coming. How do you like the study of China? Did you know that China is one of our Allies? They're fighting Japan with us. Daddy's keeping busy down here and misses you very much, but I hope I can come home in 3 or 4 months, and if this terrible war ends, maybe sooner.

Honey, as to where my battalion is sent—including overseas—there's still a glimmer of hope I won't have to go. I base this on the questioning of pre–Pearl Harbor fathers by the Sgt. And today the Lt. said that fathers would be the last to leave the country. However, things change rapidly in the Army and just don't hope too much for anything.

How is the shopping situation now, Dear. I hope you're doing OK with car and gas.

Down here the meals are on the porky side. I'd say in about 80% of our meals pork is used. Sunday dinner is about our best meal—chicken or turkey and ice-cream.

Today we were learning how to use the bayonet and hand grenade. God! Can you picture me putting a bayonet through another man? But they tell us—over and over again—if we don't, they'll do it to us. (Goodnight and pleasant dreams!) Sometimes all this seems so unreal and mixed up, I hope I could wake up some morning to find it was all a bad dream—a very bad dream.

With all my love.

19 April

Just got in at 9 P.M. after a tough day. An awful lot of instruction comes from films, and after you've just hiked a few miles with full pack at fast pace in the hot Florida sun, then go into a dark room to witness a film, you just about fall asleep. Consequently, the officers, who are aware of this, switch the lights on repeatedly throughout the film to see if anyone is sleeping. It's hard as the devil to keep awake and every time the lights go on they get at least one or two guys asleep. But they're easy on them because they realize it's normal. They keep saying, "Don't fall asleep because you're going to miss something that may save your life when and if you go into battle—remember, we know it's hard to keep awake but it's important." I tell you this as I just returned from the movie instruction and fought with all my might to keep awake, but fell asleep. However, I wasn't caught since the officers probably fell asleep, too. I know one did.

Received your most welcome letter at noon, and believe it or not, was on the go till late afternoon before I could read it. I got a kick out of David's reaction to the dog-doll. I miss him so much and your accounts of him fill my heart with joy.

Had a few letters from friends today, and one from Ben B. who writes the Company is offering an interesting financial set-up for men in the service. According to him, with what we get from the Gov't., the Company will supplement the remainder to give us three-fourths of our salary, for the duration. This, if true, sounds great and sure will take a load off my mind.*

We changed huts recently and I'm bunking with another bunch, and nothing like the original group. However, we do manage to get together in our spare time—which isn't often.

Now that I'm eligible for a pass next weekend, have no desire to take advantage of it. Will just enjoy lazying around all day, resting. Dearest, I can appreciate your gnawing feeling as I get it often. I notice it disappears temporarily when I'm busy and with others. That's why I constantly tell you to do the same, though I know it's harder for you.

Tell Neil I'll write tomorrow as the lights are going out now. Goodnight, Dearest—with all my love.

20 April

Received your ray of sunshine today and as usual ate up every word. I especially enjoyed the poetry.

It was terribly hot today and I'm afraid we're beginning to get a taste of torrid weather. Each meal they require (not forcibly) that we take 1, 2 or 3 salt tablets, depending on the heat and amount of workout. I take them regularly as they replace the salt in your sys-

* The Metropolitan Life Insurance Company, Winston's employer, did indeed help its employees who were in the armed services in this fashion.

tem lost by perspiration. At least the evenings are comfortable here.

For the first time this week we were free tonight and of course you know I'd head for the movies. Am getting a G.I. haircut since we're having inspection tomorrow. There's a barber in our platoon, so it's convenient.

Now listening to Major Bowes program.* Remember, when I'd be finishing up my account Thursday nights, I'd be listening to him, and you used to wonder how I could do both at the same time without making errors? I feel a wave of nostalgia just thinking about it.

They had us double-timing (running) today with our rifles and complete packs, and believe me, it's no stroll in the sunshine. But it's good training and so far I'm holding my own and doing as well as any. In fact, I think we older fellows do better than the young boys.

Also, we studied military maps, how to read them, and explanations of the various symbols. And a gas-mask drill which trains us to put our gas masks on in 8 or 9 seconds while holding our breath. Later, we'll hike with them on, a prospect I don't look forward to with great relish. Furthermore, to test our adeptness we'll be put into a gas chamber where you have to get that mask on damn quick—or else. That doesn't seem to bother me too much, but the hike with the mask on does, somewhat.

How are those two boys of mine? While I was waiting at the dentist's last week, a little girl and her mother were waiting for their soldier daddy. I was looking at her, and she at me, and smiling at each other. All of a sudden I felt a tear run down my cheek. I'd been thinking of the kids as I looked at her, and it hit me with some impact when I realized I was so far away and unable to see them.

That obnoxious Captain—the guy who was so ruthless when we started training—was just promoted to Major. He must have something. What it is I wouldn't know, though.

---

* Major Bowes' Amateur Hour was one of the most popular of all network radio programs during the 1930s and early 1940s.

22 April

Couldn't write yesterday, Friday, as we have rifle inspection Saturday A.M. and it requires many hours to get the rifles in shape. Our Lt. has the reputation of being the toughest in our Bn. on inspection and if you don't pass you lose "pass rights" for the weekend, besides being hit with an extra detail. You can't begin to imagine the importance they attach to this, and I must admit that I and all the others were worried we wouldn't pass.

You see, the rifle is rather intricate and has to be just so—not one grain of sand can be found (down here there's only sand—no dirt), no rusty parts—just the proper thickness of oil on certain parts, etc.

After he inspected mine he said, "You have a good rifle." That, from him, was like a commendation from a 5-star General since he rarely says a good word, and you can bet I'm a happy soldier today.

Well, 2 weeks of training are over—one-third—and we're not unhappy about it. It seems to go quickly in spite of the pace. Will put this letter in the mail now, Sweetheart, and hope to write again tomorrow, Sunday, when we sleep about an hour longer. Mighty decent of them don't you think!

25–26 April

Received your daily booster and as usual it took care of me for the entire day. I had a good laugh reading your account about the 4-F.*

Yes, you hear all sorts of stories about the Marines, and here in the Army, too, you hear all sorts of incredible stories. One guy I know has rheumatic fever, and another fallen arches and really bad feet. Physicals are a joke around here.

---

* Mrs. Winston had included in a letter to her husband the following anecdote: "Lee's husband was deferred as a 4-F for 2 years. However, 6 months ago he was called in again for a physical, and this time classified as 1-A. When he was asked what branch of the service he preferred, he replied, 'Either Army or Navy'—so they put him in the Marines. The poor guy is afflicted with an ulcerated stomach, asthmatic condition, varicose veins and sundry complications—and now he's a Marine! Now don't let any Marine tell you they're the cream of the crop!"

Just got back from the gas chamber and it was an experience I could do without. They fill the room with poisonous war gases and march us into it. We must get that mask on instantly or suffer the consequences. I got through OK but we all inhaled plenty of gas. As an added fillip we were ordered to walk the two miles back with our masks on. Not only is it tough breathing, but it's hot and uncomfortable. However, don't worry, I made out fine.

Tonight another goodie is in store. They're taking us way out into the woods, give us a compass and instructions and then we must find our way back. Of course, we already were taught to work a compass so we shouldn't have too much trouble.

Today we were put through two hours of bayonet practise, and it's the meanest, toughest grilling I've been through yet. Savage is a better word for it. You feel like you're in training to murder another human being—which you are—and the thought is sickening. But in this pretty game of war you have to gear yourself for about anything. And as I told you before, I can take it along with the rest.

Overall, things are going fairly well, and physically I'm feeling better than ever—and stronger. Been getting dark (tanned) and, I guess, leaner. My muscles seem to be loosening and I can take strain pretty well. Besides, my wind is better than ever.

27 April

I'm now at the dentist awaiting my turn, and anticipating the "wait" I brought along some writing paper. My appointment is for 7 A.M. so you see even the officers (dentists) have to be on the "ball."

To tell you a little more about last night, we hiked 2½ miles, and they walked us into the dense woods, gave us a compass and ordered us to find our way back in the dark. Unless instructions are accurately followed, it's easy to get lost—but we managed to make it back in good order, and when we returned at 10:30 P.M., they gave us coffee.

Clean clothing is a problem. Could you send me all the T-shirts I have at home? They're most important, and I'll buy extra socks and shorts here. If I stop this letter abruptly you'll know I've just been called into the dentist's office and I'm sure I won't feel much like writing afterward.

It's now 10 hours later and I received your delightful letter #16, with Rose's note enclosed.

We might as well forget about the furloughs. It hurts to say it, but I'm in a class which goes through a 17-week cycle and if I miss over 6 days, I've got to start all over again. Besides, only an emergency furlough would be granted.

I want you down here in the worst way, but I don't think we should figure on your coming till the 6-week period is over. I even hesitate to encourage your coming at all. This is why. I couldn't spend much time with you except perhaps a Saturday evening and Sunday (if I'm not on detail) for my time is completely taken up, even to 9 and 10 in the evenings 3 and 4 times a week. The pace is so fast here and so much to be done, that your presence would, in a sense, be frustrating, as I could hardly get together with you and it would be painful, knowing you were around and our not being able to get together.

It's terribly hard for me to talk this way. If I didn't think it through, I would say, sure come on—I can't wait. But for a night or day—I wonder. Yet with all my "thinking it through" the idea even for a night or day seems to be worth all the trouble. I'll analyze it further and look into the possibilities but don't figure on it till the 6 weeks are over.

Thanks for the offer of cash. You're like I am. I give you candy, and eat it up myself! And you offer me money a few days before pay day. But kidding aside, if I find myself short I'll let you know. I'm getting by OK.—All my love, Sweetheart.

30 April

Just got back from Jacksonville, and while a bit different, it wasn't that much but what I think I'll stay in camp hereafter over the weekend. You were saying you thought I was through at 5 P.M. Well, Dearie, it's not quite that simple. We have precisely planned

Basic training, Camp Blanding

activity. By checking with the bulletin board Sundays we're aware of our schedule for every day of the week. There is so much they want to teach us; if it takes 2 or 3 extra hours in the evenings, there's no argument, we just do it. In addition, there's KP or Policing (cleaning the grounds or huts for inspection) or anything that has to be done. The Army has no "hours."

Feeling a little low. Probably because I was in the city and saw a touch of civilian life, though actually civilians in Jax are a rarity. I stayed at a private home, through USO. Cost, $1.50 including breakfast and well worth it, especially since there was a warm, homey atmosphere. These folks had 4 sons in the Army and we were able to understand each other. It was a nice change.

About the USO—they're doing all right with the boys, making every effort to make them comfortable, such as weekend accommodations, checking packages, serving coffee, cookies, and among other things, giving them a comfortable place to write letters, read, rest or listen to the radio.

1 May

Two more letters and gobbled up every word. Right now I'm in the Company game room, waiting for my call to come through. So often I get a sudden urge to phone you, and when the operator tells me there'll be a 4- to 6-hour wait, I tell her to forget it. But tonight I was free and put the call through. And now I'm waiting. Dear, you warm my heart with your accounts of David. You can't write enough about him.

As you know, we're learning to shoot the rifle. You have to give them credit for their expertise in teaching us how to fire, and if this preliminary instruction means anything, they tell me I'll be an "expert," an appraisal which somehow failed to rouse my "sporting" blood under these conditions. Anyway, to give you an idea how it works—there's a movable bull's eye 200 yards out. The soldier looks through the rifle which is placed in a permanent position, and by signalling another soldier 200 yards away, the bull's eye is moved up, down, over, etc. until the rifle is aiming perfectly at the target. Then he signals the soldier that he has focused, and a mark is made in the center of the bull's eye. The bull's eye is moved twice more and the same procedure is repeated; if the three marks almost coincide, the novice rifleman is considered a candidate for an "expert." While I was told mine was one of the best, when we use real bullets next week it could change the picture. Rifle practise is like a sport until the thought hits me that this isn't shooting at carnival targets, but is aimed at shooting people and it leaves me cold.

Wednesday our Co. is scheduled to march and drill at the retreat parade—which means we'll march with band music and be reviewed by the General. It's amusing how excited the officers are about it, like kids, ordering us to practise every spare moment.

Today our Sgt. told us he was promoted and will be leaving us.

You might recall, from the beginning he commanded our respect, and we felt bad to see him go as we all thought the world of him— unlike that swinish Captain who only aroused our contempt.

Got paid today—$9.85. How they arrived at that enormous figure I'll never know, and there's not much you can do about it.

Just spoke to you, Sweetheart—how I enjoyed it. I felt so good to hear your voice—and there's one soldier who's feeling a little better tonight!

6 May

Sunday. Received a great 8-page letter from you. Sundays are anathema to me for with not much to do I revert to being blue and homesick. Such was the case today until your letter arrived.

Very pleased about our first apple blossoms. Looks like we'll be having some apples this year. And that mock orange should be pretty if it blooms. I enjoyed your account of all the greening.

Taking in a movie tonight. *Up in Mabel's Room.* The boys say it's very funny. Could go for a few laughs. Goodnight for now, Dearest.

7 May

Am back to the rifle range which we'll be hitting all week— eating out here but returning at night. We walk out and back—6 miles. And this time we're using real bullets. Am writing this letter in spurts as the day is long and busy. I want to get one off to you tonight even if it's abrupt or nonsensical.

I really have a sweet job today. How would you like to have 75 men shooting all at once at you? My job is what they call "pit detail." I and 40 other men are in this big pit with targets—and 75 men shooting at them. We're safe enough—the bullets are flying about 2 or 3 feet above us and we're well protected. We constantly change targets.

After lunch. (We ate in the woods where they brought out a hot meal on trucks.) Today I'm getting my first chance at shooting the rifle. Will continue later.

Well, Dearest, am now in bed—very tired after a hard day which will be duplicated the rest of the week. I was pleased with my first results. Friday we take our official test. Under normal circumstances this rifle practise could be fun since it does require a certain amount of skill.

Dear, the linen service is lousy. If you haven't mailed the stuff I asked for, please add towels, pillow cases, a sheet, swim trunks, shorts and dusting rags. I need these extras.

10 May

It's surprising how much money I spend down here—every night will find me at the PX. After a hot, weary march we all look for refreshment—ice-cream (a pint no less), drinks, cake, and always something extra like writing paper, soap (plenty, too), foot powder, shoe polish, brush, movies. However, I believe I'll make out when I receive my first full pay—about $13. net. Your enclosure of $5. sure came in handy.—This past weekend in Jax convinced me to stay right here unless I've a definite thing to do or place to go. It gives me a chance to rest and I'm ready for what Monday brings.

We're really stepping—up at 4:45 A.M. and on the march by 5:30—4 miles and speeded to about 140 long steps per minute. (The average civilian steps 80 per minute.) And then a long day on the range—and the 4-mile hike back, speeded to 150 steps per minute in the hot, blazing sun. Yesterday, 12 men fell out—one of which was not me. However, I'm not boasting as it was sheer guts that kept me going as was the case in 95% of the others.

After supper I usually lie down for half an hour—go to PX to refresh a bit—then spend two exciting hours cleaning the rifle. Finish about 10 P.M., then a bath, clean mess kit, wash socks, shave, and try to hit the bed by 11, but it's usually closer to 12. Then up again at 4:45. That's just this week, but so far with half gone I don't feel any the worse for it. If I miss writing I know you'll understand.

The above was written this morning in the target pit while awaiting the fog burning. Right now I'm about ready to turn in.

11 May

I'm glad we decided to number our letters. This way we'll know if any haven't been received. Just finished reading #30 which is my shot in the arm for the day.

We took our marksmanship tests today. I qualified as marksman with a 161 average out of 210. Four more points and I'd have been a sharpshooter—but I don't seem destined for such "glory." Forgive me for this abrupt ending, Darling, but I'm very tired. Our platoon is a day ahead of schedule and tomorrow should be much easier. All my love.

12 May

Today is Saturday. Inspection day. If it weren't for your bright letter I'd be feeling even lower than I am. Why? From what I've told you, you know the platoon put in a tough week, and as a result our huts weren't in such hot condition due to our leaving for the range after rising. But there are no extenuating circumstances in the Army, and when the new C.O. inspected the huts the 1st Sgt. was bawled out plenty. As a consequence, the Sgt. who can be really tough when he wants to be, took it out on the men (what they call displacement in psychological jargon) restricting the entire platoon to the Co. area indefinitely. We all feel like prisoners around here, especially because of an idiotic whim.

Yesterday was relatively easy. Outside of a 2-hour hike—and a slow one—we cleaned our rifles (a requisite after firing). When the Lt. came around for inspection only 15 men out of the 60 had perfect rifles, one of which, fortunately, was me. We were allowed off and I hotfooted it to the movies, but the rest of the poor guys were restricted till 8 P.M. And now this.

Monday we're slated to use a carbine. It's a rifle one-half the size and weight of the one we carry daily. That's the rifle I'd carry as a clerk in combat. It's almost as good as the regular rifle but weighs about 5 pounds.

We'll be started on speed marches soon which usually begin at 2½ miles daily and work up to 10. They're done partially in double-time and fast quick-time, alternating 1 minute double and 2 minutes quick.

The weather down here has been delightful, the sun somewhat strong but we get a good breeze most of the time. So far, the evenings are incomparable—very cool, and boy does that help!

It might interest you to know how we dress for training and daily details. We have 2 sets of fatigue uniforms—pants and shirt made of heavy denim material. Leggings fit over the pants, bagging at the knees. When on duty this set-up is used with a helmet at all times. Many nights we're so bushed when we return to the huts we don't change to our dress khakis, often going for a week without getting into these trim outfits you see a soldier wear.

14 May

It's Sunday and we're still restricted, so you can imagine how low I feel not hearing from you today. Dearest, I'd give anything to be home for good—not just a furlough. How much heartache would be over for everyone if this war would suddenly end.

And to top it off, today is Mother's Day and the camp is literally filled with soldier's wives, mothers, girl-friends. You can imagine what I'm feeling—but I'm at a point where a little temporary pleasure would not satisfy me.

Gee, talk about loading troubles on you. I'm the guy who should be keeping your morale up and I'm debating whether or not to tear this letter up and start another. But really, Dear, things aren't as bad as I've painted them—probably just due to my inactivity and immediate circumstances. During the week we're so busy we hardly have time to think. And this week we're to get some school. About 4 hours of typing and a few hours of instructions on Army forms.

Since our Co. had so many intricate forms, I don't think I'll have much trouble there.

Today, to lure volunteers for the paratroop school (you don't get in except by volunteering—no assigning) there was an exhibition of parachute jumping. We were ordered to attend this as our group was one of many that acted as guards to keep spectators back. However, it turned out to be interesting and thrilling—24 jumpers and no mishaps. Until later.

16 May

Am now awaiting a truck ride to a firing range. The purpose: to acquaint us with firing at unknown distances requiring accurate estimation as to yardage. For the various ranges the rifle has to be adjusted accordingly. It's quite a learning experience.

Since I wrote the above I've been on the range and back again. We had another taste of the Captain's ruthlessness. We'd been working hard in the hot sun for 3 solid hours, and finally given a rest. When we started to drink from our canteens, the water was literally hot so very few boys could take it. However, set aside in a shady spot were three 5-gallon cans of cool water for the officers. The guys saw this and about a dozen went over and filled their canteens.

When the Captain discovered it he questioned the men but no one would admit to their "guilt." He turned blue with anger and ordered us all to walk back in the hot sun—a distance of 7 miles— even though we were slated for a truck ride back.

I showered immediately to revive myself and got dressed but was too tired to eat so went to the PX for a quart of milk and crackers.

Tomorrow again in the field all day and will be having our first taste of C rations. They come in cans, and the boys say they're very satisfying.

23 May

When we returned from a speed march tonight, the huts were so dirty, according to the Lt., we were compelled to "G.I." the huts—which means a virtual overhaul. And since the previous night we had guard duty, we were damned tired and dropped off to sleep at 11:30—the sleep of the dead. Today I pulled KP for 16 hours—rising at 4 A.M. I'm not telling you this to induce your sympathy (not that it would help) but to assure you I'm able to "take it." But I'd like to hit the guy who asks me what I do in my "spare time."

Today I received 3 letters, #'s 41, 42, 45 and they're the shining lights of my days. They help me more than I can tell you.

25 May

Have half an hour between classes and want to get off a few lines. First, I'd like to say that as of today I feel better than ever before. I never told you this, but all during my physical basic the pace was brutally exhausting. I felt stiff and worn-out almost every minute of every day, and going through the paces was little less than agonizing. I was no exception—we all felt that way. But now, with a limited amount of physical training and more rest (not at night, though) at the classes, I'm beginning to feel great. Never, in the beginning, were we able to rest.

And yesterday after returning from a speed march, I felt looser and better than I ever did in my life.

Devoured every word you wrote of our little fellows, and there are few things I enjoy more than your completely graphic accounts of them. Will continue later, after class.

Just got in and awaiting chow, but we'll have to wait till the first platoon gets in—in about an hour—so I think I'll shower and eat at the PX, then head straight for the movies.

Later. Back from the movies—saw *Dr. Wassell* with Gary Cooper. It was about a Navy Lt. Commander whom the President commended a couple of years ago on one of his fireside chats. We listened to that speech together shortly after the war began. The story was inspiring—particularly to a soldier who has been taught and (learned) military discipline, like me. My love to you all.

27 May

After chow today, our Company was called on to witness something that will be difficult to ever forget. Two companies of 360 men came off bivouac last week—which means 2 weeks of maneuvers. They eat and sleep there for the entire period.

It's a strict rule that empty ration cans are to be gathered and brought back to camp by truck for salvage. The purpose—to discourage wild pigs from inundating the area. There are hordes of them and they seem to be everywhere. Well, anyway, one of the boys dug one of his cans into the ground—probably eating between meals and tried to get rid of it some way.

That was the last day on bivouac. Early the next day, as soon as the group returned, the Company was informed that a hole four feet deep was dug by pigs immediately after they left. Well, the whole group, one by one, was questioned and since the "guilty" man would not own up, the entire 360 foot-sore, weary men and 10 officers were commanded to walk the 34 miles back as punishment.

In order to impress upon us the need for proper disposition of these cans, our Company Commander ordered us, in military formation, to watch this group start off on this needless, brutal hike— 6 platoons, officers, a chaplain (a Red Cross truck for possible casualties), all marching off as if to slaughter. Thirty-four miles because of one man's infraction of rules. Being forced to witness these desolate men starting off was a searing experience I'll long remember.

I got socked again this Sunday with KP but it's all part of this game and we all get hit with it.—Again I got so much joy out of our little cherub through your vivid explanations. How I miss my fellahs.

School work is interesting. The myriad of forms and complications keep you alert and on your toes. Next week will be easy—no speed marches. You won't believe this but I'm really getting a kick out of them. After the war I'm going to continue exercising to keep in trim. Weatherwise it's been almost perfect.

The boys here are a great bunch of guys, and the more I see of them the better I like them. You've never seen a group from so many walks of life that seem to have so much in common. For instance, business men, lawyers, clerks, laborers, farmers, men of position and money, men with little or nothing, but there's a genuine bond—you might call it survival—that brings every type of man together. With few exceptions, everyone is a gentleman.

29 May

It's early in the morning and I haven't yet received your daily letter. Mail call is immediately after lunch and supper. Here's the procedure: the mailman blows a whistle and all the boys make a bee-line down. He calls out each name, and as the boy says, "Here," he walks over and picks up his mail. Besides chow it's unquestionably the most popular thing we have. Sometimes I think it's even more popular than chow.

The 1st Platoon in our Co. left for bivouac this morning at the unholy hour of 2:30. They'll walk 18 miles to their area, and for the next two weeks will eat, sleep and simulate actual field problems. I heard the clerks actually get to do clerical work out there, even use a typewriter. I can't say I'm looking forward to it, but it appears to be the one thing that is a must before training is over. And I assure you I AM looking forward to training being over.

I'm learning there's a definite difference between being a trainee and not. A trainee is under strict discipline—a schedule to keep up—rain, shine or whatever circumstances might turn up. And it will be completed. Incidentally, the word will is a demand word in the Army. When a superior officer gives an order he usually says, "Your shoes will be shined," or the equivalent, but always the word will is accented. Even soldiers throughout the camp, when speaking to each other, might say, "You will meet me at the PX," etc.

Well, lunch is over now and I received your welcome and expected letter. Am enclosing another test paper for Neil. When I explained to the boys that I was exchanging test papers with Neil it created a good laugh.

31 May

I continually hope for a climax to this war, but some days more than others I get completely fed up. They pile it on thick and the worst of it is that so many orders and demands are asinine and senseless. Some officers feel the same way, but they too are following orders equally stupid. I'm fed up with regimentation. You know my feelings about dictatorships, and the Army is a classic example. While it does have to be run on some sort of authoritarian basis, a closer look at some of the directives in relation to the total picture would be in order. And especially at some of these 2nd-rate officers who implement these orders with the flair of a Hitler. It's not easy to swallow—and the fact that you can't get away from it, even for a few hours, doesn't help. Even when you do get a pass to escape the surroundings you see more of it than at camp. It seems to be an incurable disease you have to gear yourself to live with.

Something that's a paradox around here: Our instructors, all with years of teaching experience and doing a fine job—all are privates. They entered the Army 17 weeks before we did, completed their basic and then were appointed as instructors with no promotions. One in particular has a great sense of humor and is as thorough as they come—yet he's still a private. His class is one you enjoy looking forward to. He says, "I'd rather be a live private than a dead Captain." And that's about how they all feel.

How did the asparagus come through? Can you cut enough for a meal? And the rhubarb? Did it take? I imagine the beans are coming along, aren't they? I could use some fresh-cut asparagus here. Although the meals could be a lot worse they're still porky. The "beef" comes from the soldiers—about the seasoning. It's so strong you can't tell what you're eating. On the subject of food, while you generally get as much as you want, all you hear at the table is "pass this" and "pass that" and "pass this"—and you're lucky if you're able to get a mouthful in between passes!

On these very hot days when you and the kids do a lot of perspiring, try to get enough salt in your systems. Take it in the form of pretzels or plain table salt—but take it. We find it does wonders in relieving you during the hot spells.

Well, well, just received letters 50 and 51 in which you tell me of Rose's visit.* About early discharges for fathers, tell Rose we refer to hearsay as "latrine" rumors in the Army. After a couple of months we've learned not to assume, anticipate or hope until the command of execution.—Dearest, you take a load off my mind with the swell job you're doing. All my love.

3 June

Here it is another day, and I just can't seem to get used to "Army." I've been thinking about some of the letters I've been writing and you may be getting the idea that I'm continually griping. I don't mean to be—only, as the days go by, my desire for my family is such that my patience is at a low ebb. Sure, I know there's a job to do if ever we're to get out of this war, but I can't kick this awful lonesomeness.

Just was handed a special assignment in typing which included a particular job for the General. He handed the work to the typing instructor who turned it over to me, so I'll make this letter short. But not before I tell you how much your account of the rose bushes and the perennial beds does for me. All we see here is sand, sand and more sand and it gives me a lift to think of gardens and moist, fertile earth. Until later.

* Rose is Keith Winston's sister-in-law, Mrs. Nathan Koenig, of Washington, D.C.

Time out

4 June

Just returned from an invigorating swim in the lake. It's a beautiful one and anywhere you can see bottom, the water is that clear. Sundays are generally pleasant around here—come and go as you please—good meals and everyone relaxed.

It seems that every soldier takes news of the war subjectively—how it might affect him personally. First we were pleased, then disappointed about the invasion news. As the fellows say, if it did get started and things were looking up, life around camp would certainly go a little easier.

This camp has the reputation of being one of the worst in the country. According to Walter Winchell it's a concentration camp with the General's wife running it.* I have no basis for comparison, and since clerks are in a somewhat different position, it's hard for me to really know. However, my guess is that it's probably a bit of

---

* Whether the radio commentator and newspaper columnist Walter Winchell had ever said any such thing is dubious, but almost precisely the same comment was attributed to him about every infantry basic training camp in the United States during 1943 and 1944.

an exaggeration. Many believe the rumor started with the officers, as the General is very harsh and strict with them. But that's just my guess.

We're now enjoying one of those refreshing rain storms. It's quite a phenomenon—it comes in torrents and almost at once the sun comes out strong, and that nemesis, the sand, is dry in minutes. I'm planning to see a movie tonight. Until later.

Just back from the movies—saw *Make Your Own Bed*. Exceptionally bad, but it certainly got my mind off Army for awhile. It was strange—I forgot myself completely for a little while, and then the movie ended—I realized where I was and such a disheartening feeling came over me.

Darling, I hate to close for the same reason you do—I feel so much closer when I write and when I finish a letter it's like saying goodbye. But just let's make it goodnight. With all my love.

On 6 June 1944, American and British forces went ashore at Utah and Omaha beaches on the Contentin Peninsula of Normandy, France. By the close of the day, nearly 155,000 Allied troops were ashore, and a beachhead of almost eighty square miles had been established, but at the cost of from 10,000 to 12,000 casualties.

6 June

Darling! Today is D-Day and I'm so happy I could bawl. The invasion will be a success—it has to be. None of us see it any other way.

At 5:45 this morning there was suddenly a lot of loud cheering outside but we paid little attention. Then someone from another hut ran in yelling, "The Invasion is on," and five guys, as one, jumped up to turn the radio on. It was true—and I wasn't the only guy who hid a tear. This is the day we all dreamed about. And now that it's here, we're all going about our duties—which continue come what may—with lighter hearts and a renewed hope, for the Invasion will not fail.

The above was written early today. It's now 11 P.M. and I just returned from the movies. Saw *The Eve of St. Mark*. I urge you to see it as it gives you some idea of Army life—what the men do and think and feel.

Well, it's been quite a day—all around. Goodnight, Sweetheart.

8 June

Ordinarily, today's stretch which started 4:45 A.M. and ended 6 P.M. would have knocked me silly during the first part of training. But today, believe it or not, I took it like a "trouper" and actually enjoyed it. Obviously there's a big improvement physically—and I'm no exception—the whole platoon feels it. In fact we've been buttered up by the "brass" throughout the camp for everything we do. They tell us we're much better than average and have "spurt." We're reacting like kids enjoying a pat on the back.

Today Jim had an accident, not too bad, but requires a minor operation. A tiny piece of shrapnel pierced his neck and has to be removed. I went to see him tonight. Incidentally, it was purely a freak accident and very, very rarely happens, so don't worry about me. If it were something to be concerned about I wouldn't have mentioned it.

Today we spent the day out in the field learning how to operate the bazooka gun. Remember Bob Burns' bazooka? Well, this gun is named after that because of its queer, cylindrical shape, and is able to penetrate several inches of armor plate—the idea—to destroy tanks and other armored vehicles.* Nice thought, eh?

From here on we'll be having field work thrown in with our schooling, but personally I welcome it as I do get tired sitting inside all day.

* The "bazooka," a handheld rocket-firing weapon, was so called because of its resemblance to a large horn made out of pipes on which the radio comedian Bob Burns used to play certain tunes, notably "The Arkansas Traveler." The weapon itself was extremely effective against German tanks.

10 June

It's Saturday and am in a good frame of mind. Why? I passed inspection. Half the guys didn't and it ruined their weekend.

You couldn't begin to guess what goes on during inspection. Your rifle is inspected as if it were a rare gem, and PERFECTION is the word. One tiny grain of sand or one piece of lint means you don't pass. And that's just part of it. Your appearance must be immaculate. There's no such thing as an alibi.

After that we were taken to an obstacle course. As the word implies, it was just that—a course jammed with obstacles.

We jump off high structures, climb high contraptions, leap over fences and large, deep holes; we cross logs placed over huge dugouts, etc.—all this with our packs and rifles. How you endure all this, I'm learning, depends on your mental attitude. You must acquire the proper attitude to survive. The plain fact is, if you don't think this way you can go bugs.

We're to go through 3 more hours of the same and I'm not looking forward to it.

Last night we got a few laughs out of our extra detail of pulling weeds that surround the hut. How they thrive in sand I don't know, but they do. They flourish. Our Sgt., an old Army man from Arkansas, with a thick drawl, is as dumb as they come, but mighty tough on inspection. He orders, "Git that Johnson grass out now an' fill up the foxholes." The "foxholes" are small cavities left after crabgrass is pulled out. So the boys go about saying, "The Johnson (why Johnson we don't know) grass *will* be removed—and the foxholes *will* be filled." We all get a kick out of it and life is just a bit more pleasant.

Did I tell you we have a new Commanding Officer? At first we didn't go for him but he's turning out to be a prince. He says very little but tries to make the trainees as comfortable as conditions will permit.

For instance, throughout the camp, at 5:45 A.M., every soldier rolls out of bed, gets dressed in 3 or 4 minutes, and without shaving, runs into formation where a roll call is taken—then back to the huts for washing, etc. That's what's called Standing Reveille.

Well, now our Co. doesn't stand reveille, due to the C.O. no doubt, and that's definitely okay with me though most of the men hardly appreciate it. The fact is, the guy who stands reveille and the one who doesn't still eat at the same time. But the guy who doesn't has extra time to do little things or—as they do in our hut—sleep an extra 10 minutes. A few extra minutes is a luxury and I'm one guy who appreciates it when I get it.

I see on next week's schedule that we're due for our "overseas physical." While I don't think fathers over 30 will be going, we all go through this "physical." Please note quotes around physical. It's a farce. If you're warm, breathing, have both arms and legs, you've passed the test and are ready for combat.

Am going to the hospital tonight to see my sick buddies. Well, I didn't say much but it took a lot of space to say it. All my love to you and the boys, Darling.

11 June   *Our Anniversary*

Darling, received your lovely, moving sonnet written for our anniversary. I read it a number of times and with every reading like it even more.

I can enjoy it doubly as I rest comfortably on my bed listening to the radio. It's so peaceful on Sundays.

Bought a pair of sunglasses and a box of vitamins. We get few fresh vegetables and what there is "ain't fittin' to eat." Besides, we pay 25¢ for a box which costs 49¢ in civilian life.

The PX's are non-profit and everything is cheap. Candy bars, 2 for 5¢, ice-cream, 20¢ a pt., razors 15 for 10¢, cigarettes 2 for 25¢ (17¢ a pack at home) and so on. All profit goes to the boys in the form of a big party at time of "graduation." Our Co. has over $200. now from PX profit.

Just received a wonderful letter and again I tell you that on Sundays they're doubly enjoyable.

This afternoon 3 of us from our hut went to the movies, then to the hospital to visit Jim, who will be getting out tomorrow, I'm glad to say.

After the visits we took a pleasant walk along the lake, reminding me of our walk around Andover Lake in Conn. Then we stopped over to watch "Dress Parade"—an outdoor show put on by the boys in camp each Sunday evening. They're really good! The weekend is about over and already I'm looking to the next one!

Thursday is Infantry Day throughout the U.S. and thousands of visitors are expected to view us.

12 June

Darling, did you hear Walter Winchell last night? He said Germany's position is much worse than it appears and he predicts they'll be out of the war within 6 weeks.* I didn't hear him myself, but that's what the boys told me and I hope they got the facts straight.

Lately we've been chewing over the possibilities of where (what section) we might get placed—such as personnel section of a company, battalion, regiment headquarters or even field cadre. The general feeling among the men is that they'd like to be shipped out of here and take their chances on a location closer to home. The way it works now—all men are shipped to Fort Meade or Ord, and then reclassified. After this training, my classification should (and little doubt will) be Army Clerk–Skilled. Then you're shipped to camps where you're needed—if not out of the country. At the present writing, men over 32 years of age and those with families are not shipped out. My pipe-dream is that the German part of this war comes to an abrupt end and the government starts discharging men fast— and that I get transferred to some point up north where they have huge administrative sections and need thousands of office help. Even if kept in the Army, which is far from unlikely, and at one of those points, it wouldn't be so bad, would it?

Of course all this is just thinking out loud—and if you were in the Army you'd know what I mean. It seems they take the most

* Although at this point the Allies had expanded their beachhead and landed large numbers of troops, the war was still far from over. The invasion forces were still bottled up in their beachhead, without a breakthrough, while far to the east the Russian summer offensive was moving steadily westward, but was still well to the east of the Nieman River.

logical idea, turn it around and do exactly the opposite. They discourage use of common sense, insisting you take orders as given, no matter how crazy or absurd they may sound—and then tell you there's a reason for it—but nobody ever knows the reason. But we learn to adjust and try to find the "humor" in it.

13 June

Lots of commotion this morning triggered by the speed march yesterday—chiefly because men fell out—something unusual in our platoon. The cooks' platoon that lost 30 men didn't help any, and the whole battalion may suffer as a result. The Colonel is considering cutting out passes on weekends when a speed march is scheduled for a Monday. It will hit the guys who leave for the weekend, but it will only affect my peace and quiet, which I enjoy on Sundays when everyone is away.

The announcement of 4 openings in the OCS School created a flurry in our platoon yesterday. A huge number filled out applications. In case you're wondering if I'm applying—no—I'm not.

Here are my reasons and you might agree there's some merit in them. In the first place, out of 50,000 men, 4 will be chosen. Just 4 . . . Then each candidate is interviewed by the Company C.O.— and right off 4/5ths are eliminated. The remainder of "lucky" ones go to the Battalion C.O., and he in turn sends 4 (from the entire Battalion) to the Regimental C.O. who might choose two. And those from the other 10 regiments send their 1, 2, or 3 candidates to the General of the Camp who then chooses the 4.

If you're lucky, by the time you get past Bn. you'd be a candidate for a heart attack. As it is, I wouldn't stand a chance and it would take a lot to convince me that the 4 final choices got it completely on merit. There's usually someone behind pushing.

As for me, I hope the war ends immediately and I'm still a private. Knowing you, I'm sure you feel the same.

Just got your letter telling me my anniversary gift to you arrived. Now I'll tell you my little secret. First, I took a pass to Starke with the express purpose of getting you a gift, but that town is lousy—I mean *lousy*. It's a honky-tonk hot-dog resort. No prices marked, inferior junk and sky-high prices, run by civilians trying to get rich off the soldiers. I gave up in disgust. Not knowing just what to do I hit on the idea of writing Jerry, gave him several items to choose from and asked him to have Gimbels mail it directly out to you with a gift card from me. So if you've been wondering about it, now the "mystery" is solved.

Today is about the hottest day of the year and we were ordered to hit the obstacle course again this afternoon. Not only were we played out from yesterday's march, but hardly anyone could function because of the intense heat. Well, to make it short, one of my hutmates fainted, and when we got back nearly everyone was sick, including me. We heard the hospital was full of heat-prostration cases all day. But I'm feeling fine now and definitely no cause for alarm. A few salt tablets and shower usually do the trick.

15 June

The range all day again, shooting the machine gun. It was hotter than yesterday but cooled down somewhat this evening.

By the way, Honey, you'd better deduct the check I mailed to Jerry. It's pretty nice when you pay for your own anniversary gift!

One of my hutmates got a $30. M.O. from his wife—10 for his birthday, 10 for their anniversary and 10 for Father's Day—which all fall in June. She must love him! You know I'm kidding. But of course my hutmate doesn't receive sonnets from his wife. Just cold cash.

Since I'm writing this in the latrine with all the lights out, I'll say goodnight, Darling. All my love—always.

16 June

It's a tough week, with the weather and rough training conspiring to make it so. But it's Saturday tomorrow, and after inspection, a little rest will be forthcoming.

Navy rumors are referred to as "scuttlebutt," but ours are "latrine" rumors—usually originating in the latrine. Well, the latest is that our whole regiment (radio men, clerks, cooks, messengers, motor mechanics, etc.) will be shipped to a camp in New York known as Pine Camp* (sounds like a summer resort) by the end of the month. Of course I've learned to pay no attention to latrine rumors but like to give you an idea of what we think and talk about in idle moments.

Another rumor—and they sure float around—is that our Bn. of 4 companies—until now 2 for clerks, and 2 for cooks—will be made up of 4 companies of clerks and the cooks shipped to Ft. Benning.

Still another rumor is that the Marines gave this camp up a couple of years ago because weather conditions were too hot for their training—well, how do you like that, if true, which I doubt.†

Actually, a day under that hot, merciless sun can do more to tear a man down than anything I know. Good physical condition means little to the sun.

Our Bn. has a softball team, but when your ball-playing husband doesn't play after being invited—you know he's had it.

The sun must have really gotten to me. I'm dreaming of 2 weeks of complete rest. Am thinking of a hotel at the seashore—some private beach—with no one around, only you. I can dream, can't I?

Well, here's a new one fresh out of the oven. Just got in from class where I heard that Bn. Headquarters don't think we're active enough though we get a full morning of classroom work. So instead of giving us the usual 10-minute break each hour, as is the custom throughout the Army, they've cut it down to 5 minutes and the 15 minutes "saved" are used in double-timing us around the block 2 or 3 times. In this terrific heat it does things to you. Some sadist sitting in a cool room behind a desk must have thought this dilly up.

Speaking of the 10-minute break, it gets to be a joke around here. An officer will, during a serious discussion on the rifle or other subject, of a sudden look at his watch and say "Take 10." But the guys, who are continually tired and sleepy, feel the rest time is over be-

* Pine Camp (later Fort Drum), New York, located near Watertown, was anything but a summer resort.
† Rumors such as these, most of them without foundation, were commonplace throughout the Army at all times. Veteran GIs soon learned to discount them.

fore it's begun. When they're just beginning to unwind, the officer yells, "Break's over." So now the boys mimic the officers, saying, "Take a 10-minute break's over."

18 June   *Father's Day*

Today, being Father's Day, I hear a lot about it over the radio and naturally it's been getting to me. Your letter helped considerably. That gnawing, homesick feeling grips me every so often. Writing you seems to help me feel better. Dearest, I miss you every minute and all day long my thoughts are homeward.

Just finished chow, and the best I've eaten in the Army—Southern fried chicken that melted in your mouth, and all the trimmings. And to top it off we're planning a trip to the movies 2 P.M. where it might be a little cooler. The theatres have a pretty good blower system. Today I went to Chapel for a change but the heat drove me out.

Heard over the radio Cherbourg Peninsula has been taken and that's good news as it will provide an undisputed channel for supplies and men.*

Later: Took a walk around the lake this evening by myself. It's an area not frequented by G.I.'s and that in itself helped make it more palatable. It was beautiful. The air was cooled down and being completely alone was a great feeling. Guess who was uppermost in my thoughts!

19 June

Today a very long and wonderful letter—and its effect could be classified as a morale builder for a very low and lonesome soldier.

---

* The port of Cherbourg was not actually captured until 26 June 1944. Its capture, following extensive repair work, gave the Allies an invasion port and ended dependence upon the artificial breakwaters and docks that had been installed at Omaha Beach, and had been all but demolished by storms on 19–21 June. Another such artificial "seaport," Gold Beach, used by the British, was much less severely damaged by the storms.

Now this soldier's morale is not so low; he's still lonesome, but feels better.

Again on the range today with the machine gun, shooting at a mechanical plane (no one in it) controlled by radio. It's amazing how it worked.

The heat continues—today we walked only 2 miles in it and rode the rest of the way by truck.

Now 6 weeks—and 4 days left to finish training, and believe me, we're all counting the days. Heard the 9-mile speed march will be eliminated and you know no one is shedding tears over that. It was tough enough doing 5. I'm sure the decision was reached because of the intense heat. The first platoon made it last week (9 miles) and only half were able to finish. Others dropped along the way from exhaustion and heat prostration.

You know, Honey, it has always been a secret desire of mine to study medicine some day, and I feel I could make out well in it. This might surprise you but I'm writing for college catalogs now. I'm crazy—there go the bonds!

Your letters are my mainstay. I haven't realized their significance until recently—for without question they do more to keep me going than anything else. Goodnight, my family.

23–25 June

I'm writing in the field where we've just finished our C rations, and resting awhile. Earlier we fired rifles as we would in actual combat—part of a 12-man squad—each doing his job under simulated battle conditions. When the leader signals we fire at an imaginary enemy line 200 yards away. Later today we'll do it again, only this time with moving targets.

Your 8-page letter came just at the right moment and was just what the doctor ordered. David's hide-and-seek game with Neil was a joy to hear. I want so to see and hold him.

The 1st Platoon graduated Saturday—and pre–Pearl fathers are the only ones receiving shipping orders. They get a 14-day furlough—I hope it works that way with us. Also, they don't return, but head for Ft. Meade to be classified again, then sent to a permanent location.

We start our 12th week Monday—and I hear it's OK, mostly classroom work. The next two weeks aren't bad either. We go directly to offices throughout the camp getting practical experience. Then 2 weeks of bivouac and the last week, cleaning up, readying for shipment.

If a furlough is granted I'll want a solid rest, without visiting or entertaining. What visiting I'll do will be over the phone, and I know you'll understand.

Re: Ft. Meade. After reading this you might get the idea that being sent there means being shipped. Not now. Before, yes. Meade is now a reclassification center where they analyze each soldier's service record, and ship men where needed—age, family status are all evaluated. The single rifleman will probably go; the clerk, father, probably won't. All my love to my little family.

26 June

I'm finding that the 20 odd minutes right after lunch can be about the most relaxing throughout the day. And so it was today when I got your letter which I zealously took to my hut, sprawled out on the bed, and with strains of light, soothing music, read your most satisfying letter. As a result, my spirits are high and I feel generally fine.

We're getting mimeograph stencils to type now—will continue later.

Back again. I truly enjoyed your letter—and reread it over and over. That's funny about the hornets nesting in the mailbox. Well, I've been wanting to get rid of that shabby looking mailbox anyway.

I didn't tell you about our Corporal, did I? He's an interesting guy, rather young and was going to college when he entered the service 15 months ago. He has an engaging gift of gab, but throughout the platoon he isn't too well liked—probably because he spouts off a little too much at times, and doesn't seem to use his head sometimes. But my reaction is that he's a soldier's soldier, a normal human being who reacts like any other man under stress, who's worn out by a speed march, who can only take so much exercise, and who can be knocked out by the sun, too. Yet he has plenty of guts. On the other hand, some of these young, stupid non-coms don't seem to be affected by all this, or at least hide it so they can be regarded as supermen. Personally, I like the Corporal for his simple, honest qualities and I think he has the potential of a first-rate officer.

The Colonel just walked through. Several times a day one of the "brass" walks in appearing from nowhere. He makes the rounds, checking up chiefly on the instructors. It puts pressure on them, and for their sake every soldier is at his best. In fact, when we spot them coming we call out "BRASS"—the signal for everyone to be on his toes.

Are you following the Republican Convention on the air? I bet one of the fellows in my hut that Dewey would not be nominated.* A pint of ice-cream, too! I hope Willkie gets it again. I don't consider Dewey presidential timber. Even if he gets the nomination I don't think he'd accept it, knowing too well his slim chance with Roosevelt running, and his defeat would probably void his future chances. He'll probably be a sure bet for 1948 if he lets it go this time. That is, to run. Getting elected is another story.

How are you making out on groceries? Any shortages at home? If by chance you have any extra ration stamps, send them down. I'd like to buy a few staples to take along on bivouac. I hear you're always hungry out there. Not many stamps, though. Don't rob yourself. Also, if you get a chance, mail me the extra cannister set which will keep edibles safe from ants and bugs, and will provide for quite a few of us.

28 June

It's early in the morning and a dozen boys of the first platoon, who graduated Saturday, left for home. You can't realize what we

---

* Governor Thomas E. Dewey was nominated for President by the Republican Party in 1944; his running mate was John W. Bricker of Illinois.

were feeling, watching them leave for the train, happy as kids, in direct contrast to the gloom of those watching.

Well, our day is coming. After I go to the next camp I'd be eligible for a furlough in addition to the "delay on route" but I'm still hoping things will be over by then.

Eighteen-year-olds are sent to Alabama (Camp Rucker), but I think pre–Pearl Harbor fathers are sent to Camp Meade, reclassified, then sent wherever they're needed.*

If I'm sent to Meade, wouldn't it be great if I were stationed there. Everything in the Army seems to be HOPE and LUCK. One of our group whose eyesight is not up to par, but otherwise as good as the best of us, was classified "Class C" and permanently assigned here. He's one of the lucky ones as he lives a couple of hundred miles from here, and his wife often visits.

Went to the movies last night and fought like the devil to keep awake. I had to wake up the fellow I was with.

Another 5-miler tonight, but things are tapering off somewhat. One more 5-miler (speed march), one 9-miler, crawling through the infiltration course under gun fire, and throwing hand grenades.

I'm learning why some sergeants and corporals are so viciously unreasonable. Usually, when a platoon completes its basic, some 18-years-olds are kept in the camp for "cadre"—meaning, assigned to aid in field training, and in a month or so are promoted to Corporal if they make good. (They all "make good" whether they do or not). I heard two of these kids talking last night—not to me—but within earshot.

One said, "If they keep me on cadre here, I'm going to take it out on those new guys, I'll make their life miserable."

The other says, "Yeah, when we came in they treated us like hell and I'm going to give them the same."

The first one: "You're goddamn right. If these new trainees weren't here, we wouldn't have to be here—and they're going to suffer."

"Same here. Boy, am I going to make them bastards suffer."

Now you see the mentality you're up against in the Army. Of

---

* The armed services were under considerable pressure from Congress and the press not to use eighteen-year-olds as replacements overseas without a year's training. As the needs of the invasion increased, however, it proved difficult to adhere to this policy.

course, a large percentage are OK but in the meantime 60 new homesick trainees are put through Hell when they need help most. These young idiots soon realize you can't get very far that way, but they keep trying.

Remember about the men from my platoon who tried for OCS, and how I felt what you had to buck against wasn't worth it all? Well, most of the applications were OK'd by the C.O. very highly, but by the time they went through Regimental Headquarters none were accepted. The boys really felt let down.

We bivouac tonight at the end of our speed march. By that time we're soaked to the skin; then we set up our tents and go to sleep in our wet clothes. It's pure misery sleeping that way. However, this time I packed an extra fatigue uniform in my field pack.

30 June

I'm happy to say that we went through the bayonet-assault course this morning for the last time. It wouldn't be so bad, but they get us up at 4:30 and boy, could I use that extra hour's sleep. Reading the *Record* the other day I was amused to read: "Tom Dewey made a very fine speech, and to think he only slept 6 hours the night before." It would be the height of luxury if we got 6 hours sleep.

One way I try to keep my mind stable around here is to think of home and make plans for the future. Perhaps we can work together on this. How about making a landscape plan of the back lawn— where you want flower beds, trees transplanted, etc. Maybe the Home magazines could give you a few ideas—then send them to me. It would be very diverting for me. Perhaps I might add to it, or subtract. It sure gives me a lift just to think about it.

3 July

Monday, and the start of another week.

Have I ever told you how it feels getting up at 4 A.M. to go on some scheduled detail? This morning was typical, and I think interesting. We went on the bayonet obstacle course two miles from our area. Well, we're awakened at 4, have breakfast, and head back to our hut to get prepared. It's pitch-black outside, and this morning a steady downpour, but rain or hail or storm never stops an army on a scheduled mission.

There's not a word among the men as they're getting ready. They're still sleepy and have their hands full getting into the proper regalia (light field pack, raincoats), filling canteens, etc. There's grim silence—as often pictured in the movies right before a group heads into battle—waiting for the zero hour. The total darkness helps to produce that effect.

Then, 5:30 we're on our way—marching through the dark. I can't quite describe how it feels—our minds are hazy and unclear—and you almost imagine you're in Italy or somewhere heading for the front. As light begins to appear we start snapping back to reality. Despite the raincoats we're drenched, but by this time it doesn't matter. We march along like zombies—and the strange, weird thing is that regardless of the obstacles we march right through them. This morning we pushed through puddles up to our ankles as if it were clean, dry land.

Not many latrine rumors lately but I'll keep you informed. It seems the bunch of us eat, talk, sleep "delay on route" time. We're taking it for granted that we'll be shipped out—basing it on the many new boys pouring in, and the fact that everyone under 35 not in Class C is being shipped out.

The general feeling around here is that the boys want the furlough, and want to get out of this place come what may.

I received the ration points and will make good use of them over the weekend—also the package from Gimbels. It was just like a grab-bag—one box cookies, one of crackers, a glass jar of chicken, one of turkey, a can of sardines, jar of peanut candy, stuffed olives. Thanks very much, Sweetie.

4 July

If it weren't for the radio, I'd never know it was the Fourth of July. I'm bleary-eyed after guard duty last night but it's a comparatively short day, finishing up at 4:45 P.M.

Everything we do around here requires a different uniform. Checked the schedule and found we change our uniform 5 times Thurs. Not 5 different uniforms, but on and off 5 times. The schedule informs us what to wear and we dress accordingly.

I learned I'll be getting credit for my experience on the mimeograph. The Army has a complicated filing system. It works this way: trained clerk-typists are rated 405, in addition if you can mimeograph you're rated 408. That means if a call for a mimeograph operator comes from Podunk, they may pick me! However, Ft. Meade might need one, too, so be patient. It can work either way—or might not have the least effect whatsoever.

After coming in from guard duty last night we opened up the jar of chicken. We planned it before supper—each bringing back a roll—and the five of us had a good-sized sandwich which was delicious. Another evening, another snack.

After supper: well, well, an unexpected treat in the form of a letter you wrote Sunday. Good girl, or shall I say, good driver. I see you're getting confidence behind the wheel. Great.

It's not quite as you think, Hon. I couldn't sleep till noon now even if I wanted to. However, if I can get 8 or 9 hours for a few days I'll be back to normal. Even more important, I'm dreaming of falling asleep with my arms around you.

Just returned from the movies—*Marine Raiders*. It gives me a pain in the neck how they glamorize these officers, when it's the G.I. Joe who deserves the glorification.

New fellows are moving into the platoon and it reminds me of my first day 13 weeks ago (to the day). My sympathy goes to these guys.

6 July

Dearest, I want to correct one thing before you build your hopes up too high. Only when I finish training here and get an official "delay on route"—only then can you figure me due home—*not until then*. You already speak of my coming a certain time; I wish I were that confident. Let's just hope I'll be home around the 10th of August, and not figure too heavily on it—OK?

Work now involves mimeographing Special Orders—involving shipment of troops after training. From this camp the boys, in most cases, are shipped to Ft. Meade or Ft. Ord—and I need not hide the fact that the latter is for the So. Pacific theatre.

Today we witnessed an orientation film entitled *The Negro Soldier*. I enjoyed every part of it—there's no doubt such a film is a must. You can readily hear a Negro say, "If we're fighting for democracy, why don't we begin at home." You and I know he's right, but it's damned hard to convince an ignorant southern soldier, or for that matter—northern soldier—or worse yet, supposedly intelligent ones, too. A film like this should enlighten a few.

Guess it's mental telepathy—as we both listened to Phil Baker Sunday night we were thinking of each other. Miss you, Sweetheart, and can't wait till I see you.

10 July

I can't tell you how thrilled I was with our phone call last night. It was wonderful to be able to speak to you, and you'll never know how much the sound of your voice touched me. I might try again before the week is out.

Spent the weekend in St. Augustine after all. The town is truly picturesque, and the beach—where I spent a lot of time—is beautiful. The Army provides for beds and bathing suits, making it a fairly economical holiday. We (Jim and another soldier) hitched in and out and we had good luck. Sat. night we were guests of a friend of Jim's. Sunday, we swam and took a long boat ride.

When I got back—there it was, your letter, waiting for me—and the perfect finish to a nice holiday. Thank you, Dearest, for coming through.

We haven't seen each other for 3 months, but it seems so much longer. But I guess we shouldn't complain too hard. Last night I was speaking to a Sgt. from Darby, Pa. He's been in the Army 3 years and just returned from Italy. In all that time he was only granted one furlough—when he returned from overseas. His wife is pregnant now. (Maybe the furlough wasn't so good after all!)

It's evening now, with two of your letters before me. I had to hold back the tears when you related Neil's remark about how much he missed me. I was happy he took it so well, and that is some solace.

About our grading—getting A's means nothing. When the course ends—regardless of grades—we're classified 405—expert typist-clerks. "A" or "E" doesn't even enter into it. But for those who get bolos—flunk—it's really bad. It means one of two things—repeating the course which is highly improbable or being transferred to a rifle or heavy weapons outfit—God forbid!

11 July

Retired earlier than usual last night as it was so cool and I slept well. In our hut of 5 men, we have 5 different personalities, and consequently 5 different bedtimes. Three of us, around 30 (age), and a little more thoughtful of the value of sleep, try to hit the bed at a reasonable hour. Even at that, one of us gets in late frequently— and one of the three is very noisy and wakes us up. Then after we get to sleep again, the young boys come in. One in particular has no regard for anyone, and again we're awake.

I do notice now that training is not so vigorous, I sleep sounder and don't wake as easily. You can't be too hard on these kids since life is so unnatural under these conditions.

The Post Commander of the permanent camp has been replaced. We don't know why—possibly transferred. I'm under the jurisdiction of the Infantry Replacement Training Center (IRTC), in itself a training school located on the Post but running independently, with its own Commander.

It all might be compared to a large market—the Post, in this case. And a "concession," which is the IRTC. The concession has its own boss and rules, but to a certain point is regulated by the rules of the "market."

Speaking of Colonels, Majors, Captains—brass in general—they are, in many cases, going to have a rude awakening after the war. They're treated like gods by the enlisted men, through enforcement. "Yes, sir," "No, sir"—saluted under compulsion. One word from their "godly" mouths is law, regardless of reason or logic. Many are kids who got in at the right time and are beginning to think they're "somebody." But in civilian life these same kids are not going to be able to understand that when they say something, why every civilian in hearing distance doesn't double-time to listen. Our C.O. is an example of what I call a real officer. One who says little or nothing, always trying in his quiet way to make things more comfortable for his men. Of course, the set-up of the Army is such that strong discipline is an integral part of it, but it takes a real man not to take advantage of the situation.

Well, here it is evening, and a pleasant surprise, a letter from my Sweet One. I got one last night and didn't expect one today.

12 July

Twenty-four more days and the course will be over. I count every day, and every day seems to be longer than the one before.

Another new ruling—some new goodie every day. Now we get up an hour earlier and finish our day one hour earlier. What next? But we can take it, I guess. All the more reason I'll relish some rest on my furlough.

Did I ever tell you about Special Orders, and how they work? Let's say that Washington, D.C., decides they want 100 men—50 riflemen, 25 laborers, 15 cooks and 10 clerks sent to Fort Dix. They telegraph our camp which houses an elaborate filing system. They push a number, 610—that's the Army file # for riflemen—and also 50 which gives them the first 50 riflemen, and so on down to #40 (clerk file #) and get the first 10 clerks available.

The names, rank, serial number, Company and file number of occupation are listed in this general order with instructions as to what camp they're being transferred to, and dates, etc. My special order will be somewhat different. The Washington telegram will probably read—send 200 trainees who have just completed basic to Fort Meade. And at Meade the above procedure would follow after I returned from the furlough.

Right now I'm at my practical work office where I'll be mimeographing General Orders, as 2700 men are to be shipped. Have a feeling that orders for our 2nd platoon will be included—they're in their 17th week—graduating in 3 days.

Later.—As I thought, the special orders came down from the 2nd platoon and they're due to ship Tuesday, 3 days after graduation. I hope I'm that lucky.

When I see my name on such an order and am safely ensconced on the train, I'll feel like a new man. Until then, I'm just anticipating.

It's cool and pleasant with rain each day. Yesterday while reading the Philadelphia *Record* I saw you had 97-degree heat, and could hardly believe it.

13 July

Two beautiful letters today, especially long and newsy. By all means continue to talk from your heart, and don't apologize for anything you write. I appreciate your talking that way—never get the feeling you're complaining.

Am using the typewriter now but from here on you'll be getting penned letters from bivouac. About our phone call, your feelings were exactly like mine, but I actually did break down after I spoke to you. Luckily, it was dark and I was the only one around. (The game-room lights go out after 11 P.M. but you can sit up there in the dark.)

The little lazy one is quite a guy, isn't he? Can't wait to see him. The big lazy one isn't so bad either—is he!

I thought I partly understood Neil's and your problem, but after your explanation I can see I didn't really understand it at all. Well, hold on and we'll hope to improve conditions when we get home.

We hear about your heat and drought and I feel very badly about it. Fortunately, we continue to have cool weather and a daily rain.

By the time you get this letter I'll be on bivouac and well started on week #15. Every day is a milestone—and I'm getting anxious.

Went to the Camp Commissary today and was surprised to see the large market they have—just about everything. Sorry we just learned of it or we could have made good use of it during our cycle.

Do want to get to bed now as tomorrow will be rough. Goodnight, Sweetheart.

15 July

It is now Saturday evening. Thought I'd go to the Service Club and write you but instead, decided to go out on the lawn and sit on the grass and write till it gets dark.

Miss you tonight even more than usual. On this spacious lawn surrounding the Service Club, there are scores of soldiers with their wives or girls and that always makes things a little harder.

Tried to catch up a little on sleep, but it's not easy—what with the noise and so many things to be done (washing clothes, etc.). We're getting prepared for our bivouac trek. We carry a heavy pack consisting of a tent, accessories that go with it, blanket, raincoat, mess equipment, helmet, shoes, rations. It weighs 55 pounds besides a 10-lb. rifle. We start our 18-mile hike Monday 3 A.M.— breakfast at 2 A.M. Well, after this it will be practically over, and if that's the case—bring it on.

Thought I'd tell you something of the infiltration course while it's fresh in my memory. Yesterday we went through it twice. I wasn't the least bit concerned until a day or so before, when the Corporal (in trying to assure us everything was OK) kept telling us to be sure and keep our behinds down, and if we bumped into anybody who was hurt or petrified (literally) from fright, don't stop—and if a bullet "ricocheted" (hit something and bounced back) on us, it would only burn and couldn't hurt us, etc. Then I became somewhat nervous. Our new Lt., in an effort to raise our spirits, told us they used to shoot bullets 18 inches off the ground, but too many men were being killed, so they raised it to 19 inches. Kidding, of course. But now that it's over I can tell you that occasionally some soldier does get killed.

Well, we were finally led to the slaughterhouse and given the signal to "go over the top." To say I crawled, is putting it mildly. I practically dug a hole and crawled along like a mole. It finally got to the point where I was so fagged out that I forgot all about the bullets whizzing overhead—and just concentrated on pushing on to the end. It wasn't just plain "crawling." We had to maneuver through a tangle of barbed wire and climb over logs. I was soaked with sweat and covered with sand, which was everywhere, and the only way I could get out of there was to complete the course, for if you stand, it would be for the last time. So, exhausted or not, you've got to inch on. Well, I'm writing this letter so you know I finally made it, but it took a few hours to recoup from the ordeal. It was one of the toughest grinds we were ever put through.

To make the "run" more realistic they kept blowing off dynamite charges that just about deafened you and shook the ground like the rumblings of an earthquake. The main effect was to unnerve you, but I realized that keeping my wits was the essential thing, and, believe me, I worked at it mighty hard.

At night it was easier physically, but harder on the nerves, chiefly because in my lane (there were 10) was a row of dynamite charges and boy, when they went off, every few seconds, it was murderous.

In a grim sense it was thrilling, too, because they use tracer bullets which leave a trail of smoke and fire, and at night, skimming overhead, it was a fascinating sight. I believe if it weren't for those hellish dynamite charges, I might have lain out there a bit just watching the bullets.

We have a new Lieutenant—and in the day or so we've had him he's turning out to be a gem. He's young, looks 10 years older, comes from Alabama, and in a thick southern drawl, keeps telling us he's amazed at how good we are. He says when he was at West

Point (he never saw the place) they didn't march that good, and that while he's been a soldier for 12 years (he's 25—guess he always looked older) ever since the first time they called "Attention" and the rifle "was taller than me" he couldn't do as well. He's really a buffoon in the best sense of the word, keeps telling us to work with him, meaning, "Put on a good show when the higher brass is around" and we'll have nothing to worry about.

He came up the hard way. Evidently enlisted as a kid and looked old enough to get away with it, and was a private for 2 years. He says he enlisted because the "Star-Spangled Banner" got him. He's a good Joe and gives us all a lift.

They tell us now that we've been through infiltration we're "real soldiers" and ready for combat. How encouraging can they get! Going through infiltration is important to them and is really the first obstacle where they call your name from the roster as you start the course—I guess to check if you're still alive after it—after which it's entered in the Service Record.

Received one of your sweet letters at lunch today in which you tell me that David can drink out of a glass now. I liked that very much. Gee! that guy Neil and his Mother and the bee stings!! Hope his foot is OK now.

I hope you've gotten rain by now. It's still pleasant here but missed rain today for the first time in awhile.

It's getting late, Dearest. I'm looking for a nice letter tomorrow—Sunday—to bolster my 18-mile hike.

God bless you all.

P.S. Wanted to phone you tonight but the lines are broken down and no calls can be made outside the camp.

16 July

It's Sunday today and your letter was particularly appreciated. The day has been one of preparation for the big event—our two-week "vacation" trip they call bivouac.

Very glad the drought was broken and I hope you get plenty of rain. I'm sure those flowers and bushes are pretty thirsty.

About Neil and the piano—use a little psychology and be sure he wants to make the start. I hate to push a youngster into something and then find it a waste of time and patience, as happens in so many families. So glad he shows an interest and maybe it'll work out. As to sending me anything while on bivouac, I'll let you know. I have 5 cans of sardines and one of Spam. We can't accept anything except for immediate consumption, unless jarred or canned, as the wild pigs out here will tear the camp apart while we're away to get some food if they smell it. I'll wait a day or two before writing you, concerning this.

Well, I got a little extra sleep last night but still need more to catch up—but with all the noise around tonight, it's probably wishful thinking.

Until later, with all my love.

19 July   *On Bivouac*

Yesterday, in the midst of my letter to you—and in the dark, too, some of the officers staged an "attack" and we immediately had to get into "battle formation." Thus the sudden ending, but I still wanted to get it off so you'd know all was okay with me.

Had a few minutes to start another letter yesterday, handwritten, and will copy it word for word—even if some of it is repeated. First of all I received a beautiful letter from you—one of the best ever. I'll say more about it later.

Yesterday was truly tough. We arose 1 A.M. Monday and while my body took the hike very well—my feet took a beating. We marched on a quickly made macadam road with lots of jagged points and stones bulging up above the surface—over 18 miles of it. The nails of your shoes are bound to come in contact with these protrusions—thus pushing them into the inner part of the shoes. Consequently, my heels were cut all over—not seriously—but enough to be painful. In spite of this I was surprised I took the march so well.

With no rest or refreshment, we were immediately put to work digging slit trenches—2 feet by 2 feet by 6 feet—and then setting out tents—and finally lunch. Immediately after we ate, the clerk-school instructor took over by ordering another slit trench dug—and a tremendous foxhole beside it for our field desk for clerical work in the hole—with various levels for sitting and placing our equipment. Its size—6 x 6 x 6.

Now that the office is dug, we're required to sit here for hours at a time, not permitted out—this is supposed to be war. Of course, we have a long and tedious problem to keep us busy, but we don't believe in rushing it—we have important letters to write—such as this one. Everything we do is as we'd do it on a battlefield. We're not permitted to congregate with more than one person, and must stay 5 yards away from anyone else—doing no, or very little, talking at all times. Fortunately, our instructor is swell and loosens up considerably. But, he, too, is checked a hundred times daily, it seems, and has to be careful. Some fun, eh?

I don't like all this and can't wait till it's over. It could be much better, as we have a beautiful lake close by and a fine campsite—but the discipline is harsh and rigid.

Don't bother sending me anything, unless you can put your hands on a set of foot pads—full shoe size—as they may come in handy.

Dearest, we're living out of a barracks bag now, and it's terribly hard to keep things right. Our filthy, dirty clothes and underwear are crushed in with our few clean clothes. Toothbrush and extra pair of shoes are together in the same bag—and if I want to write you a letter, I've got to dig down into the bottom of the bag to get some stationery. I mention all this as I just realized I left 2 of your letters at the camping site.

You must know how consoling it is to know you will be thinking of me out here, and I'll try to write as much as I can. I don't know what they've cooked up for us, but I do know a lot of it is surprises—such as the "attack" last night—and this morning—a tear-gas bomb hurled at us and we had to get those gas masks on in a hurry. Tonight, another problem that will keep us going till midnight. C'est la guerre!

We'll swim awhile this afternoon, I'm glad to say—but we tote our rifles and gas masks to the lake's edge. We're eating exceptionally well, and will only get C rations two days.

Now that Neil is visiting Rose for a week, how does it feel without your little big man around?

It's gotten rather hot down here—too hot yesterday, but we had a refreshing shower last night and it cooled off—but today's another scorcher.

20 July

Only glanced quickly at your letter last night as we had to get right back to duty—where we simulated the execution of an order. We left the present area for one farther up to the "front," with our field desks and typewriters, dug another foxhole and set up a field office about 2 miles from here. We waited for darkness since that's what the problem called for. There was no moon, took our field desks to a designated point close to our present foxholes, left them there, then walked about two miles through the woods. If I'd been alone, would have gotten lost. We dug no more holes, but returned to our present area and lugged our desks back to our holes. Even had trouble walking the 50 yards to find the holes. Well, after a few more details, we got to bed around 11:30—very very tired.

I see that you miss Neil already, but as I said before, it will do you both good. About his returning, I was thinking: when I come home (I'm taking it for granted) the Army takes me as far as Washington, and I'll leave my barracks bag at Rose's. If Neil wants to return with me, fine; otherwise—after the furlough we could drive down to Washington together, and then over to Fort Meade. If I found I could get out each day, I'd keep the car at Meade. Otherwise you could drive over daily. How does that sound? If it sounds too good I'll probably get orders to ship to another camp. That's the Army way.

Yes, I've followed [Drew] Pearson's predictions and columns, and always like his logic and honest reporting. Willkie would be a swell running mate for Roosevelt, but that just can't work in politics.*

---

* Wendell L. Willkie, the Republican Presidential nominee in 1940, had taken an increasingly "liberal" position on domestic and foreign policies, and in 1942 had traveled around the world as President Roosevelt's special envoy. His 1943 book, One

Both Willkie and Henry Wallace talk straight and in simple language to the public but that doesn't jibe with politicians who are expert at "double-talk" and "trimming"—thus, it's not a question that the nation thinks they're good men, but whether they'll play ball with the political machine. If they felt they stood a chance of winning without Roosevelt, they'd get rid of him, too. Politics, generally, is a rotten game and rarely does the best man get in. And the public is always the loser. I believe Wallace would make a fine President—and appears more liberal and public-minded than Roosevelt.

Today we eat rations again. Remember that story I told you some time ago about the ration can buried by a soldier and the harsh consequences handed out to two companies? Well, now they check every can—by roll call—to insure their proper disposal.

Tomorrow will be our last working day as clerks. Saturday we fill up all foxholes, walk 3 miles to another lake—set up tents—dig more foxholes, and Monday we start 5 days of soldiering. Sunday will not be tactical—we do what we please, as we please, within bivouac area, of course.

Our platoon is the only one here this week: the cooks are on practical work in other areas. It makes things a little better for us. However, they'll be back next week.

Again our platoon seems to be breaking precedent. Each day heavy brass comes out for inspection, and each day we get a "Superior Rating." The Battalion has never received such a rating, but we've come through 3 out of 3 times. Our Lt. is simply crazy about it all. He says, "Ah've been in the Ahmy a long, long time and never did I see a platoon to compare with ours." Well, in the Army you try to get a kick out of whatever comes along—and while I don't go for this rating bit, I'll admit it does feel good.

Two men sleep in a tent and pair off together throughout the whole period—even do our clerk problems together in the foxhole. The boy I bunk with, Marty, is a fine guy and comes from Ft. Mon-

---

World, was strongly anti-isolationist. Apparently Roosevelt had made some overtures to Willkie about accepting the Democratic Vice-Presidential nomination for 1944, but nothing came of it. To strengthen the Democratic ticket Roosevelt jettisoned Vice-President Henry A. Wallace, who was much disliked by party conservatives, and Senator Harry S Truman was nominated in his stead.

mouth, New Jersey. He's 31, too, and has a 5-year-old daughter, and very much a family man. We have a lot in common and he makes the time spent here so much more pleasant. He, too, counts the days and tells his wife to be looking for him soon. We take lots for granted, don't we?

The Philadelphia *Record* arrives each day and it's a great source of relaxation. I look forward to it, and will want it to follow me wherever I'm stationed.

Last night I received your letter and devoured every word. Reading your letters, I often find myself checking on the number of the sheet, and if I'm on the 2nd or 3rd page of, say, a 6-page letter, I relax and enjoy it more, knowing there's still a good bit to come!

After 5 days out here now, I must admit I don't mind it nearly as much as I did the first couple of days. Although we ate rations yesterday, the meals have been superior—good in any restaurant. And while I can't sleep too well on the ground, I find I'm getting better rest than expected. Have run into only one mosquito, but many flea-like insects that buzz around but don't seem to bite.

A funny thing happened Tuesday night. I was slated for guard duty at 2 A.M.—but the Corporal of the guard didn't waken me. Marty's guard duty was from 12:30 to 2 A.M. When he was wakened for his turn, I woke, too, but knowing I was to follow him, I settled back to sleep. About two hours later he walks into the tent and wakens me to ask, "Hey, Keith, I walked my hour and a half, didn't I?" I was still half-groggy and in a fog and said I didn't know. So he continues on his march. About an hour later he comes in again and says, "What happened to the Corporal? What's going on? The cooks are getting up now."

Finally, at 5:40 A.M. the Corporal shows up and tells Marty he's through. Marty was sore and complained about being left out for five continuous hours. The Corporal then informed him that instead of 12:30 when he was to have been awakened, he was actually called at 3 A.M., and only had 2 hours and 40 minutes of duty—and did he mind "terribly much" putting in the extra time as he, the Corporal, hated to wake a new relief for only 40 minutes of duty? Having a decent guy for a Corporal—no complaints were registered—especially from me!

One thing we all miss is that little extra something to eat around

Guard duty, Camp Blanding

9 or 10 P.M. at the PX. Last night, however, the Lt. let up a bit and the packages came through, and I did manage to get something.

Last night it started to pour during chow—but we just sat there eating as though the sun were shining. Today our fatigues are wet and foul-smelling. Where is my other pair? It's just as wet and stinking. Hope to get time to wash them Sunday. Goodnight, my Love.

21 July

Today another letter and it was the one with the pictures, too. Just can't keep my eyes off them. That little doll baby seems to be oozing with personality. He fills me up each time I look at him.—I get this awful urge to want to be home and start working on the house—just the thought of it lifts me out temporarily from all this.

Tonight I'll be alone. Marty and 12 others had appointments at the dental clinic. That's the only way you can get off bivouac, into camp. They stay the night—see the dentist 8 A.M., then back here again.

22 July

The rain is still coming down hard and I'm in my tent awaiting the order to move on to another area late today. First week is over and I've had enough—but who has a choice. At least we're at a point where we can almost count the days on our fingers.

This afternoon I'm feeling one of my low days and the teeming rain doesn't help. Despite the weather we've been filling up foxholes and cleaning the typewriters and field desks—and I'm just plain exhausted. Had an early morning guard stint and that didn't help.

Marty should be back anytime now. He planned on bringing some candy and I'm aching for it. Just looked at that little sweet one again (picture) and he gives me the biggest lift. It's hard to wait the days out till I see him.

We live in little pup tents—ideal to put up in the back yard for the kids where they can play even when it rains.

Quite often the Lts. throw a tear-gas bomb in the middle of a group to give us practise in putting on our gas masks, which as I said before, must be with us at all times. Last night one bounced within two feet from my tent. I jumped right out and made it OK. However, some of the boys were fast asleep and rudely awakened. This sort of thing isn't too smart but we have two kids for Lts. who don't know any better.

24 July

Don't know how far I'll get with this letter as we're away from the bivouac area, supposed to be having artillery fire over our heads.—Yesterday, Sunday, just as I sat down to write you, I was put on KP in the afternoon. I wasn't due, but one of the boys wanted to go to church and I was glad to relieve him.

Sat. night we moved to this new area and the only thing in its favor is the lake which is simply wonderful, clear water, and clear sandy bottom.

Today wasn't bad. All about rifle formations approaching the enemy. This section of Florida, they say, is very much like the wilds of Guadalcanal, and after today's experience I must agree. We pushed through swamps, dense brush, mud and sand and wilds—the purpose—to get an area closely simulating the South Pacific. And they sure did.

25 July

Last night I saw a spectacle that will be hard to forget—the working of an Infantry Battalion on defense. They shot tracer bullets (impressive and noisy), and demonstrated in action, cannons, rifles, machine guns and mortars—separately—then simultaneously. After witnessing that display it's not hard to understand why our boys are doing so well.

Again this morning we watched an Infantry Battalion on the offense—and boy! when you see those riflemen out there in the midst of fire, you begin to feel mighty good about being transferred to the Clerk School. A rifleman has a very important and dangerous job, and believe me, every infantryman in battle is a real hero.

Next day—26 July.—I dug a foxhole 2 x 3½ x 6 feet deep in the sweltering sun—and fast—with gas attacks all afternoon; and after all that, had to fill it up again.

Only 3 more days out here and you know I'm not sorry. Seem to be having a hell of a time sleeping on this ground. I have yet to get the first good night of rest.

Again today worked on "rifle squads in action" and another foxhole dug, another simulated attack, and again, filling it up. Then a swim—ah, a cool refreshing swim. We've been lucky swimming almost every day and it gives me a chance to wash up.

They got us doing 101 things. We tackle a 4-hour "problem" to-night—starting at 8 P.M. Goodnight, Sweetheart.

30 July

It was so good to hear you last night. The day is getting closer, isn't it. It could be 8 or 9 days, maybe sometime next week.

You can see by the letterhead that I'm in a hotel in Jacksonville. I slept well, rested during the day, showered, and all in all didn't regret the money I spent. I hitchhiked to and fro and was lucky. The M.P. car picked me up going in—and a Colonel drove me back.

Went to the movies last night. Saw *Gaslight*, Charles Boyer and Ingrid Bergman—superb acting, but terribly depressing. Do not see it under any conditions.

Everything is relative; it feels so good to be back in the Company area instead of out on bivouac. Thank God it is behind us. I want you to know how much your letters meant to me. They were so newsy and inspiring, and I fully realize the effort it is for you to write so lengthily. Please know, as you're writing, that they're so appreciated.

I don't think I wrote you about our homeward trek, back from bivouac. We rose at 1:45 A.M. and started walking at 3:30, reaching camp 6:45. Two bands were out to welcome us—and boy—when the music played you wouldn't have believed we came off an 11-miler, heavily ladened. The boys marched beautifully. Our Commanding Officer told us he was very "proud" of us for the fine showing—and again, our Lieutenant told us, without exception, he's never seen a better platoon than ours in the Army. The boys eat it up as we know we're good! If ever I felt a chauvinistic twinge it was then. But, really, all that mattered to me was the symbolism of the music—the finish of a long, grueling training period.

The lights are going out now, Dearest, so, until tomorrow, all my love to you and the kiddies.

2 August

Good news today. I'm on order to ship out of here next Tuesday, August 8 at 8:30 A.M., as of this writing. Jim J. at "classification" sneaked a pre-view. Tomorrow morning when I get it to mimeograph, I'll have all the facts.

Am to get 13 days, including travel time, but there are a few more details I don't know of yet. My next letter will tell you, I hope.

Received your very thoughtful letter which you wrote Sunday evening after having written the long one in the morning. What it means to me, no one but you can know.

This morning we made our 9-mile speed march, and I actually enjoyed it. Felt fine at the end and could have gone 9 more—I think. Perhaps it's the thought of home and you that gives me vitality!

I've been reading about the PRT strike in Philly, re: the first trial run of eight Negroes being trained as motormen. I hope by now it's settled. The world is full of prejudice, and it doesn't seem that it will ever change. It's very sad, but I'm afraid, true.

I'm thinking about next week when I'll be home! Maybe we could spend 2 or 3 evenings out, at some good hotel, dining and dancing with some friends. It would be nice to see friends that way—and not have to entertain them on my few precious days at home. Perhaps another evening, a show or movie?

Don't mention anything to the family about my coming home, otherwise they'll be planning to entertain me, which I absolutely won't accept. We'll drop in on them, with just short notice, and I think it will be best all around. Again, until tomorrow, my Love.

3 August

Well, Sweetheart, I just spoke to you and feel so good. The peculiar feeling I now have is that I can't wait until Tuesday. Until now I've taken the days in stride—but since our conversation, I feel like an impatient kid.

Don't go to any trouble, now. As for food, I have no special desires—just simple meals—and the house will look good no matter how you fix it, so don't waste your energy.

Tomorrow we graduate. Saturday we're having a party paid for by the Company. I imagine Sunday will be the longest day. Monday will be spent finishing and getting ready for the big day!

4 August

I got my diploma today and we had quite a ceremony—band, Generals, Colonels, speeches—the works. But I enjoyed it all even though I knew it was a lot of bunk.

Tonight I'm going to the movies with a hutmate, Mort. I don't think I ever told you much about him. He's married, about 30, spent 2 of the 3 years of his married life in Greenland on a construction job. Soon after returning to the States he was drafted. I didn't take to him in the beginning, but gradually we've developed a strong friendship. At present his wife runs the large oil business he headed when he left.

Later—Saw John Garfield in *They Made Me a Criminal*—so-so.

Sorry to hear of Lee's illness. Dear, when you're in the Army you're always on the go—and it's rough. It's a wonder more boys don't get laid up. Incidentally, if you're not suffering too badly, being in the hospital in the Army is considered a good deal. You get plenty of freedom—permitted throughout the hospital grounds—PX, movies, etc. However, I prefer being well!

We're more anxious than ever to get going now that we're "graduates." It's amusing, but in the last 2 days we've had at least 4 lectures on what AWOL means, and its consequences. It seems that some of the boys have trouble getting back after their first furlough. (Can you blame them!) We were told that 10% would go AWOL—which means away over 24 hours, or overdue in reporting—regardless of excuse—and the consequences are really outrageous. First, a dishonorable discharge, then imprisonment from one to twenty-five years—or even life—Army law even permits death. So you see why I'll never be AWOL!

The 18-year-olders in our platoon are being shipped to Texas—after their "delay on route." Eventually they'll be part of the Army of Occupation.

Incidentally, Dear, never mention to anyone—regardless of whom—things like the above. It may sound so innocent to you but some guy could be looking for just such information.

I presume you'll get this letter Monday—and the next day I'll be on my way! Goodnight, Dearest.

5 August

It's really chaotic today. We began as usual—inspection, and at 9 A.M. a formation, with orders not to leave the area under any conditions. An hour later we're told the Company is to be de-activated by 1:30 P.M. And since then we've been in a frenzied rush and transferred to another Regiment, chiefly to eliminate the specialist trainees—clerks, cooks, auto mechanics, radio men, etc.—and hear this—re-group them as riflemen. That means our camp will not, in the future, train any more specialists—only riflemen. It also means that our increment was the last Clerk outfit to be trained—thank God for that.

This change could be worse—but it seems home (even in the Army) is home, and you sort of miss the old hut. But we'll be here only two more days, and then a real home which will mean more than anything in the world.

Unfortunately, it also means that those clerks and specialists who have not completed their training, will all be made riflemen—and I know that will hurt many—it certainly would have almost killed me.

Again your lovely letter today and you can't begin to realize how much they mean to me. I know I keep repeating myself, but I appreciate them more than words can tell.

Dearest, remember not to say much around of my furlough, since I'd like a quiet time. Okay? I'm a little tired—and also tired of all this war atmosphere too, and looking for some relaxation.

The lights are due out in 2 minutes. Goodnight, Sweetheart.

2. 100th Infantry Division

Fort Bragg, North Carolina– Camp Kilmer, New Jersey

August-October 1944

*F*ollowing completion of his basic infantry training cycle at Camp Blanding, Florida, Pvt. Keith Winston was ordered to report to Fort Meade, Maryland, for reassignment, with a ten-day "delay on route" to visit his family. Fort Meade was only two hours from Philadelphia by railroad, and it was briefly possible for him to return home overnight on a military pass.

On 28 August 1944 he was shipped out of Meade to Fort Bragg, North Carolina, near the city of Fayetteville, where he joined the 100th Infantry Division. Activated in November 1942, at Fort Jackson, South Carolina, under the command of Maj. Gen. Withers A. Burress, of Richmond, Virginia, the "Century Division," as it was called, was made up predominantly of troops from the northeastern United States, Virginia, and the Carolinas. Following basic training in 1943, the division was engaged in advanced combat preparation, but its ranks were several times massively depleted when over-age soldiers were transferred out and other troops were assigned as replacements in divisions being alerted for shipment overseas. In the late fall and winter of 1943, the division participated in winter maneuvers in Tennessee, and was then moved to Fort Bragg. Extensive combat training went on during the winter and spring of 1944. The division lost additional personnel sent as replacements to other units, but in March its ranks were filled by 4,000 men who had been stationed in Army Specialized Training Program units at various colleges and universities during 1943–44. Before the 100th Division received its overseas alert orders in August 1944, there were more losses of personnel, and Keith Winston was among the final group of replacements sent to the division to bring it up to full strength again. The 100th Division consisted of three infantry regiments, the 397th, 398th, and 399th, plus headquarters personnel, Division Artillery, the 373rd, 374th, 375th, and 925th Field Artillery battalions, the 325th Engineer "C" Battalion, and the 325th Medical Battalion.

29 August 1944   *Fort Bragg, N.C.   Tues. night*

This is right after my call to you and I know it isn't fair to try and make myself feel better by burdening you with my troubles and heavy heart—but what is a wife for?!

Already, I'm feeling a little better after having talked to you. I left Meade Monday at 3:30 P.M., on a troop train similar to other troop trains—draggy and slow—arriving at Ft. Bragg Tuesday morning. We hung around all day, then the Division (15,000 men) was separated this afternoon—all into rifle companies, regardless of previous training—typical of Army organization.

The entire Division is scheduled to move out for overseas duty by the end of September, which means, everyone attached to it will go. That's about all the details I know.

Don't know the set-up on passes but I hear in general the camp is very "scrimmy" (bad) on them. I think I could make Philly with a little time to spare on a 3-day pass—and you know I'll do everything in my power to get it. I'll write you daily, as before, and keep you in touch with everything that may develop. *Don't figure too much on a pass, though.*

To tell you something of the camp—it's tremendous, and as someone said, it would take a weekend pass to get out of here. Haven't met any of the fellows I will live with—and may feel better then.

I miss you dreadfully already, and should tell you that the furlough and Fort Meade days spent with you were the happiest days of my life. We must actually pray that this war will end almost immediately so we can get home and have one long furlough for the rest of our lives.

You've been a wonderful "soldier" up till now—and your reaction to this must be taken in the same spirit as you've taken other difficulties. If you continue as you are, it will be an inspiration to me.

I'm not in the frame of mind to write too much now, Sweetheart. Please try to write each day—I look for it more than you'll ever know. I'm very happy that you're home now.

NOTICE OF CHANGE OF ADDRESS
(Sufficient cards will be distributed to each soldier when his mail address is changed to permit
him to send one to each of his regular correspondents and publishers.)

Date _____ AUG 28 1944 _____, 194___

This is to advise you that my correct address now is— 33927725

Pvt _____ Keith Winstn _____ (Army Serial No.)
(Grade)   (Name)

100th INF DIV   FT BRAGG NC

(Company or comparable unit)   (Regiment or comparable unit)

APO No. _____ ℅ Postmaster _____
(Strike out if not applicable)   (Name of post office)

Signature Keith Winston

NOTE.—Newspapers and magazines may need your old address for correct processing.

My old address was _____

W. D., A. G. O. Form No. 204* (1 November 1943)
*This form supersedes W. D., A. G. O. Form No. 204, 8 April 1943, which may be used until
existing stocks are exhausted.   c16—33987-3 GPO

30 August   Wed. morn.

I'm thinking of you all morning and feeling a little closer to you as I write these few words.

Yesterday, the Captain told the boys that when we leave for the P.O.E. (Port of Embarkation) we may get a few days off. I merely tell you this—as little as it might be—since something to look forward to makes all this a little easier to take.

I can't tell you I'm happy here, but when I become acquainted a little more, I'm sure I'll feel better. As I learn about the camp I'll tell you more about it. May go to the movies tonight.

Will drop this in the mail now, and plan writing again tonight. Time is short now. My love, Sweetheart.

30 August   Wed. eve.

Every time I think of the way I write you, always in a melancholy tone, I feel I'm not doing right by you. You have all the trouble and responsibility and heartache (if you feel like me, and I think you do) you can handle, and then I add a little more of it in my letters.

Another "physical" today—a little more thorough than the usual one. Tomorrow we go to the Personnel Office. Why? I don't know.

About the toughest thing I have to face now is the fact that I have little or nothing to look forward to.

I'll probably say very little in my succeeding letters about the things I do tactically (military) because it will only be a repetition of the things that happened in Blanding, unless of course, something special occurs.

I'm going to try and find Jim tonight—it'll be a job, but if I do locate him I know I'll feel much better. I really don't know what else to say now, except that I'd do anything in the world to be with you. I think that furlough and Meade spoiled me. I forgot I was a soldier and it makes it harder getting back into the rut (I mean just that).

31 August

This morning the clerks in our regiment took a test at the Personnel Office. I don't expect anything to come of it, but I might classify it as a straw, although a very thin one, to eventually shifting back to clerical work. Of course, that wouldn't keep me from going over, since when a Division moves, everything and everybody concerned with it moves too.

I've heard something about this Division—perhaps some rumor and some truth. It was activated about 2 years ago in Camp Jackson, S.C. A Division is a complete combat unit and is geared to operate solely on its own in any theatre of war. Well, 2 years, during wartime, is a long time to train a group of men who've already had their basic, I thought. It seems I was right, as I learned that the Division was not up to snuff militaristically, so the Army has been drawing the men out as replacements—so much now, that probably only 25% of the original men are left.*

* Since the 100th Infantry Division's commanding general, Maj. Gen. Withers A. Burress, headed it from its activation in August 1942 until the war was over, this

A main purpose of a Division is teamwork. In this case, with a General constantly removing and replacing, teamwork cannot be accomplished. And with the Division moving shortly, most of us have been concerned about the kind of job and area we'd be shipped to.

Those of us who have been trying to figure logically (which is a mistake in the Army) thought that since this outfit doesn't appear to be a good fighting one—we'd be sent to a zone as an Army of Occupation. *But who knows what.* We may not even go across, although those prospects are pretty slim.

I'd like to get out of this outfit since the boys are all jitterbug types, and most of the non-coms are horrible—young, dumb, quick-tempered goons. There are a few nice ones, however. I met another clerk who came in with me—trained in Texas, and about my age. He comes from Iowa and a very nice boy.

Think I'll drop this in the mail right now as it might get off today.

31 August   *Late Evening*

Received your lovely letter and assure you it was a great help to this homesick soldier. I admire your wonderful spirit, and for reasons explained in previous letter, I'm getting to a point where I don't think we'll play a combatant role—that in itself seems encouraging.

Had a fine evening with Jim tonight. After a pleasant talk we went to a movie in another part of the camp—the Army Aviation Section.

Tomorrow we shoot the carbine, also the M-1. It's necessary in every camp an Infantryman is stationed.

Give my love to our boys, whom I miss more than ever.

---

seems unlikely; had the division proved sub-standard during its early training under Burress, the odds are that he would have been replaced by someone else. A more likely explanation is that the 100th was an entirely new division; unlike the older divisions that had existed at least since World War I days, or the National Guard divisions, the 100th started from scratch, with its cadre transferred in from other units and in most cases promoted in rank for the occasion. It is probable, therefore, that the War Department chose to schedule such a division for late deployment overseas, and used its ranks to provide replacements for divisions that were closer to being sent into combat, until the time drew nearer for its use in battle.

1 September

Will continue where I left off last night, as I just returned from the transition range, and have a little time for writing.

The war news still continues to look pretty good—but it has to look even better, doesn't it, so we can always be together again.

This Camp is tremendous and unless you have a car, it's just about impossible to see it all. The Division area I'm in, houses between 7500 to 10,000 men. We have one Service Club and 2 theatres—and that seems inadequate, especially since the same picture plays in both theatres the same night, necessitating leaving the area if you've already seen it.

This happened last night so Jim and I went to that area 3 miles away. An M.P. gave us a ride over in a jeep. Well, honey, this area is like a country club and unlike any G.I. place I've ever seen. No crowds. No waiting in lines at movies, Service Club or PX. Jim and I decided to visit it more frequently.

There's no training here at camp. Schedules are issued from day to day, e.g., today they raked through the records and listed those who hadn't fired the carbine or M-1 rifle on the transition range (there are numerous types of ranges) during the last six months, and the Army requires it every 6 months.

Other days we have lectures, and exercise almost daily, but in the form of games—baseball, football, etc. I just mention this to let you know I'm not overworking. My only problem is being away from home. Think I'll close now, Sweets. All my love.

3 September

Yesterday received your 3rd letter, and if my letters make you a fraction as happy as yours make me, I'll be pleased.

I was thrilled with David's "Da-Da" after I left. Show him my pictures occasionally so that he won't forget me. These next six months he'll be picking up a lot of expressions. Today is his birthday and I just feel that something lucky is going to happen between his birthday, and Neil's, on the 21st. I hope it's lucky!

You ask where I'd be reporting if I go across. From here we'd go directly to a staging area, where specific training, adapted to the type of work (combat or occupation), would be slated—lasting from a week or 2 to three months—or—go directly—and probably this is it—to a P.O.E. for a long "boat" ride, taking up to 6 or 7 days, depending on the boats, supplies and size of Division.

The P.O.E.'s are located chiefly in New York and New Jersey—and let's pray, maybe Fort Dix. Our Captain who is no more informed than we are, suggested that we hold on to our pay, as we may get a few days off at the P.O.E.

You know, today is Sunday. And only last Sunday I saw you, but it seems like months. This week has been tough adjusting, but I'm feeling considerably better now.

Last night Jim and I went to the Post Theatre and saw a double feature—the 6th in 5 days. You know how I like movies, and I get plenty of it here—and it does get my mind off things. However, all good things come to an end, and I'm anticipating details next week—KP and the like. We'll see.

I'm writing at the Service Club, as I like to get out of the Company area whenever I can. Besides, our Blanding group has an agreement. Every free moment, we're to gather at the Service Club, and then take it from there.

Did I tell you of the splendid group of boys that came down from Meade with me to Fort Bragg? Only six of our platoon, but 250 specialists, typical of those we had in our platoon, and practically all from Blanding. We have much in common and took to each other immediately—90% married, with children, specialists in civilian as well as Army life, above average in intelligence, and probably most important, we're all in the same boat—we're all to be made riflemen. It seemed to create a strong bond between us, and we all meet here and exchange views and experiences—something like bull-sessions. It's probably the reason my morale has improved.

This weekend I get a 36-hour pass, but am not going anywhere. If we're here any length of time and I learn to get around better, I might be tempted to go home. It's a 12-to-14-hour train ride to Philly, and could give me about 10 hours home, but I think I should save that for a time when I'd have been away from home longer. However, I might just turn up one of these Sunday mornings around 6 A.M.—but don't even think about it—it's wishful thinking at this point.

4 September

Just returned from the hospital where I visited Jim. It seems he's getting a pretty good deal—even though an operation is part of it. First, he stays there for 10 days before his operation (minor). Then 30 days of convalescing. All this time will probably save him from moving with us. I hear there's an Army rule prohibiting moving overseas for 6 months after an operation.

Expect news any day about date of our leaving. The supply rooms are already busy packing up.

The heat has been bad; I can take it, but I do miss the cool evenings we had in Florida. I perspire continuously.

The PX's here are putrid. To begin with, they're filthy. While there's plenty to drink, it sells so fast it's unusually warm. Jim and I have been staying out of them, getting our drinks and snacks at the Service Club.

5 September

I'm contented now, as your letter is before me. With it, my morale is lifted as high as it's possible under these conditions.

You ask if Jim is in my Division. Yes—although in a different regiment. There are three—397, 398, 399. Although closely aligned, they're divided for administration and training purposes.

Neil's observation of your "worried" look touched me so much. He's really a great little guy, with all the little problems he creates. Re: the Infantile Paralysis scare. By all means send him to school. I don't believe in overcautiousness, as that often turns out to be just as bad.

It burns me up the way the Army operates. All a G.I. has to look forward to, is evenings and weekends. Why, then, do officers and non-coms just wait for those periods to pile on the extra details, especially with little or no training around. They hold those few free hours over your head and practically make you sweat for them—after they've shaven it down to a minimum.

Try not to worry, and always remember I'm thinking of you, and love you.

6 September

Received your letter at noon and must say it was the most beautiful letter I have ever had. Your big soldier's eyes were wet when he finished reading it. I wish I could tell you what it means to have someone who misses you, who is concerned with your troubles—who likes to hear the little trifles that happen throughout a long day. It's the richest thing a man could own.

About the war news, I feel as you do. I don't anticipate an immediate return home should the war in Europe end, but as you say, it could lift some restrictions and relieve a lot of our pain. It had better end suddenly, though, if I'm to stay in this country—and even that is questionable.

This P.M. we've been firing our rifles. I don't have the least interest, but merely go through the motions. With all that, I'm amazed at my improvement. Last week I shot a perfect score with the M-1 rifle (standard 10-lb. rifle). It seems, with my disinterest, my quality improves—probably because I'm relaxed when firing, whereas in training, I was tense.

There are a few positive things in this camp. At Blanding, everything you did was scrutinized, as if we were babies. Here, with 400 guys shooting on this range—no one watches or raises the devil—yet the men do very well. There isn't someone always whipping us into the proper step; we talk in ranks everywhere we go, and our clothes are not examined through a "magnifying glass." These are the "pro" elements. I could tell you plenty of the "con," too.

Later—at the Service Club. I have a call in now, and will add a few lines if I get through to you.

Just spoke to you, Dearest, and it was wonderful. The time flew so fast. About the weekend, don't figure too heavily on it. I could be on detail, or I might not get the extra few hours that is needed to make it. If things work out, maybe there *will* be something to look forward to.

6 September

This platoon gives me a pain in the neck. As I said, they always infringe on the little free time you have. Supper is over at 6 and most of us want to take off for the evening. No—it can't be that way. We must report back to barracks and wait till we're released— which was 7 P.M. last night. I had planned to visit Jim at the hospital. Visiting hours are over at 8; I couldn't catch a ride so I started to walk. By the time I reached the theatre, a half mile before the hospital, it was 8 P.M., so I just got in line and waited to get into the movies.

Sometimes, pleasant things happen, too. While waiting in line a soldier struck up a conversation with me. We sort of took to each other. He's 34, been in the Army 20 months, married, and has a 14-year-old son. He's thoroughly disgusted with Army life, but has an excellent deal. He was transferred from California a month ago and has been home 6 times in 20 months. He's in a contingent of 60 men the Army is at a loss to know what to do with, since they were part of the searchlight brigade of the anti-aircraft which was recently de-activated. They bum all day long at the Service Club. He lives in a big stone barracks on the post, much like a College Hall and it reminds you of a campus. Some guys get the breaks; I plan on seeing him tonight after I visit Jim.

I try to get out of this "hole" the first minute I can, and return as late as possible since it's so dirty, smelly and hot and a good percentage of the boys, especially non-coms, disgust me. If you think that sounds like a gripe—well, it is, and I'm sorry to burden you with it.

7 September

I'm extremely happy tonight. Just heard a rumor, confirmed by good authority, that we get 3-day passes starting late Saturday. But I'll still need an extra few hours to make it home.

Now that it's over, I can tell you that today we were hit with the infiltration course again, and while tough, I came through much better than before. Tonight a 12-mile speed march. I must have gotten my facts wrong about things being easy around here. However, I don't worry about these orders now and it really comes easier.

Excuse the short letter, Dear. I'm just content to know I'll be seeing you soon and the letter seems secondary. But, boy, how important a letter is when "in person" isn't so imminent. All my love.

8 September

Still cling to hopes of seeing you this weekend. The 3-day pass isn't sure yet, but it looks pretty good.

I'm enclosing letters and pictures as we're not to carry anything to help identify us. Though they don't know when we're going to move, we must be ready at a moment's notice.

Received your 2 letters today, and happy as usual to get them— one with a $5.00 bill, and as I was practically penniless it was very helpful.

Will call you Saturday if I can't make it home. Dear, I hope I see you before you get this letter.

11 September

It sure was tough saying goodbye to you, Dearest, and I was pretty low all the way back. I'm glad you came down to see me off, though. It was tough, but having you with me till the last moment felt so good, and in the future, if we can we'll do it again.

Standing and lying down in the aisles most of the way was worth it just to be with you all—even for the few short hours. It was funny how quiet the boys were throughout the trip back—whereas on the way up they were noisy as hell.

Got in just on the dot of 6 A.M. The train was two hours late, and then because of the huge mob of boys I had a long wait for a bus to camp. Here's a bit of irony. After I got in I heard there had been a train wreck on my line somewhere, and all passes had been extended eight additional hours. How do you like that!

I called Rose from Washington and spoke with her about ten minutes. She made me feel so much better. She always comes through—one way or another.

Something happened today that may indicate something's in the air. After lunch the 1st Sergeant called me into his office (30 of us, one at a time). He asked if I liked the Infantry, and I said, "No, I'd like to get out of it." He asked why. I said I didn't think it fair to the Army since I wasn't helping in the best way I was able. I further told him that shooting people was not my line, regardless of how much I hated the enemy—and that combat conditions tended to unnerve me. To which he replied, "That's only natural."

I went on to tell him there are many jobs suited to my training and background which would be far more beneficial to the Army, but a rifleman was not one of them. All he said was "Okay"—made some sort of a mark and told me to send the next boy in. I have no idea what it's all about but will let you know when and if I hear.

About the significance of the confab, I believe if it were really important the Captain would have conducted the interviews, not the 1st Sgt. Since our Company is about one-third overmanned I think they're trying to eliminate men. The interviewees were over 30 and under 19. Don't know exactly what to think except that we're being considered as transfers out of the Division—which I wouldn't mind.

A rumor—purely so—is that all C and D men are being sent to Fort Meade and Fort Dix as permanent cadre. However, I know nothing of my being anything other than Class A. If I learn anything, I'll write immediately.

I'm looking forward to my next visit home, which somehow doesn't seem impossible now.

13 September

Your letter was truly a gem. You put into words exactly how you felt—and I felt exactly the same. Of course, you don't have to "appreciate" my visit since it was for my benefit, too. As I told you before, I'd make the trip regularly, despite travel conditions, if I were to remain here.

My trip back wasn't comfortable either, since again I couldn't get a seat. However, I made good use of the Sunday *Record* and slept on it in the middle of the aisle, with a barracks bag as my pillow. It wasn't half bad—and to prove it—Monday wasn't too tiresome a day. The rush for seats in Washington was little less than bedlam. I didn't even go for a seat. I just wanted to get on that train—but that jam was something I won't forget so soon. Yet, with all the discomfort and lack of sleep, I'd do it every week if I could get off in time.

Speaking of "the luxury of a good cry," I'm afraid that is a luxury no mother as busy as you are can afford, though I know it would help to "let go," occasionally. At least, the kiddies got your mind off things temporarily and I hope that helped a little.

David sure looked good. He constantly improves. It warmed my heart when he jumped up and down and stretched his little arms out to me in recognition. And Neil looked better than I've ever seen him. Keep him drinking milk. How did he make out in school that first day?

I know you must have felt badly disappointed when you realized I forgot that fine lunch you prepared for me. However, I question if I could have eaten it, as I had a lump in my throat throughout the trip and—my appetite, nil.

Today they got me in the kitchen—but not for KP. The Company barracks are due for a check-up by the War Dept. Friday, so they're scrubbing everything up—and I'm scrubbing. I hate the kitchen, would prefer anything to that—but that's where I always land.

13 September   Wed. *night*

The 3-day pass chances seem to be getting better, since they're rushing to fill all overseas requirements before shipment, and when they're filled the pass is upcoming.

I was called before a board today to determine the possibility of putting me in Class C or D. Reason—when interviewed by the 1st Sergeant I told him of my intense aversion to killing people, and my tendency to become ill at the sight of blood. He seemed impressed enough to send the report up to the next echelon. It appears they're prepared to take me out of Class A, but want a doctor to talk to me first. That's scheduled for tomorrow morning.

Class C means I'd stay in the States as station complement to some camp—perhaps Dix or Meade. It would be along the lines we'd like—but first the doctor's report. If something happens, at least I won't be in this Division which I've disliked since entry. All the newer boys feel the same. You see, it's an established organization, with all its cliques—officers, non-coms, clerks, etc. and it's next to impossible for a new man to break in. Besides, the new men seem to be shunned and far from welcome. My hope is to get to Dix as a clerk of some sort. But this is Army—and never plan on anything.

Dear, after our long talk, now you know that I want you to write me just exactly how you feel, and what you're thinking—if your lonesome, or your morale is low. I let you know, don't I, and usually feel better for it, too. So don't hesitate as it makes me feel closer to you.

14 September

Already I miss you, and the week isn't even over. The possibility of a 3-day pass will be determined by the results of the War Dept. inspection tomorrow, Friday.

I'm awaiting a further interview on my Class C status, which was due this morning, but haven't been called yet. It seems that in the Army all there is, is anticipation and hope.

I don't think I ever told you about Class C men. C men out of the Infantry—the roughest and toughest branch—usually means they fall out of the marches, and not because of ailments. In my case, I told my interviewer I could make the marches, but not on my physical prowess, but on my "guts." At one time it would have hurt my foolish "pride" to be Class C, but there are an awful lot of better men than I in that class. And I realize that with "pride" and "guts" go a rifle—(and a military specialty of rifleman). In my case I was being prepared to function as a Right Flank man on a rifle squad, and issued a "sniper rifle." Now, how does that set with you?

It's 10 P.M. now. Just came off the infiltration course at night— everything OK—no trouble.

This afternoon a Major interviewed me relative to all that's happening, and said I'd hear the results of the interview later on.

Something else is afoot—but not related to this Class C business. I must report to Battalion Hdqs. early tomorrow. It may mean a transfer to Bn. Hdqs. which is a better break than what I have—but first let's see. I'm sure it has no connection with the other, though.

So far I've written a lot but said little. Tomorrow should be a day of reckoning. Maybe news on the pass—or news of a change of classification.

Take good care of yourself, Dear. Hope to call you at my first opportunity.

15 September

I guess I was thrown on that order to report to Battalion. After all that conjecture, guess what it turned out to be! A mere detail— which I'm on now.

Later—Am now at the Service Club after seeing Jim. He had his operation and seems to be doing swell.

Got paid today—$17.70, and Jim paid me the $3. he owed me. Do you want me to send you any? I'm rich!

My classification has now been referred to the Corps area and I have an appointment 7:30 A.M. with another Major. There's an order right now—don't know if I'm on it—transferring all C men to Pope Field—the Air Corps here at Bragg.

The 3-day pass is turning out to be a farce. From Sat. 4 P.M. till Tuesday 4 P.M., only 20 men in each platoon are permitted out. Then they have a 36-hour pass for 20 more—similar to a weekend pass. Don't figure on me, as these passes will, no doubt, go to the regular clique.

Furthermore, the High Holiday possibility* is out—despite efforts from the Chaplain who's been told by the Army Ground Forces in Washington that our Division is about to move, and would not sanction leaves in such bulk.

I'm writing as I'm waiting for a phone call to you to come through. Despite the above reverses, please try not to feel too badly, and as your mother says, "every dark cloud has a silver lining."

It could be that I'm moving with the Division, but I'm pretty sure I'm not. But even tonight I'm talking of indefinite things. I haven't been told that I don't get a 3-day pass, or that I'm going to Pope Field, or that I'm out of the Division. I'm merely guessing—but who knows.

After the call: I enjoyed talking to you, Sweetheart, terribly much. You're a wonderful sport. Disappointing things you take so well in stride and it makes me feel so good to know you "can take it."

17 September

It's Sunday morning and I'm taking it easy at the Service Club. Things have been happening in the last 24 hours that seem to have a bearing on us.

First, I think I can reassure you that I won't be with the Division. I'm classified as "Q.S."—Qualified Service. This means, from what I can gather (and I find it hard doing so) that I am not Class

---

* Winston is referring to the Jewish Holy Days of Rosh Hashonah and Yom Kippur, which occur within ten days of each other in late summer or very early autumn. With many of its personnel drawn from the Middle Atlantic states, the 100th Infantry Division's ranks included a large number of Jewish soldiers.

C or D. However, it seems to be a classification that exempts you from combat. I've heard two different stories: First, that all Q.S. men go to Pope Field where they'll be quartered until reclassified. Another—that Q.S. men will travel with the Division to the P.O.E. in the not too distant future. I hesitate to name the State in the letter. Furthermore, the story goes that this camp keeps Q.S. men— which is just what we'd want, isn't it. The date the Division is set to move is 2 days after Neil's birthday—but you'll know before then if I'm moving to the P.O.E. or not.

An interesting thing happened yesterday regarding my reclassification as a Q.S.—and it shows how the Army can, because of one officer's attitude, ruin the life of an enlisted man. It might not have been so in my case, but could have hurt me. I'll try to be brief.

It stems from the fact that my horror of killing and my weakness at the sight of blood seems to have a bearing on my new classification.

Anyway, the Captain who interviewed me said, "Do you hate even German blood?" I replied, "Just as much as any other." This seemed to steam him up, and he said, "I'd like to bathe in it." It went back and forth in that manner, and then he said, "Oh, you don't like to see Germans killed!" I said, "If it meant saving the lives of our boys—yes—but I don't want to do it, and furthermore, I'm not asking for any special privilege. I want to fight, but in the way I'm most capable—and not with a gun."

He *burned*, and made a note of the interview with *one* word, which at the time I was unable to decipher.

Then, yesterday again, I was interviewed by a committee of three—this same Captain, a Major and a Colonel. It was the same Major who had interviewed me a day earlier, and for whom I had a good deal of respect after our session ended. Well, the Major, who seemed to control the committee, had a copy of the Captain's notation before him—and the three were to arrive at a decision as to my future in the Army.

At this point I was pretty close and could easily see the record across the desk—and beside my name, the Captain had vindictively printed "psychologic."

The Major said to the Colonel—pointing to that word with his pencil, "Colonel, this is all wrong." Then he went into a lengthy detail of our previous interview, how impressed he was, and added, "Shall I cross it off?"

The Colonel replied, "Now, wait a minute," and proceeded to ply me with questions relative to all I had said. And then, looking very scornfully at the Captain, he said, loud and clear, "Major, cross that off!"

I looked the Captain square in the eye and he turned away quickly. I'm sure he must have been laid on the carpet after that, because both the Colonel and Major were seething with anger.

Now you can see how one individual can ruin a man's career, even his life, for in the Army, that word "psychologic" is a dirty word and if entered on my service record—and it would have been if allowed to remain on that form—it would take a Congressional order to remove it.

After seeing Jim, who seems to be doing well, I went to the movies last night. I'm going back to the barracks for lunch now, and anticipate another letter from you. Until later, Dearest.

21 September   *Happy Birthday, Neil!*

As you know from the telephone call last night, I'm in Raleigh, No. Carolina. Came over to the USO chiefly to write you and was pleasantly surprised they had a typewriter I could use.

Before leaving camp yesterday I'd started a letter, telling you that it would probably be the last uncensored letter I could write. After Thursday, all mail will be censored from Fort Bragg. Of course I'm still hoping I don't leave with the Division after it reaches the P.O.E.

There seems so little to do in this city. I often think as I visit these towns and cities, even camps, how I'd enjoy them if you were with me. Army life has succeeded in teaching me something—that regardless how good—or terrible—something is, how it affects you is influenced by your attitude. "Attitude" is crammed down your neck and with good reason.

Right now I'm thinking of this interesting city, and I'm not enjoying it the way I could since I miss you so. But attitude is influenced by feeling and you can't turn off your feelings as easily as you do a faucet.

Neil is doing so much better. He seems to be developing into a strong little guy. Am glad you spent time with him on his subtraction. Once he catches on, he holds on to it. Since today is his birthday I bought 3 jerseys in a department store and had them mailed. Still looking for that wedding band I told you I was anxious to get for myself, but as yet haven't been satisfied.

I'm here with my friend, Earl, from Iowa.* We'll probably take in a movie tonight and head for camp about midnight.

23 September

Well, Honey, things have started to pop and at first glance you may not be too happy about it all. I know I wasn't. But first with the story—the pros and cons afterward.

First, there's little chance that I'll be leaving the Division, as I am now attached to the Medical Detachment of the 398th Infantry.† Now, sit down—that was given to you a little fast.

It was very hard to swallow at first, but there are some good points, I've found. In the first place, I don't carry a rifle—no medics do—enemy or ally—because the terms of the Geneva Conference make such a provision. We wear a white band around our arm—and we're not supposed to get shot at. (I'm laughing.) This, at least, will eliminate our see-saw hopes and anticipation. It's all been settled for us—our concern about being transferred out of the Division, and if, or if not, I'll remain in this country. With the stroke of a pen they took care of it all very expeditiously—my future, our lives. Every soldier in the Army is manipulated like a puppet and you just have to take what's handed out.

One bright spot—the Lieutenant and Sergeant and boys are turn-

---

* Sgt. Earl V. Campo, of Chicago, Illinois.

† Winston's assignment to an infantry battalion medical detachment meant that he would be a combat medic, working as a part of a front-line infantry battalion, engaged in rescuing wounded riflemen and administering first-aid and on-the-spot treatment. Severely wounded men were evacuated from front-line aid stations to regimental and divisional medical and hospital units.

ing out to be really swell guys, and you can't begin to understand how much easier that makes it.

Dear, even now, for the love of me, I just can't see that we're going over—I really can't. My guess, which I emphasize is my opinion, is that we'll end up at the P.O.E. and stay there—at any rate, for quite a while.

It's ironical they put me in the Medical Detachment, without a single day of training. I spoke to the Lt. about my predicament—my reaction to blood, the whole bit. I assured him I wanted to cooperate to the best of my ability—go anywhere the Army sent me, but this would make me sick and I couldn't do the right job.

All he could say was that he sympathized with me, that he'd heard me talk with that Captain, and understood just how I felt—that he, too, was inclined to react that way—but what could he do. He said I'll have to learn to get used to it, that he knew it would be a hard dose to take, but could offer no encouragement.

It all seems so incredulous and irrational. You see, if we were in combat and some poor guy was depending on my ability as a medic, which is nil, I don't feel capable of performing what would be expected of me. Also, my ineptness could mean the loss of life for some wounded soldier. Not only would I be incompetent, but the thought bugs me that I could be instrumental in the death of some boy or boys. It's so illogical—and typically Army thinking; they put you in a job you're not qualified for—yet your training and expertise in many other areas is completely disregarded. There are scores of places I could be assigned, right here in the 398th Infantry where I could be an asset.

I will say that the boys have made this easier to take—a much better bunch than the rifle crowd. Don't write till you hear from me. From this point on—I'll probably call you.

I hope I haven't been crying on your shoulder too much, and that you don't feel too badly about it all. Perhaps things could be much worse. (At this moment it's hard to think of something!)

At least that awful suspense is over with—and I *am* happier here than in the other outfit.—It's so comforting to know I have someone I can let my heart out to. I love you, Sweetheart.

24 September

Today, Sunday, I received a sweet letter from you—and as I'm in new surroundings, I doubly appreciate it. I'm not bursting with joy, but I really do feel happier here than in the rifle outfit—and that is some solace.

Last night I met Jim, who is out of the hospital, and he, too, is definitely going with the Division. It doesn't seem humane—taking a man just operated on—but P.O.E. will give him another physical, supposedly rather rigid—but you know how rigid these Army examinations are.

Your letter was full of hope for a "decent break," but by now you know the "break" doesn't appear so decent. But I know you're able to take it by this time—and furthermore—don't cross any bridges till you come to them.

The boys are already talking about not wanting to be part of the Occupational Army—and they're writing their wives to put the pressure on their political representatives. One guy said, "I told my wife that if she doesn't form a 'Bring the Boys Back Home' Club, I'll never speak to her again." I don't mean to be putting ideas into your head—but I thought the above amusing.

Incidentally, as a member of the Medical Corps, I'm not in the Infantry anymore. I'm attached to an Infantry regiment, but could be transferred to any other outfit without formality, but this isn't too probable. One thing I notice here—if there's nothing to do, we just don't do anything. But in the rifle Co. they never gave you a minute's respite—we were always kept busy at unnecessary, senseless details.

Well, Sweetheart, today we're confined to the Division area for *obvious* reasons. Jim left 3 days after Neil's birthday; for me it will be 4 or 5 days after.

Was just talking to a boy who went to the P.O.E. we think we're going to, and he tells me the transportation accommodations are perfect, and knowing the section up there, I can see why. This all may sound vague to you, but you realize we are not to give even minor details.

Received my First-Aid equipment today and I reminded the Sgt. I don't know the first thing about it. They don't hear anything, or don't want to. He said I'd learn gradually. They're always very agree-able, saying, "I know, I know," probably realizing that "honey" will get them further than vinegar.

I don't have an awful lot to say. I'm getting very anxious to get out of here, since it will mean getting home for a few hours, anyway.

27 September

As you are probably aware, things are happening—and fast. We have moved, but I can't tell you where although I think it's per-missible to say [censored].

We've all been promised passes and are counting the minutes till we get them, but am disappointed I'm not allowed to phone you.

Please don't be alarmed at all this secrecy, censoring and restric-tions. You must realize it is for our protection. I assure you it's not nearly as bad as it sounds; it's just that the Army goes all out to keep secret the movements and whereabouts of this organization. They don't put us in a cage, I assure you, as we're given unlimited privileges, i.e., passes.

You're probably anxious to hear more about my transfer to the Medical Corps. And as I said before, aside from my reaction to blood, which is the least of it—but this reaction might be the cause of a loss of life, and my conscience would never be clear. I still can't understand the rationale behind the transfer to this branch since the officers responsible were aware of all this—and repeated to 4 different echelons.

However, since the boys here, the non-coms and Lieutenant are very easy to get along with, I wouldn't mind staying with the Medi-cal Corps—if only in a capacity that would not put me in constant contact with the wounded.

I find it difficult to write you, knowing my letter is being cen-sored—and also knowing how you like to hear of my activities in detail. But censor or not, I know I can tell you how much I miss you and Neil and David. Have you tried feeding David ice-cream again? Isn't it odd he shows so little interest in it, whereas Neil liked it so much at his age. I ache so much to see him. I was thinking of the recent weekend I came home—how David, so early in the morning, joined happily in on the family reunion.

Someone in the barracks has a radio and I just learned today is Yom Kippur. It didn't have too much of an effect on me until I noticed, while Jewish music and observances were coming from the radio, that the boy below my bunk was crying and reading his prayer book, and for his head covering, he used his helmet. It moved me deeply.

By now you must realize if I've neglected to write certain things— and I know there's an important explanation you're looking for— it's because I'm not permitted to write about it. But if I say every- thing is okay—it could be a lot worse.

Miss you terribly—and it's not too impossible that you may get a surprise soon.

Note new address:

Pvt. Keith Winston 33927775
2nd Bn. Hq. Co. 398th Inf. APO 447
c/o Postmaster, New York, N.Y.

I'm sure you're writing, but because of my change of address I've not been getting any mail—nor has anyone else.

We've been promised passes, and the anticipation, the worry that I'll be eligible for one is making a nervous wreck of me. To be with you will mean more than anything in this world. I feel like a balloon growing bigger and bigger, almost ready to burst at the slightest provocation.

Last night I took a walk around the camp. It made me feel con- siderably better, although the "balloon" feeling still persists. Don't have an awful lot to say, since what I'd like to say isn't permitted. I'm always thinking of you, Sweetheart. Kiss the boys for me. I want you to know you're forever on my mind. At the risk of sound- ing corny, keep the "home fires" burning—I feel certain everything will be okay soon.

3 October

It hurts me to tell you I probably won't be able to see you Wednesday as I'd hoped. I try to tell myself we shouldn't feel too badly since we were fortunate in seeing each other as much as we did. I shall always cherish the memory of our last meeting, and in the days ahead I know it will be my one great source of comfort. Remember what I've told you—we have much to live for, and look forward to, and a real foundation on which to plan our future.

Today was a little different and rather interesting. I was what they called the Emergency Man, and my job was to stay at the dispensary for a 24-hour stint, sleeping here, too. (This letter is being written on dispensary typewriter.) I've got a pretty good idea of how this place works. I don't have any ambitions here except to perform my job as private in the best way I know how. I get along well with the officers here and that makes things pleasanter.

Saw Jim tonight and his presence as always made me feel good.* I've always been sorry we didn't land in the same Regiment, but at least it's the same Division. Call Alice up (his wife) as she may have *something* to tell you.

The more I'm with this outfit, the more I like it; therefore, unlike before, I hope that's one less problem I'll have. Little to say except that already I miss you. Will write daily—unless impossible—and hope you do, too. My love to you all.

* Tec 4 James N. Johnston, Jr.

3. En Route

Atlantic Ocean–
Mediterranean Sea

October 1944

By 27 September 1944, the 100th Division had arrived at Camp Kilmer, New Jersey. Nine days later, on 5 October, the full complement of 762 officers, 44 warrant officers, and 13,189 enlisted men traveled by rail to New York City and went aboard troopships. The next day a convoy of eleven ships, guarded by a destroyer and four destroyer escorts, passed the Statue of Liberty and headed for Marseille, France. Aboard were the 100th, 103rd, and advance elements of the 14th Armored divisions. Six days out of New York, the convoy was hit by a tremendous storm, and for forty-eight hours battled ferocious winds and sea that at one point forced a change in course. Another storm struck the convoy after it had entered the Mediterranean. On 20 October, after a fifteen-day journey, the convoy dropped anchor at Marseille, which had been liberated during the Allied invasion of southern France in August. Port facilities had been almost completely destroyed, and the 100th Division was ferried ashore by landing craft. The division set up quarters at an area twelve miles from the city and awaited arrival of its heavy equipment.

The war in the west, meanwhile, had become a war of movement. In late July the American forces in Normandy had broken through the encircling German lines, and a headlong German retreat from northern France had followed. Close to 300,000 Germans had been killed or captured. Spearheaded by the U.S. Third Army, American forces drove toward the Siegfried Line along the German border, while to the north British and American armies shoved the German defenders beyond Antwerp. From their landings in southern France the U.S. Seventh Army and the French First Army swept northward up the Rhône River valley and approached the German border near Switzerland. For a time it seemed as if the war could be won that fall. But then the German defenses stiffened. The northern swing through the Low Countries was blunted at Arnhem, and the U.S. First and Third armies ran out of gasoline and supplies and were forced to slow down; during September and October further progress toward the German border was slow and heavily contested. By late November the line of the western front stretched from Arnhem at the north along the Roer River and southward to the Saar and the Vosges Mountains to Switzerland.

At Sea

I received your letter, written after you were convinced I was going over, and your reactions were identical to mine. You know, Dear, I never realized that my family would be the only thing on my mind when leaving. I knew it would be uppermost, but surely I felt I'd be thinking of the boat ride—would I be seasick—where in God's world were we headed—would I ever come back. And once on the boat I was sure I'd be constantly worrying about the crossing hazards—the subs and mines.

But strangely enough none of that seems to bother me—in fact I'm hardly concerned.

The only thing I can think of now is that every day and every mile on this boat takes me farther and farther away from you and our boys.

On the day we were leaving—I don't think any of us realized the significance of it too much. We all seemed to be rather numbed by the final turn of things. It was weird—not until retreat, when the National Anthem was being played did the actual impact hit me— and I realized I was leaving my homeland, and that this would be the last time I would hear it—for a long time—on native soil. And for the first time I knew well what the Star-Spangled Banner meant to one who was leaving his country. And it hit hard.

Another thing that touched me deeply was the warm way the Red Cross handled us as we were ready to march up that gangplank. What a wonderful feeling to know that somebody cared—even strangers—and on hand to say goodbye. Besides the liberal refreshments, each of us was given a large pouch with a number of useful things in it.

It was good that we had discussed the probability of my leaving when I was last home. And the clue that I would give you if I couldn't call you, so I was pretty certain you would "see through" the bouquet of roses I wired home. I felt so damn helpless, being so close, yet unable to talk with you. But as I think back, maybe I would rather have said goodbye as we did—I shall never forget you as you stood outside the train window. You were so beautiful, so refreshing a sight, and such a pleasant thought to look back at.

We haven't learned where we're headed for—officially—although

—cartoon by Bob
Clarke, from The Story
of the Century

I'm sure it is the [censored] theatre, if my deduction is correct as to the way the ship is headed in relation to the sun.

By the time you get this letter you will know, I'm sure, since this letter won't be mailed till we reach our destination, and I'll probably have others to go along with it then.

I've had a case of seasickness all the way, so far, although somewhat relieved this afternoon. If I write few letters on this trip you'll know why.

The above was written the 2nd day; and from then on until this writing I've been seasick. Now that I'm feeling better, and I assure you I am, I'll get back to writing you.

There's absolutely nothing to do on ship. We sit on deck when and if we find the room—no comforts whatsoever. If I'm not talking with someone I'm thinking of you and the children, and yearn and yearn and yearn, and as I realize the ship is taking me farther away from you, it becomes unbearable. I've read your letter over a number of times—the one I received on the ship—and being the only real "home touch" I have among my possessions—it means so much to me. While I'm thinking of it, mail me copies of those two pictures I like so much of the three of you.

Lots of things are happening here that I can't talk about, but have made indelible impressions on me, so rather than forget about them, I'm jotting down a few things—my impressions, etc. that someday we can read together.

Jim is not on the boat but will no doubt see him at the destination, which we already know, but still not permitted to reveal. I plan to cable, if allowed, as soon as I arrive.

There seems to be some argument as to whether airmail or V-Mail* is better. Of course, you can't enclose anything with V-Mail, and must use the prescribed envelope. Also, it takes extra time to photograph V-Mail. So the consensus is that airmail is faster. I'm going to mail a V-Mail letter—marking it #1, just as I have this letter—and take special note of the difference in receipt.

For the time being, mail airmail—getting the 6¢ airmail envelope. If you don't have one handy, just put the same postage on and in large print—add OVERSEAS AIR MAIL. Also, rather than wait for the mailman to pick it up, put it in the mailbox immediately as a delay of one pick-up could mean a delay of a week, more or less.

Now that I'm overseas-bound I have a keen desire to learn how others of our original platoon fared. Via Jim and Ed Crim, I heard 18 of us are heading overseas—don't know about the rest.

Another Day

Oh, Dearest, they go so slowly, and I miss and love you more than ever before. Just read your beautiful letter again, and each

---

* A V-Letter was written on a single sheet of special stationery, which was on sale at post offices, and was photographed after mailing; the film was sent overseas by air, and the letter was then printed in reduced size on photographic paper and delivered. Supposedly the procedure reduced delivery-time for mail, but as we shall see, this did not always work out.

time I read it, it touches me just as much. I was thinking of Neil and David today. How much I'm proud of Neil's maturity, and what a little gentleman he's becoming, and praying and hoping I'll get home before David learns too many words. Just as you say, "Thank God I have Neil and David"—and I say the same, as just thinking about them gives me so much pleasure, and pain, perhaps.

I think you should have the car fixed as I suggested, since winter is approaching. What's the news from Papa and Rose? Also, keep my mother informed of any developments.

Perhaps the little I'm permitted to say about the boat ride may be of interest. First, while we only eat two meals a day, they're pretty substantial. It seems cooking goes on all the time as there's always an odor of food. Now that I'm over being seasick, I don't mind it too much, but while sick, it was absolutely horrible, and good reason for my continued "mal de mer" siege of nausea and the whole bit. Even on deck, where troops are permitted, the odor is drawn out by a number of kitchen exhaust fans.

In the "holes"—the troops' quarters—it's disgustingly sickening, since air is lacking and it's so crowded you can't move without bumping into some soldier. All this makes it hot and putrid smelling since we have such poor facilities for bathing—and the clothes STINK.

We're under strictest supervision, even in the closest quarters on deck—and herded like cattle. Where we can go, and where we can't go seem to be of paramount concern to the officers. Don't get the idea from the above, the ship is small—ONLY, naval officers MUST have a private dining-room, and a private lounge, and troop officers MUST have their private lounge as well as private dining-room.

From what I can see, the small percentage of officers on board have as much room as the combined troops. I have not seen one solitary chair where an enlisted man can sit down to write a letter. He sits on deck or his bunk to write. I tell you this since it's about over and you need not worry—but it has aroused a resentful feeling, not only within me, but in everyone around me. I wonder if things like this come under the heading of military discipline (officers are not to mingle with enlisted men—to instill respect and dignity). If this is so—that thinking is way off base as it has created the exact opposite effect, a complete lack of respect for the officers and the System. I could say much more—but what's the use. It doesn't bring us any closer (in spirit), and to me that is the main purpose of our letters.

This letter is extended because I have been adding a little more to it each day and will all be mailed at once on arrival at destination. Never doubt for one second that you are always on my mind—I love you.

Still at Sea

My Sweetheart, I haven't written you for the last few days, a little seasick again and very depressed. Then last night, at the sight of land I was somewhat cheered and more in the mood to write this morning. I'm so anxious to get off this boat that's stuffed to the hilt with human cargo; then perhaps I'll be able to think more clearly. What we have been sent to do here will be made less hazy, and whatever it is we'll learn to adjust to. We're pretty well geared by now to know it won't be too pleasant, nor will we be living under comfortable conditions—conditions with furloughs and passes to visit the [censored] as is common belief in the States, but at least I'm resigned to the worst.

On this deck where we're packed like sardines, and this is no idle simile, I have to stand to write you. However, the spirit all around seems to be pretty high—what with the sight of land, a beautiful day, and the calmest of waters. Activity on the deck consists of roving from place to place looking for a place to sit (no chairs, as I've said—just a small empty space on the floor), reading and card and dice games. When and if I lay my hands on a periodical I read it from cover to cover, advertisements and all. Lately, I've gotten a kick watching the dice games, which at times run to pretty high stakes. The gamblers have plenty one day, and nothing the next. I'm thinking of one who just cleaned up $225—but yesterday he dropped $250—and that's how it runs. Don't have the slightest desire to get into a game, but watching them is one means of passing the hours.

I've become friendly with one of the boys, Harry, who was in the old rifle outfit with me. He's 29, unmarried, a graduate of Boston U., native of Boston and a very likeable character. He, too, likes to gamble, and whenever he wins he insists I hold some of it, so when he's on a losing streak, he won't lose it all. So far the plan has worked well because each day he can start again with what I've held from the previous day. Watching him, I've realized more than ever what a wonderful wife and family can mean to a man with the difficulties we're now facing. Thinking of you, praying for you, waiting for you and loving you means more than anything in this world to a man. That is something I have and thank God for it. He doesn't have it—and misses it. He's written to about 20 girls—many of which he knows are probably going steady with men, but craving feminine contact, writes them. As he asks me to edit them all, I can get a pretty good idea of what he's thinking (between the lines). So you see, with all our heartache, we have something we should derive a great deal of happiness from.

The chief subject on deck is the "chow" situation. The boys are hungry—me, too. We get but two meals each day, and while the seasickness siege was on, food was the last concern. But now with everything pretty well back to normal, 2 meals don't seem to be enough, especially when some meals are skimpy. Many of the boys couldn't hold out and started eating their K rations, which are supposed to be held for another date. Until today, with a little hoard of chocolate I brought from the P.O.E. I got by—but it's all gone. I did save a couple of hard-boiled eggs from breakfast today and that will probably save me. I'm sure we'll all live, however, and fortunately, for the most part, we manage to be well fed. I'm sure the sea air has something to do with our enormous appetites, too.

Until tomorrow, my Love.

4. Into Combat

Marseille, Vosges Mountains

October-December 1944

By 29 October 1944, only nine days after arrival at Marseille, the 100th Division had managed to get its heavy equipment unloaded and assembled, and began moving out for the front. Following overnight stops at Valence and Dijon, the motor convoys reached the staging area near St. Gorgon, at the edge of the Vosges Mountains near the easternmost tip of France. There they became part of the U.S. Seventh Army, under the command of Lt. Gen. Alexander M. Patch. Their assignment was to relieve the veteran 45th Infantry Division and join the attack on German positions in the Vosges Mountains. On 1 November a field piece of the 925th Field Artillery Battalion fired the division's first shot of the war. By 8 November the division was fully committed in replacement of the 45th Division, and the assault on enemy positions was under way.

During the succeeding eighteen days, the 100th Division was involved in heavy fighting as it outflanked and captured Raon-l'Etape, fought its way across the Meurthe and La Plaine rivers near La Trouche, then drove through the towns of Senones, La Vermont, and Champanay. The 398th Infantry Regiment halted at the town of Salm. Meanwhile Winston had been transferred from the 2nd to the 3rd Battalion medics.

19 October 1944* France—V-Letter #1

We are here at last. Where I am, and what I am doing, and what I have seen—I cannot say—but it has been a revelation.

I have always said how much I appreciated my wife and children and home and community and American way of living. Today I say it again, but my appreciation comes from a fuller realization of what it all means. Seeing boys, as young as our little Neil, begging for money or something to eat. Tears come to my eyes, at first in pity and compassion for a world so torn up and terrible that it could reduce itself to such horror—then in thankfulness that our boys

* Winston's letter is dated 19 October, but the 100th Infantry Division convoy did not arrive at Marseille until 20 October.

would never have to resort to this because we live in America—because we happen to be fortunate enough to be living in America.

God has been good to us. Don't feel too badly that we're being asked to give up just a little of our happiness, temporarily, so that other people just like us who are not Americans, can have a taste of what we're having.

We haven't been told yet how much we can say in our letters home, but I'm playing it safe and saying little regarding location. I hope Neil and David are well. However brief, I'll do my utmost to get a letter off to you daily.

My deepest love.

21 October   *France*

As usual, today I'm thinking of you and longing for you terribly. Perhaps even more so, as some of the boys received mail from home. I know you're writing, and as all mail received was airmail, and I suggested you write V-Mail when I left. I'm sure that is the reason. Now we'll try airmail unless that proves unsatisfactory.

From the above date and location, you know we're permitted at least to say that much—but not the part of France we're in, at present. However, where we are, I assure you there's no activity.

24 October

It gets dark so quickly here, my Dearest, and sometimes you start a letter and find it impossible to complete. There is no light (electric, etc.), after darkness sets in. We live in tents, bivouac style. I don't enjoy it—nobody does—but once over here, with all the discomfort you see among civilians you realize that all this is part of accomplishing our ultimate goal.

We've had so much rain, rain and more rain, and French mud is really mud. Our shoes and leggings are always muddy, but our tents are dry and that means everything.

My Sweetheart, I'd go through all this every day for the rest of my life if it meant being with you. My only real discomfort, my only real heartache is being away from you. But then I start to rationalize—we could be in the States, in a camp like the IRTC—and I'd be unable to see you for 5 or 6 months anyway, and maybe it won't be more than that, maybe less, in this situation. Keep yourself busy, it helps so much.

My tentmate is a young boy from Springfield, Mass. While only 23, he's been around—looks much older. Unlike the average G.I. he tries to be so considerate, and I sure appreciate that. At present I'm involved in a "Mr. Anthony" dilemma.* He's been married 3 months—after knowing his wife only one week, and has been with her one month out of three. She's Protestant, he's Jewish, and like most newly married couples trying to adjust themselves, have innumerable arguments. These continued through the mail, and her last letter suggested divorce. Naturally, he was terribly upset at the thought of losing her, for he does love her—and at my suggestion, which he solicited, wrote her a beautiful love letter. He said I made him feel so much better. So now, I'm watching the outcome with much interest.

How are my two big boys? I'm so pleased and proud when I think of all the fine things Neil is doing to make things easier for you, and for me, too. And I have so much confidence in David, since Neil seems to be a good example.

Dear, did I write you that I made out 2 checks at Camp Kilmer (our embarkation point)? One for Jim for $5. and the other for $10. to myself, as I was short of money when we sailed. It did little good, however, since my wallet was lifted out of my pocket on the boat, ten dollars and all. It bothered me very little in this situation, as you begin to realize how unimportant money really is—agree?

Don't send any money since we use French currency, and will have no use for it. And by the time I'd get it, I'd be paid for October. You might send me a few blank checks though, as I might want to send for something in the States. You probably already know the regulations concerning packages being sent overseas.

* "Mr. Anthony" was a radio show in which persons would recite their problems and receive advice, frequently on affairs of the heart, much in the manner of today's advice-to-the-lovelorn newspaper and magazine features.

There are a few things I could use—candy, nuts, plenty of it, but make sure they're packed in cans. Perhaps once a week, but I'll have to write a written request each time—these are the rules. Also a jack-knife and a few bars of soap. Cookies, too, the kind that don't crumble and get any worse with age—and a plum pudding from Horn & Hardart's would be welcome. Call P.O. to learn exact size and regulations. We're outdoors all day and I get very hungry—often eating C and K rations.

The villagers are interesting here. Cigarettes are practically nil, and they'll barter almost anything for them. They have plenty of wine, and that is their chief source of exchange. Since I don't go for wine much, I've traded for grapes and pears which are delicious—the only food items there's no scarcity of. A franc is only worth 2¢ in American currency—used to be about 19¢.

25 October

Today received your first letter—the first V-Mail! It's been a long time en route, so in the future use only airmail.

We're not working too hard, and our little Medical Group is turning out to be quite friendly. The Captain and Lt. are decent, democratic guys, and pleasant, and don't go around pulling rank. When work comes up it's shared cooperatively. Much happier here than in the Infantry.

We still have rain, rain, mud, mud, mud but manage to keep dry and warm in our tents or in the First-Aid Tent. I meant to go to town today for a bath (16¢ in American money) but it's rainy and cold, so if weather permits will go tomorrow. Don't expect a letter from me daily, Dearest, even though I write, as the mail doesn't leave each day, so you'll probably be receiving a few at a time. I'll try to number my letters as you do so you can read them in proper sequence.

26 October

Today your 4 V-Mail letters made me a very happy man. As yet no regular mail, which is due by boat. However, I'm relieved and happy now that mail has started coming in.

On pass, today, we spent in the large city near our bivouac area—intensely interesting. Wish I could tell you the name of it. The French are a unique breed. Bargaining is the rule—not the exception. There are no places to eat—not even refreshments, except for drinks or grapes or pears. Rumor has it that the Army will allow us an extra C or K ration to compensate for the meal we miss on pass.*

While I referred chiefly to the soldier or transient—it's almost impossible to get anything to eat. Civilians have limited rations; and even these are insufficient. Whenever they can they bug the C and K rations from the boys for fancy prices. They go for cigarettes the same way, but mostly in barter. There are lots of junk things to buy, but nothing interesting enough to get you and the boys.

Just got back from town where I'd been writing this letter in the Red Cross Club. It was a treat to be indoors for a change—the first time since getting off the boat a week ago. A number of American women direct the Club, although the help are French. It's no cinch for a woman to be here and they're much appreciated.

Saw a wedding band I liked in a window; it was after store hours but I expect to go back in a couple of days and purchase it. It will be a constant reminder of our solid union.

---

* The Army issued two basic types of packaged field rations to its troops. The K ration came in a waterproofed box, approximately the size of a Cracker Jack box, and its contents were dried. It could contain crackers, candy, dried and preserved food, and other items such as matches and cigarettes. The C ration was canned; it came in several varieties, and was designed to be eaten either cold or heated. C rations could contain meat, vegetables, cheese, and other items. All field personnel carried mess kits, which when opened up provided two oval pans, sectioned, into which hot food could be ladled. One pan was slotted, and the hinged handle of the other fitted into the slot underneath, to allow both pans to be held in one hand. Army cooks tried to serve at least one hot meal a day to troops in the field, but under combat conditions this was frequently not possible. Each soldier also carried a canteen, the bottom of which fit into a cup. Even when cooks could not get hot food to forward positions, they usually sought to move up under cover of darkness to front-line foxholes and entrenchments to provide hot coffee, though often enough this too proved difficult of accomplishment. As we shall see, Pfc. Winston and his comrades were highly appreciative of the efforts made by their unit's cooks.

—cartoon by Bob Clarke, from The Story of the Century

27 October

Again I'm in the "big city" chiefly for a shower and the wedding band. I got both and am particularly happy over the ring and its significance.

Today I had an opportunity to go through one of these famous vineyards. It was small but meticulously cared for. The grapevines twist around low wooden frames and it's amazing to see how little space a properly tended vineyard requires. Roughly, there were over 1000 vines. The local grapes are the green, sweet seeded ones and they sure are good.

28 October

Yesterday's meeting with the boys set me up and my spirits are pretty good.—And what do you know, today is my birthday! Next year you'll have to make up for the cake you're not baking this year!

Today no mail, but maybe tomorrow. It's been windy all day and we anticipate a cold winter but we're prepared for it.

I may be over-optimistic but I feel that the near future will bring an end to all this.—Will continue later.

30 October   *En Route*

Now that we're on the move I can give you a few details of our trip not permitted earlier, as every move is secret. Now that we've left, I can tell you the "big city" I kept mentioning was Marseille. We landed there October 20th after a long, miserable 15-day voyage.

We sailed through the Gibraltar Straits getting a good view of the famous Rock. North Africa lay to our right, and Spain to our left as we coursed through the 22-mile-long, 8-mile-wide straits. Despite the distance of 8 miles, the two coasts were surprisingly visible. We sailed 2 days on the Mediterranean Sea which was like glass—glistening, warm, beautiful. But late in the second day we ran into a raging Mediterranean storm and went through a night I shall never forget.

We docked in Marseille, a city about the size of Baltimore. Effects of bombing were visible in some areas but in the main sections you'd hardly know it was a war city, except for the constant presence of soldiers—Allied soldiers from all over the world. Wine is the chief industry, and with U.S. cigarettes the boys are stocking up plenty. After dark the city suddenly becomes quiet and by 9 P.M. the streets are clear of American soldiers.

You'd probably like to know something about the "famous" French girls. It's not fair to make a blanket judgment but in the short time I've been around here I find the French a highly immoral people by our standards. It's said there are 41,000 licensed prostitutes in Marseille—so if that figure is correct—it appears that almost every woman in this city is a whore. I'm sure this damned war, with people half-starving, contributed to this sad state—and I'm afraid our boys didn't lose much time sampling their "wares."

Oct. 31st—still en route. The trip, boring and uncomfortable as it was in the beginning, is turning out to be most interesting. First, I should retract some of the things I said about French women, as apparently what I saw and heard was common only in Marseille, but the farther we get from the city, the finer the people seem to be, and less mercenary. Scenery is breathtaking—comparable to any I've encountered—anywhere. Being mountainous, it reminds me of the beautiful Skyline Drive in the Shenandoah National Park.

The French vineyards are exciting to see—usually located on the side of a huge mountain, and divided off into parcels about the size of our land. Then each section is leveled by a dry wall. Looking at a mountain and seeing hundreds of these parcels, each with their little dry wall, is extremely picturesque. And I study these walls closely as I can visualize how easy it will be leveling our ground with them. Everything you see is stone—no wood—stone walls, stone homes, etc.

I hear that during the ripening season, grape-growers do a good bit of worrying. They watch the mountains carefully, for a storm rolling down from the heights of a mountain can ruin a season's crop.

All this, despite their interest and beauty, can't be fully enjoyed when I realize under what conditions we are here.

I'm writing while traveling, thus the unsteadiness of my pen. Right now you and Neil are probably exchanging your morning "greetings." Oh, Sweetheart, how I wish I were home to hear it.

For security measures I suggest you use plain paper when you write. No name or address like ours has. You might cut it off. Envelopes are OK because I'll just burn them—but I like to keep your letters a few days and I'm not to carry any identification on me.

That gnawing, heavy heart feeling is returning. Maybe everything will turn out better than it presently appears. Please try to be a good "soldier" whatever that means.

2 November—Another day and we've finished travelling. We're bivouacked in a rather nice area. You know how the countryside looks this time of year with its change of colors—well, I'm right in the midst of this beauty but can't enjoy it, hard as I try. I have so much to come home to, and it makes all this so much harder to take. Exactly one month ago I saw your smiling face saying goodbye at the station. It seems like a year.

There's hardly anything to say—we're not permitted to write of our activities here, but writing brings you so much closer. I'm returning two of your letters—one in particular (Oct. 3) when you realized I was sailing. I've read it at least 20 times and shed more than one tear. It was the only tangible thing to bring me close to you throughout this past month.

By the time you receive this, Election Day will be over.* I hope you voted, as our man needs all the support he can get. I have every confidence he'll be re-elected. God only knows how much he is now needed.

We've been eating rations the last 3 or 4 days. Expect something hot tonight and it will be welcomed. While the rations become monotonous, they're substantial and that's what counts. We all favor the K rations.

We're supposed to be paid November 1, but I'll have little use for money. Darling, I look forward to your letters.

4 November

Church bells were ringing when I awoke this morning and for a split second become excited and full of anticipation, half-dreaming half-hoping it could mean the cessation of hostilities. Somehow I feel the war could end just that simply and suddenly.

The *Stars & Stripes*, an Army newspaper, was supposed to arrive daily but we haven't seen one yet, consequently we know nothing about what is happening. The one thing we *do* know, however, is

---

* Incumbent Democratic President Roosevelt won reelection to a fourth term over Republican Thomas E. Dewey, 25,602,505 votes to 22,006,278.

that the European War is still very much on, and right now all other news is secondary.

Censorship is pretty strict and I can't tell you of my whereabouts. However, I'm willing to bet our location was already published in U.S. papers. Read the papers carefully and you'll probably find out where we are before you find out from me. You remember our Division—I can't mention it here—nor should you when you write. Don't hesitate to let me know anything you learn about us—and I'm not kidding.

5 November

Your four sweet letters did for me what fresh water does for a dying plant.

Demobilization is the main topic of conversation around here, so would you send me a copy of the plan Rose sent you in your next letter? And I could make good use of a French textbook. Knowing the language is an asset. The other day two French women told one of our boys who speaks the language, how much they'd like to do for our group, but it's so difficult to understand each other. They offered to wash and press this boy's dirty laundry and insisted he come up regularly for a bath and hot meal. A little French is very helpful!

6 November

Received 9!!!! V-mails late last night, and between the 4 regular letters, my letter to you, I was busy with mail all day—and happy about the whole thing.

More rain today but we manage to keep dry. The leaves are falling and the colors are beautiful. Remember the gardener who sold us our perennials? He took pride in adding "French Gardener" after his name. Seeing how neat and efficient these French people

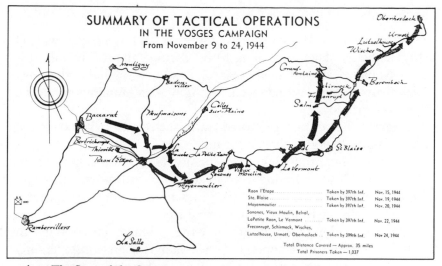

—from The Story of the Century

are with their lawns and gardens and fields, I have a better understanding of his pride.

Your news of U.S. commentators predicting an end to the European war before Christmas was encouraging. You might call the *Record* for their overseas edition if they have one—if not, try the *Bulletin. Time* magazine has an overseas edition which I'd enjoy getting.—I laughed when you wrote of Bunny planning to take time out for a nervous breakdown after the war. Her husband is now in Hawaii, isn't he?

Your poem I enjoyed immensely. I'm so proud of you, Sweetheart.

Don't worry your little head about me trying to be a hero. I don't believe in that in this *game*. Fortunately, my C.O.'s pet expression is "don't be a Hero," and is chiefly interested in keeping his men safe and alive; doesn't believe in taking chances unless absolutely urgent.

10 November

We've been on the go the last few days and at present writing still on the go. There's nothing to be alarmed about.* If only this mess would clear—not next week or next month, but right now. How many lives would be saved, and how many millions would be delirious with joy.

Today I heard our President was re-elected. I know you're pleased—and that goes double for me.

My new set-up, though very temporary, is exceptionally comfortable, especially after having lived in tents up until now. The small group of medics are actually living in a house—plenty of warmth, food and a chance to shave with warm water.

Conditions don't permit me to write a longer letter, but I'm well, comfortable and hopeful. I pray daily for an abrupt ending and that I'll soon get home and be able to put my arms around you. God bless you and our two children. I love to think of the glorious days we'll have together—soon—with God's help.

11 November

Today is Armistice Day, and I couldn't help thinking what it must have meant 26 years ago when we thought we fought a war to "end all wars"—and all the attending lunacy of war. And that people, once and for all, had had their fill, and realized the futility of greed and senseless killing. And that finally we'd seen the last of wars. But the world didn't count on the insanity of power-mad "leaders" who could throw civilization back a century or more— and that our so-called civilization would have lost its meaning, and make you wonder what this world's about anyway. And though I'm

* There was a good deal to be alarmed about, and Sarah Winston, back home in Pennsylvania, sensed that her husband was in danger. On 8 November, two days before, Winston, who was serving as a litter-bearer, had gone out into a minefield to rescue an injured infantryman, and exploding shrapnel had wounded him in the face. Throughout the Vosges and subsequent campaigns, Winston consistently downplayed what was going on, in an effort not to alarm his wife.

not a praying guy as you know, I did pray today, hoping for a complete rout and defeat of these madmen, and that we'd know peace again before it's too late for us and our children. It's hard to believe, Honey, but power-hungry lunatics are around in all countries, including our own—and my outlook isn't too bright for a peaceful world 26 years from now. People in our country don't begin to know the meaning of war—and don't care—until it hits them; when one of their family is killed or wounded.

I didn't mean to go on like this, Honey, but when you see what I see you begin to wonder about people and the world and it doesn't flood you with confidence for the future. Armistice Day seems to have so little meaning.

What I can tell you is still limited. I've been working very hard the last few days, and I suspect you know what that means. But no cause for alarm. My set-up is adequate with hot meals during the day, and that's something most soldiers can't enjoy unfortunately.

Re: your letter in which you ask me to confirm or disaffirm certain presumptions. All I can do is refer you to the newspaper, if and when they print it. I can't say anything—yet. It sounds ridiculous but the censorship is usually lifted through Washington, and the newspapers print it the same day. By the time we're told it's another two weeks. Then 10 days by mail to you.

About your concern over what the French are paying for American cigarettes—don't let it get you too much. They take the soldiers over plenty, too. Lots to tell you on that.

Neil and his good work in school continues to be a source of great pleasure. And David's doings delight me. I love them both so much. Darling, I'm so tired. The main thing is that I'm well. Take care of yourself and the children.

14 November   *Somewhere in France*

Some days the going is a little rough—like today—and it makes me want to be home and away from all the "murdering." Forgive me for being so dismal.

Was transferred to Hq. Co. from the 2nd Bn. My new address will be as the envelope states—Medical Detachment—instead of 2nd Bn. Hq. Co. I haven't heard from you for a few days, and now with the change of address, it may take a few days before mail catches up. Your letters are my mainstay. I'm still waiting anxiously for the pictures.

While I have little faith in the rumor, I hear Gen. Patton says he'll be in Berlin *before* December.*

Darling, I'm so homesick. Praying, hoping, writing just don't seem to satisfy. The feeling is worse sometimes more than others but I'll snap out of it. Today I'm laid low with it but please don't let it bother you too much, and know that when you read this I'll be over it.

Harry—the boy from Boston—is in this section and I'll probably be seeing a lot of him. It will give me a lift.

Just heard something new—that I'm to be transferred to the 3rd Bn. Hq. Medical Section—but write to the same address until I tell you otherwise.—You're forever in my heart—and I'll never be happy till I can hold you in my arms again.

15 November

Another day. Nothing new except my transfer to 3rd Bn.—same capacity. I feel somewhat strange, but will be closer to the original group—the rifle outfit—and seeing some of them occasionally will help. We're ready to move again, so may cut this letter short. There's only one thing on my mind—you, our boys and home. I miss you all so.

It's noon and church bells are ringing in the village. Apparently it's on old custom, but someday the bells will ring announcing the war is over—and that day I'm looking to prayerfully.

No Red Cross Clubs or the like are within reach and I'm having

* In three weeks, beginning 8 November, the U.S. Third Army slugged its way forward 35 or 40 miles to the Saar River, but was stopped at the Siegfried Line. Meanwhile the U.S. Ninth Army fought its way to the Roer River, but no further. The U.S. First Army, advancing through the murderous Huertgen Forest, suffered heavy casualties and did not reach the Roer River until mid-December.

trouble getting stationery. Could you send me some? I like pads—
easier to carry in my pockets—and envelopes.

While fixing my bedroll on the floor this morning I found myself crawling. I thought of little David and the way he crawls
around. He must be about ready to take some steps on his own
by now.

We've just been ordered to move, Darling. Still no reason for
worry. I miss you and that heavy feeling seems to be a part of me.

16 November

The rain continues, and very little, if any, sun—and the mud
continues. However, the cold, while typically late autumn-like is
tolerable. Except for the rain, it's surprising how close weather
conditions here are like those at home. And the leaves, as colorful.
We're out of doors almost all the time, but build a fire here and
there to warm us up. When possible, the Medics try to get into a
house for their work.

Your letters fill me with joy. Enjoyed every word of your account
of Ncilly's Hallowe'en party. And David's reaction to Neil's cos-
tume. Telling me about the payment of bills, and amounts, etc.
brought a touch of home. Continue to do that.

One thing we don't relish is the short days. It starts to get dark
about 4:30. About the bath situation, it's far from good. If and
when we're near a large city, we're able to get a warm bath—called
a "douche" in French. And we welcome it.

My chief request, of you, Dear, is to write daily—and plenty—
sometimes with an enclosure, a letter received from someone, a
newspaper write-up, a column by Drew Pearson that might interest me. Or the final tabulation by States in the recent election, with
names of Congressmen and Senators—or a few write-ups on a big
happening—perhaps like Wendell Willkie's death.* We get very
little news here and you're groping in the dark. What you do learn
is not detailed and I enjoy getting the facts.

* Wendell Willkie had died of a coronary thrombosis on 8 October 1944.

The set-up in this Bn. is similar to the other and I'm sure I'll have no trouble getting along. The C.O. is a young Lt. recently out of Jefferson Medical College.* He's a likeable fellow and the boys all get along well with him.

Awaiting another move and may end this letter abruptly. Well—it's here, my Dearest—we're on our way. Save this crumbled letter as there's a story behind it. I keep looking at the picture of you and the boys and it gives me strength and courage to carry on.

21 November

Missed 4 days writing to you and I guess you know why, but I feel bad because I know you're looking for a few words from me. Because of our movement haven't heard from you in 5 days. At this point could use a few of your morale boosters but neither of us can help the matter.—We're continually on the move, and while it's rough, damp, etc. it is nothing for you to be alarmed about. Censorship still limits what I can say.

You have no idea of the satisfaction I get knowing the wonderful job you're doing. We have so many good things to look forward to together.—Everyone around here seems amazed that I get a letter out occasionally—they don't seem to, as much as they try.

22 November

Just moved to another village—not too far from the one where I last wrote. It's much more comfortable—what with a little heat and a feminine touch. The lady of the house we're in doesn't seem to be able to do enough for us—especially after the boys gave her some rations. Money means little here since there's nothing to buy. On the other hand, food means everything. In fact, civilians are

* Lt. (later Capt.) Brown McDonald, Jr., of Montgomery, West Virginia. But Winston may have been referring to Capt. Joseph R. Rich.

happy to pay for it—although in this part of France, I doubt if any of the boys would take money.

After moving into this town I heard some encouraging news— news which probably is old to you. The German 1st Army surrendering to Patton, and the possible taking of Strasbourg, a very important objective.* And also, Roosevelt's probable visit to Paris. It all sounds good, doesn't it?

As I write in these homey surroundings, with the warm stove and lamp light, I look at your pictrue and say, "I love you, Darling, you look so sweet and my boys so handsome"—and it's the closest touch of home.

The courage these French women have should be a consolation and inspiration to us. Many haven't seen their husbands for 3, 4, 5 years—at present they're slaves in Germany. In addition they have to beg, borrow, steal what the Nazis leave. Yet with all that they seem—in some way—to carry on.

I feel elated about all the good news I'm hearing. It makes me feel more confident that we'll be together in the not too distant future. I get my ups and downs. Right now it is up—but not too high—as some mail from you hasn't caught up to me yet, and I don't mind telling you I'm missing it.

Tomorrow is Thanksgiving Day. I hope we'll soon have something to be thankful for.

23 November†

Dear Sonny Boy,

Today is Thanksgiving Day. I guess you and Mother and David will have turkey or chicken. I hope so. I'm sure next Thanksgiving

---

* Strasbourg fell to the French First Army on 23 September 1944. The French, however, neglected to clear a 30-by-50 mile area west of the Rhine River, containing 50,000 German troops. This area, known as the Colmar Pocket, was to create much concern at Supreme Headquarters in late December when the German counteroffensives were unleashed, and to provoke an angry confrontation between General Eisenhower and Charles de Gaulle.

† This letter is addressed to Winston's son Neil.

will be different. Right now, let's plan on going to the football game with Mother—and then home to a big roast turkey dinner. It's a promise for next Thanksgiving, Son—OK?

While we're on the subject of eating, perhaps you would like to know what we eat. Well, usually they try to give us one hot meal a day, and it is similar to what Mother might have for supper. The other two meals are usually what they call rations. Sometimes, we get "C" rations, and it looks like this—in two cans—

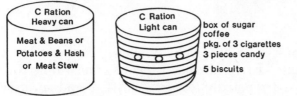

Sometimes we get "K" rations which look like this:

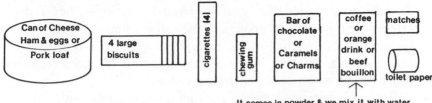

It comes in powder & we mix it with water

With love, Daddy

Its clearing of the Vosges area completed, the 100th Infantry Division was withdrawn from the line on 26 November 1944, and reassembled near Raon-l'Etape, where it underwent several days of assault training. On 2 December the 398th Infantry was moved to positions in the neighborhood of La Petite Pierre, and the day following, the 100th Division drove against the concrete pillboxes and fortifications of the Maginot Line. Built by the French in the 1920s and 1930s as a defense against future German invasion, these powerful fortifications, with underground railways, elevators and disappearing guns, had not fallen when the German armies unleashed their blitzkrieg attack in 1940. Occupied by the Germans after the fall of France, they were swiftly adapted to protect against attack from the west. During the period 3–13 December the 100th Division fought its way through the towns of Wingen, Soucht, Meisenthal, Goetzenbruck and Lemberg, and on 14 December moved out against the Maginot Line bastions of Fort Freudenberg and the heavily fortified Fort Schiesseck. By 22 December, after heavy fighting, the division had captured both, and was poised for an assault on the city of Bitche, the key stronghold of the Maginot defenses.

24 November

Today, a new house—and little activity. News continues to be good. Today I ran into Harry,* the boy I spent so much time with on the boat. He was temporarily lost from his Co. and since he speaks French, had no trouble getting along. He told me that he and the people with whom he stayed, had a real Thanksgiving Day dinner. He provided the bouillon from his rations—they the potatoes and onions—and cooked a tasty soup. And with their black bread, had a wonderful meal. Tonight we've been promised a turkey dinner—a day late, but it will be good—if it comes. I feel so much lighter with the improved war outlook.

Rain still continues, but the weather is not severely cold.

The American boys seem to have a way with the French people, who say we're generous, and while they like the British—say we're more apt to keep our word. The boys do get along well with them, and as a whole, are very much gentlemen.

My C.O. seems to be a real nice guy, and the more I see him, the better I like him. He should be a successful physician after the war.

LATER—Same Day

We're sitting around singing songs, and it really brings home close—a little too close, perhaps, especially after singing "White Christmas" when a significant hush came over the group.

Still waiting for the turkey dinner, and the last report has it that it will be ready by 8 P.M.—so now we're hungry and anticipating. Until later, with all the love it is possible to hold.

26 November

I'm feeling rather low today, chiefly because 10 days have gone by without a word from you. The mail is definitely not coming through and the let-down and disappointment doesn't help.

* Pfc. Harry H. Fienman, of Brighton, Mass., an infantryman, was wounded in action during the fighting in France and was hospitalized in England.

Today is Sunday but you'd hardly know it. War keeps no holidays. Oh, for one of those quiet restful Sundays we spent together.

Moving on yesterday we drove through beautiful countryside. While I have no desire to ever visit France once I get out of it, I can understand why so many tourists visit here in peace times.

If my letters tend to be vague or general in my remarks, remember I am aware of it, but our job requires places and duties be definitely secret. Often I find it difficult to write because of this restriction.

Our troupe (Medics) has managed to get 7 chickens and one turkey, and when we're settled for a day or two, we're ready to prepare a feast. There are 30 in our group and not too big to do things of this sort. We keep the chickens in one of the trucks.

28 November

Have been on the move again and missed your letter. This town has turned out to be interesting for me. I ran into a civilian, a man about 30, married, with a 5-year-old daughter, who speaks English, and he's done everything possible to make things comfortable for me. Through his generosity I slept on a feather mattress, and enjoyed a few home-cooked meals for a change. I like to think it was reciprocal. My presence gave him a chance to learn things about America he was eager to know. And my offering them little things like soap, cigarettes, bouillon, cheese, candy, etc. was helpful to them.

He works in an office and seemed like quite a capable individual. Showed me a picture-frame holder he devised from the waste of a product his firm manufactures, and they paid him handsomely for his idea. He owns a large "wireless" (radio), something uncommon here. They played the victrola last night and made a real effort to be hospitable.

It's remarkable how well the French make out with the little food they have. His wife, who can't speak English, made an entree of soup from potatoes which was exceptionally good. Then for the main dish—potatoes (didn't detract from the entree) and hot dogs

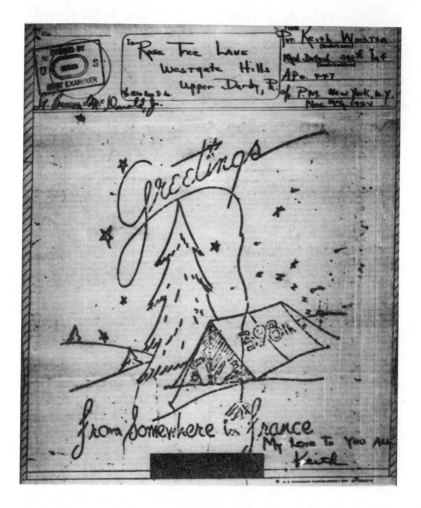

from a can of G.I. hot dogs a Captain gave them a few days earlier—and pudding and tea. Of course, under these conditions, I ate very sparingly. He told me food is difficult to get but day by day he manages to get satisfactory amounts. It's far from good, he says, but they can get by. For instance, butter is next to impossible to buy unless you pay $8. a lb. at the black market, even though the "ceiling" price is 70¢ (equivalent in U.S. money).

He was amazed to know we could get 2 pairs of shoes annually and all the clothing we could buy. Everything here is rationed, and half the time the ration points are worthless since there's no food or commodities. The town itself is a typical European village—probably the size of our Westgate, but old and rustic. I know you would love the quiet beauty of the place. It has 2 or 3 beer taverns—a principal European commodity—and a bakery still in operation. Other than that, no business places. It's close to a rather large city where most purchasing is done.

It's a pity that such splendid, historic beauty should actually be wasted since our mission here is *not* that of tourist. This charming town makes me yearn even more for your companionship, as it would be so enjoyable if you were here with me.

Well, at last five letters arrived! Hope I'll be hearing more regularly now.—We're still in this beautiful little village, and the feather mattress was again slept on last night, this time shared with Harry. I went down to his Co. to get him since I know, he, coming from a rifle Co. never gets a chance to sleep indoors. He said it was like heaven and thanked me a thousand times. We enjoyed another evening with these French people and have hopes of spending another night there.

Sorry you had so much trouble finding plum pudding—when it was fruit cake I meant all the time! I have enough soap and will give the excess to civilians since it's sorely needed.

Was happy you voted—and pleased that your enthusiasm matches mine. These French people I stayed with told us that the Germans, for 3 months, were telling them Roosevelt couldn't make it, and Dewey was sure—they were emphatic. I share your delight in Roosevelt's victory and the defeat of those reactionary congressmen.

29 November

Am having a hey-day with the mail situation. Five letters yesterday—3 today—and a chance of more coming. Do I have to tell you how I feel? I'm very sorry my mail isn't coming through as it should, but eventually you'll get it. Remember—first, I must find the time to write, then the censor must find the time to censor, then mail must be sent back to the A.P.O. This could make for a 3- or 4-day delay.

As to what I sleep on—in the tent. We cover the ground with pine needles when available, then 2 blankets, with 4 to cover us (2 men in tent). I assure you it isn't like home but after awhile it becomes easier to accept. However, being a Medic, I—perhaps 35% of the time—am in a house—even if it means sleeping on the floor. And the important thing is that it's dry.

Tonight I have a steak dinner awaiting—with apple pie. Harry suggested we ask the French family to cook a steak dinner if we provide the steak, and they were delighted. We traded cigarettes for steak—and 7 P.M. we eat—and then a feather bed to sleep in— ahem!

Rumors run thick and fast there are peace negotiations with Gen. Eisenhower, and that the President is in Paris.

We took showers in a city close by today. It's interesting how they work. They're run by the Quartermaster and moved from place to place. Despite its temporary location, it's amazing how warm and comfortable they make it.

30 November

Another day and lucky to still be in this quiet, peaceful little village.—Last night, the steak dinner was perfect, except for the steak which was tough because the meat was so fresh. They served *real* French fried potatoes—and *good*—and soup and French apple pie, so big in size and delicious, and still another pie—blueberry— which we just couldn't make room for. Tonight, arrangements have been made for a liver and onion supper. The people are grand, but we pay them well in food items, candy, cigarettes, etc.

The slow-down has been wonderful and well appreciated. Though we hope it continues on and on we expect to move at a moment's notice. I met a boy from Philly and it was nice to speak to someone familiar with places and people I know. He's a buyer for Food Fair.

I'm making a glutton of myself these last few days. First, breakfast, then candy and cake from packages, then lunch, then more package treats. Then a G.I. supper at 4:30 and supper again at our French friends at 7:30.

2 December

There is something I should tell you, Darling. About the 1st of November, one of our boys stepped on a shoe mine. He was definitely where he was ordered not to be. Even though this was far behind the lines, it takes some time for our engineers to clear mine fields. This boy was hurt and required a stretcher and 4 men to bring him in. I was one of the four chosen to get him. As we started out, one of the 4 litter-bearers stepped on another mine and was badly injured. The concussion cut my lip and it bled rather badly. My C.O., trying to be a good fellow, recommended me for the Purple Heart medal. I really thought it was a gag as this was minor to what I'd been seeing all about me.* For that reason, said nothing to you. But it wasn't a gag, and yesterday the Regiment Colonel gave me the medal. It's nothing to be proud of, and I'm only sending it to you for its souvenir value. Now I don't want you getting the idea my job is so dangerous. A thing like this occurs rarely.

Well, Dear, all good things come to an end and we finally left the quiet little village we all enjoyed so well. Harry and I said good-bye to the French family, and they said they will write one day. The man is intelligent and a product of the French upper class. God bless you all.

3 December

Today—another day—and hopefully one day closer to victory and you. At present we're located in a big hotel "sans" Bellevue Strat-

---

* Winston's wound was incurred on 8 November, not 1 November, and was, his wife says, "far worse than he described it." Doubtless it was his knowledge that the awarding of the Purple Heart Medal would be reported to newspapers in the Phila-

ford service, of course! But it's dry and we're making use of the stoves in every room.

Sent off the medal. Please say nothing to anyone about it. One reason, too, that I mentioned it was that you might see my name listed in the paper and really get upset over it. Again I say I'm perfectly well—no ill effects whatsoever. Actually, my first impulse was to throw it away, but really is an attractive thing and I changed my mind.

The Army is catching up on cigarette and chocolate rations. You see, we're supposed to get 1 pack a day, as well as a small bar of chocolate and stick of gum. Being on the move so much the rations are often missed but they keep accumulating. So in the last 5 days we've received innumerable packs of cigarettes, bars of chocolates, gum, shaving cream, tooth powder, toothbrushes, etc.—more than we can use. Knowing of the cigarette shortage back home, the boys joke about sending them back to the States.

Here are a couple of typical "funnies" making the rounds: "Don't wait up for me, General. Just leave the Sgt. burning in the window."

Little girl to little boy: "Let's play house."

Little boy: "OK. I'll be the soldier and you stay home and worry."

Every time I think of home I fill up. I dream so much about it only to be ruefully awakened in the morning.

Aside from the almost constant rain, the weather seems to be fair—I mean from the standpoint of severe cold which will come soon enough.

I'm sure you notice the paper I write on is not so hot—usually wrinkled, odds and ends, and that you assume our supply is low. Well, you're right—and they don't get replenished either. That's why I request paper and envelopes. The pen is still holding out, but many boys depend on its use and I'm happy when it comes back in one piece.—I manage to see the old 2nd Bn. crowd quite often, and it helps to take the heat of war away for a few moments.

---

delphia area that led him to mention it now. For the citation accompanying the medal, see the note on p. 252.

5 December

On the go for the last two days and missed writing you yesterday.

The home we're in now was a big hotel at one time and is quite comfortable. The family has 4 children—the youngest, David's age, and I get such a kick out of watching her. She's such a pleasant little thing, and I keep thinking of David.

The days continue short and rainy but it's not too cold yet—and the countryside is hilly and beautiful. But I'll take rain, mud or anything for Peace, and may that day come overnight.

Saw Harry yesterday. Haven't seen Jim and hope he's OK. I received 3 of your precious letters last night, and nothing, except you in person, could have meant more. I don't need money—can't spend it—so don't worry about sending any. In Marseille you can use money, but here—no. Thanks for the "Future Release" on the demobilization plan. I found it very interesting.

Last week I saw masses of chrysanthemums all over the place, but they were about finished and I know what the last flower of fall means.

We've been moving again, Dear, and I've been seeing so many kids Neil's and David's age—it kind of gets to me. I'm standing up as I write on this messy paper, around a candle for light, but I do get such a warm feeling being able to "talk" with you, conditions are secondary.

Since I felt it important to explain the Purple Heart situation, you're now aware of my particular function as a litter-bearer. I hope this hasn't caused any extra anxiety, for as far as safety is concerned, we're not foolhardy, and take every conceivable precaution for ourselves as well as the victims. Believe me, Honey, we're all happy to be well and alive and make every effort to keep it that way. The accident I wrote you about was caused by pure and unadulterated idiocy. The boy had flagrantly disregarded orders and walked into an "off limits" section heavily mined by the Germans. But you know how some dumb kids operate, they just don't use their noodles.—We don't have this problem where our soldiers are dug in.

I know it would be foolish to tell you there is absolutely no danger involved—but, Dearest. there is an inherent danger in just about every move you make in life—even in peacetime. But we try to do the best we can. So please accept all this, as I'm doing—not only will it make you feel better, but it will make me feel much better, too. Okay?

You must be wondering, and perhaps concerned about my first assignment up front. Well, here it is: Our team was rushed out to pick up a seriously injured boy. To be more explicit—to pick up a boy whose leg was blown off. You can imagine my reaction at the thought. But this was my job, and I was in the Army and I had no alternative but to go. However, as we got closer, I was determined to avoid looking at this catastrophe—and tried to keep my head averted as much as it was possible. But somehow—and this is really uncanny—the first thing that drew my eyes, as if magnetized, was this torn-off leg. I was almost in a state of shock, and I just stood there, staring, almost not believing what I saw.—But, Honey, somehow a super-strength rushes through in moments like these—and I was aware that the life of this boy depended on our immediate and careful attention. To make a long, gruesome story short, I did what I was sent out to do—and that was my first and thorough initiation. After that, I was about ready for anything.

I'm pretty tired now and this candlelight doesn't make for easy writing. Goodnight—until later.

7 December

Today is the 3rd anniversary of U.S. involvement in the war and I pinned some hope on that date for the war to be over, but the day is still here, and the war is still on. Maybe something will turn up to answer my—and millions of others—prayers.

I miss so much the daily newspapers and magazines—as you know we have no way of keeping up with home news, or even war news, except for Stars & Stripes and that paper is not much more than a school paper—nothing really newsworthy.

Though I find the native people interesting, I have a heck of a time making myself understood. You can't realize that language can be such an important factor in mixing with people. You know, some day I'd like to see a universal language taught in every school in every country, along with the native language. Then all language barriers would disappear—no matter where you might go. The way I feel now, though, once I get back on American soil, I'll probably never want to leave again.

10 December

Today is Sunday—but so different from the Sundays we knew. Last night a group of us was sitting around, discussing pre-war oc-

For the First Time in History
An Army Crossed the Vosges

Like a giant hand clutching an enormous eraser, troops of the VI Corps, U. S. Army have rubbed out the centuries-old "T" on the big word "can't" as it applies to the military conquest of the Vosges mountains.

Precedent fell like Germans as both veteran and "green" troops fought the hun, the terrain and the weather to shatter enemy defenses in a history-w acking campaign that rocked the supermen back against the Rhine.

In centuries past, military men, seeking new plans to exploit the battlefields of France, shook their heads and shouted "No!" when the Vosges sector with its pathway to the east was mentioned.

And well they might because geography seemed to be caught in a mixture of beauty and agony when the Vosges mountains were put down on the plotting board.

Beauty there is, undoubtedly — tall pines on taller mountains, rushing streams and jutting crags of sheer rock. That same picturesqueness which excites the layman is agony for the military man who has to find a new way to scale those cliffs, to push through those forests and at the same time root a stubborn enemy out of his defenses—defenses which he has had months to prepare.

Research among French officials, familiar with the campaigns which have swirled for years through their country, say that never before in history have the Vosges been cleared in a military operation.

For Centuries Military Men Considered The Vosges Impregnable. In the Fall of 1944 VI Corps of the U.S. Army Broke Thru

Thus the VI Corps has written a new page—and it was written in an autumn-early winter campaign with the mud, the rain and the snow and sleet offering practically as many problems as the buck-pedaling kraut.

The same area where Corps infantrymen and supporting troops punched through to the Rhine saw a stalemate in the first World War which extended for four long years from October 1914 right through to the end of the conflict.

The sector was the scene of bloody, vigorous fighting during part of the war but the Germans then could not be pushed off the crest of the Vosges—nor could they shove the French back from their positions in the lower mountain regions.

"Especially trained mountain troops were used in the Vosges fighting," said Col. Petit of the French Mission, 5th Army, "and the battles fought were terrible —

"Opposing infantry were separated by a few meters in trenches and dugouts. Hand grenades were tossed back and forth and pitched battles took heavy casualties.

"The objective was to win the crest of the Vosges but it could not be accomplished.

"The work of the VI Corps in its campaign which resulted in the clearing of the Vosges was remarkable—indeed remarkable and congratulations and a new place in history are due every man.

In the years gone by during military operations the Vosges were not even considered in the scheme of things. It was considered too difficult—especially during the season of rain and snow."

Generally speaking, the campaign to win the Vosges was inaugurated on or around September 21, 1944, with the cracking of the Moselle river.

That first period, which for the most part was more or less rapid in development, extended to about the middle of October when phase two got under way with the jump-off across the Mortagne river line and the push to a new water barrier the Meurthe. In between these two river lines lay more than a month of dreary fighting which saw the kraut putting up his most stubborn resistance, taking advantage of the almost continual rain, snow, sleet and natural defenses in the thickly-forested mountain country.

The push across the Meurthe — the phase of exploitation — got underway on or around November 20 and found the kraut rushing eastward with a speed reminiscent of the drive up from Southern France.

Sounds simple to put it that way —all arranged in neat phases — doesn't it?

But those pretty little arrangements don't begin to picture nights so black hat a wisp of fog could be mistaken for an enemy, of days of continual rain—day after day when the sun never peeked through. Cold

- - - The Infantry - - -

The weather was on their side. Relentless rain, snow and cold with only a rare sunny day. Civilians said it was the worst in 10 years. The Corps pushed on.   (Sig Corps Photo by Gretz)

- - - The Artillery - - -

German soldiers dreaded American artillery most. The guns of VI Corps guided by Cubs and ground OPs, ripped targets, helped pave the way for fast-moving infantry.   (Sig Corps Photo by Gretz)

Front page of VI Corps newspaper, *Beachhead News*, 10 December 1944 cupations, and post-war plans. I said little, chiefly because the boys were a rather young bunch.

Some of them spoke modestly of their future—not expecting too much, while others set their sights on making big money—and success was equated with how much money they could accumulate. You suddenly begin to realize how little money means when your health and your happiness and your future is at stake.

The Captain read that "Future Release on Demobilization," and since he's comparatively young with little or no attachments and dependents, he's resigned to being here till it's all over.

11 December

We're married 12½ years today—half of a silver anniversary. Happy half-anniversary, Dearest! I have a feeling that these next years are going to be real happy ones—with lots of activity centered around Home Sweet Home—seeing our children grow up—improving our little home, and most of all, always remembering to appreciate the little things in life. Agree?

Well, today I was transferred back to my old section—2nd Bn. Hq. They welcomed me very enthusiastically and it really gave me a lift. I'm tickled to be back with them.

I bumped into Henry, the boy who married his wife after a week's courtship. Didn't have a chance to talk much so I don't know what happened—yet, but will soon.

13 December

Another day—my spirits are pretty high in my new surroundings. This group is like a little family, and coming back was exactly what the doctor ordered.

Rumors fly thick and fast around here, you can't keep up with them. Most are unfounded—like the one going around that the

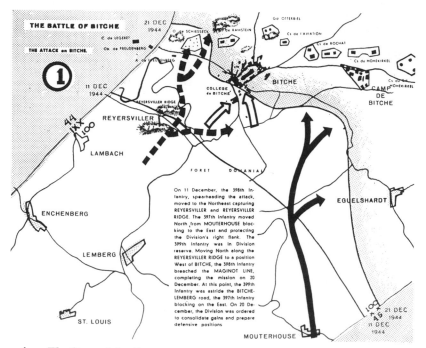

The following text appears within the map:

THE BATTLE OF BITCHE

THE ATTACK on BITCHE.

① 11 DEC 1944

21 DEC 1944

On 11 December, the 398th Infantry, spearheading the attack, moved to the Northeast capturing REYERSVILLER and REYERSVILLER RIDGE. The 397th Infantry moved North from MOUTERHOUSE blocking to the East and protecting the Division's right flank. The 399th Infantry was in Division reserve. Moving North along the REYERSVILLER RIDGE to a position West of BITCHE, the 398th Infantry breached the MAGINOT LINE, completing the mission on 20 December. At this point, the 399th Infantry was astride the BITCHE-LEMBERG road, the 397th Infantry blocking on the East. On 20 December, the Division was ordered to consolidate gains and prepare defensive positions

—from The Story of the Century

Germans would be laying down their arms on the 13th—today. But no such luck.

Yesterday we set up quarters in a tremendous French home—really magnificent. It was owned by an American. There's a powerful radio that receives stations from every country in the world—and clearly, too.

We listen to the news whenever we can, and we must have heard the same news a dozen times—probably like you do at home. And all along the front the news was cheering the day that 2400 planes in one group bombed important industrial plants in Frankfurt. I just can't see how Germany holds out with all their reversals. She may pass out completely any day now.

Again we moved last night and are quartered in a picturesque little stone home (they're all stone in France) with 4 rooms—all on one floor, similar to the $3990. homes we see in the States.

Well, well, well. I've just been handed 2 pieces of the stuff that keeps me going and how I did enjoy them!

Now I can talk a little more freely about my Division—within bounds, however, as censorship is still very much with us.

We're in the Alsace-Lorraine section of France, where the German language is spoken considerably more than French, and in the last 4 years the people have lived under German jurisdiction. Their sympathies are not too well defined—neither Nazi nor Ally, though some are strongly pro-Ally, and others pro-Nazi. These are the quiet, silent ones and you don't have to be too smart to see where their allegiance lies—Germans at heart, with hidden swastikas showing up at the wrong moment, as well as their pro-Nazi periodicals.

They drink ersatz coffee and much of the food is synthetic. One thing they welcome from us is white bread. They only have the "black bread"—comparable to our pumpernickel, and when fresh we enjoy it very much. To them, white bread is almost like cake. They can vegetables and store plenty of apples and potatoes. When they need meat, a cow is slaughtered. They have hordes of marks, but as I said, have little or nothing to buy. I enclose one for Neil.

As to the Army I'm in—it's the 7th Army under General Patch, not the 3rd as you thought. General Patch has a reputation for being exceptionally thoughtful of the men under his command—and from my vantage point, has proven it.

Speaking of the Alsacian sympathies—I have seen many families with two sons—one in the German army and the other in the French army. They seem to be indifferent to principles—they're just sick of war.

14 December

Yes, Darling, you said it right when you wrote at least I, as a Medic, am able to care for myself a little more than the Infantryman—and we should be thankful to God for that.

We should also say "God bless the Infantry" for without a doubt they're the real heroes of this war—and very little credit is given them. I'm sure you recognize the emblem of the Infantryman—

crossed rifles, and the blue piping on his overseas cap. When you see one you can be sure you're looking at a real soldier. Despite the common belief that the Infantry gets what is left, he has taken the most rigid training any serviceman gets (Marines included) and is a specialist in the particular job he is trained for.

It's nothing less than Hell to do a job under fire. And when you're cold, wet to the skin, night after night in a muddy foxhole, unable to eat, and most days cold C Rations—and all this with little complaint—with devotion for each other and their officers—then I say over and over again, God bless them. We can't do enough for these boys and I'm in a position to see just what does go on.

If you want to follow our progress—look for clippings with direct mention of the Division—a part of the 7th Army—and only a part. Incidentally, our Division is doing a great job and we're mighty proud of it. There's a sense of unity and good feeling among the men, an "esprit de corps" which is vital in a set-up as ours. Good-bye, my Darling and kiss my little guys for me.

15 December

Happy birthday, Darling! I'm thinking what a memorable day it could be if peace were declared!

I got a real kick out of David's reaction to my picture. Show it to him occasionally. A little reminder will make it easier when I return.—And Neil's football trophy—a sprained ankle. I hate to see him lose the schoolwork, but take pride in knowing he's really growing up.

That old attitude of military courtesy is nil now. In war conditions we all work together and suffer together and superficial courtesies take a very minor place.

Except for a slight cold which we all have—I am well. The hot meals—twice a day—continue to come, and we've been lucky enough to be living in a house almost regularly, with an occasional day or two where we have to dig in outside.

A rumor is floating around that 30,000 packages were burned! Hope yours were not among them.

16 December

Received three of those grand picker-uppers dated Nov. 13, 21st and Dec. 1st. Oddly enough, letters go astray but eventually catch up. Before I forget, Dear, cancel *Stars & Stripes* subscription. Not only do I get it free daily, but it's so amateurish I get no satisfaction in reading it.

Am still interested in the results of the National election—names and figures. I haven't seen Jim since Marseille. His regiment is close by, but due to circumstances, we cannot meet. Hope we will along the line, though.

I completely agree with you that this mess could be settled by a negotiated peace—and still be lasting. You see, it's so easy to follow the war behind a comfortable desk somewhere and say, "Unconditional surrender is the only solution." Surely, that's ideal, but in the meantime thousands of lives are being lost and millions are sick at heart. Without the "Unconditional Surrender" clause, the war might have ended months ago. Over here we see things from a first-hand view, and I'm with the majority thinking by far.

Darling, your birthday yesterday was a lucky day for me. I was made a clerk in the Aid Station—which means that I'll help with litters only in real emergencies—otherwise I take care of details in the Station. It's a break and I appreciate it.

17 December

I've been lucky—for the last 4 days I've received two letters each day, and today was no exception.

You're mistaken in thinking I'll be quite a Frenchman when I return. I'll never get by here in France, and for that matter, don't have the desire as long as I can make myself reasonably understood. Just want to get home in good shape and soon, and forget all about France.—And when we start feeling sorry for ourselves, let's realize that other boys have been away from home much longer, and some are having it tougher. And the people here in France. If you've witnessed what I do every day, you would get some idea of what I

Wreckage of Freudenberg
—drawing by Marius N. Trinque, from The Story of the Century

mean. When you have to dive down into the cellar to escape artillery barrage, and when shells are hitting all around and you see families huddled together in horror, women and children, you'd know what I mean. And how often I plunged down with them, trying to comfort more than one terror-stricken child in my arms.

We occupy the homes with families when we set up our Aid Stations, and when those "screaming mimis"* are hitting all around, everyone, including the animals are herded in the cellar for shelter. Believe me, Sweetheart, war is no picnic for anyone, especially for innocent civilians forced to endure it daily. I thank my lucky stars every day that my family is safe from all this devastation.

22 December

It is now a few days before Christmas and I'm wondering if the war will be over by the end of the year. By the extent of our activity here, it hardly seems that way. Try not to be too discouraged, Dear.

Your sonnet was beautiful. Thank you. And today, finally, your

* German mortar shells.

GI, 398th Infantry
—*drawing by Al Vidmar*

first package #4 arrived, so you can see how snafu* the package situation is. Anyway, it was so nicely packed—each item so acceptable and welcome. Everything went fast once it was opened.

Tonight my spirits are much higher, and though I cannot tell you why, just rest assured there's good reason. Speaking of the latest latrine rumor, the war's supposed to be over Dec. 24. Just hoping, not anticipating.

* "Snafu" ("situation normal, all fucked up") was one of the coined World War II Army words that lasted for a number of years beyond its coinage. A further refinement on the idea was "fubar"—"fucked up beyond all recognition." This one, however, did not outlive the end of hostilities in 1945.

Moved into another house today. The owners speak some English and that makes it a little easier.

Had a letter from Ben. It really gets to me when a civilian gripes about how busy they are and how tired, etc., just going about normal everyday routine, when men are risking their lives dodging shell bursts, sleeping in foxholes—sleeping! I mean trying to rest their heads a little—and walking on sore feet for miles at any hour of the night with heavy packs, constantly cold and wet for days and weeks on end. It's plain Hell and that's what the Infantry boys endure all the time. God bless them. It's our job to care for them when they come hobbling into the station at night, and you can bet your life we do our best. I know you'll be pleased your package was shared with these boys—and from other packages we fixed up a nice little spread. It hurts to see them trudge back to their miserable foxholes. And when guys like Ben complain it makes me boil.

Tomorrow we're due for baths and new outfits of clothes. I love you, Darling. Until tomorrow.

Basic training, summer 1944. Top left, on bivouac, Camp Blanding. Note desk in foxhole. Top right, Keith Winston with sons Neil and David, during Delay On Route in August. Bottom left, Sarah Winston with son David. Bottom right, during basic training.

925th Field Artillery in action with 100th Division near Raon-l'Etape, France, November 1944.—*U.S. Army*

Medics of 398th Infantry evacuating wounded soldier at 1st Battalion aid station near Reyersviller, France, December 1944.—*U.S. Army*

Forward command post, Co G, 398th Infantry, Maginot Line fortifications, December 1944.–*U.S. Army*

German soldier surrenders to 398th Infantry within Maginot Line fortifications. The American soldier is Pvt Edward Wagner, Co K. December 1944.–*U.S. Army*

100th Division troops of 325th Engineer Battalion string barbed wire close to body of dead German soldier near Aachen, January 1945.—*U.S. Army*

During the German counterattack at Rimling, these two soldiers of the 397th Infantry, 100th Division, killed more than 100 enemy soldiers. Left, Staff Sgt Alphonso J. Meyers; right, Pfc Leon D. Outlaw.—*U.S. Army*

Top left, somewhere in France; Keith Winston is standing. Right, snowy day in Germany, March 1945. Bottom, Winston, outskirts of Marseille, after 100th Division's arrival overseas.

100th Division infantryman, Pfc David O. Lukins, 399th Infantry, watches front line during German counterattack, Reyersviller, France, January 1945.—*U.S. Army*

100th Division infantrymen move through Bitche following capture, March 1945.—*U.S. Army*

An all-soldier show, "Sons of Bitche," given for 100th Division front-line troops by Special Services unit, Sarre-Union, February 1945. The female impersonator is Tec 4 Ed Hines.—*U.S. Army*

Patrol of 398th Infantry's Co K under artillery fire in woods near Bitche, March 1945.—*U.S. Army*

View from captured citadel of Bitche. Note bomb crater in foreground.
March 1945.—U.S. Army

Refugees move through American lines near Aachen. The 100th Division
soldiers laying out barbed wire are members of the 325th Engineers.—
U.S. Army

5. Counterattack, Defensive

Maginot Line, Hardt Mountains

December 1944 - March 1945

Poised to attack Bitche, the 100th Division was extended beyond Fort Freudenberg and Fort Schiesseck in a long salient when on 23 December word came to pull back. Seven days earlier the supposedly beaten German armies unleashed a major counterattack in the Ardennes Forest region, which had been left lightly defended by the U.S. First Army, and within days had punched their way well into France, with the ultimate objective the Meuse River, followed by a drive to Antwerp, which would—if successful—split the Allied armies in two. Determined American resistance at St. Vith and Bastogne, however, slowed the drive, and meanwhile the U.S. Third Army, in position below the German salient, wheeled northward and moved to relieve Bastogne and pinch off the enemy. To fill the area in the American line being vacated by Third Army units, the left flank of the 44th Infantry Division of the U.S. Seventh Army was extended northward, and the 100th Division was called back in from its extended salient toward Bitche and placed in defensive positions to the west of the Maginot fortifications it had just taken. Before departing, however, the division made sure that Fort Freudenberg and Fort Schiesseck were rendered unusable. During the period 23–31 December, there was much local fighting and shelling all along the line.

25 December 1944

Today is Christmas, and I'm feeling low, realizing today's significance when families are usually together. I hope you, in some way, enjoyed the day with the children.

Fortunately, not much "activity" and we had a rather restful day, and just about the best G.I. meal I ever had. A turkey drumstick. It must have weighed a pound—cranberry sauce, potatoes, peas, mince pie. I ate so much I just couldn't touch the pie.

And last night we had a little party. I was in charge of refreshments and everything went off pretty well. We pulled open the table, and about twice the size of our table—long like this

Through the center we ran a long sheet of tissue paper—toilet, to be exact—and on it we placed glasses for drinks. Candles were lit around a little Christmas tree in the center. We served salads of tuna, and sardines and crackers, bread, coffee. Also pineapple and fruit cake. Then we sang carols and had a pleasant time. Some of the civilian neighbors were invited in and they sang "Silent Night" in German for us. We weren't kidding ourselves—despite the outward gaiety, we knew we were hiding our real feelings of home and kids and an American Christmas.

This morning we awoke at 6 A.M. to the whistling of Silent Night by our Sergeant, and it turned my thoughts to you—and being 6 hours ahead in time, I could picture you wrapping up packages for the boys, making last-minute preparations—and it was a little tough for me to take.

The Captain (Doc, our C.O.)* said I should have been a Reverend. He said my psychology on life has made an indent on them, the boys, and it made me feel rather good to hear him say that.

Don't mind in the least you talking "war" in your letters. I like anything that comes from you—and secondly, it's good to get the news as the States get it. The G.I. way is definitely too canned and censored.

Dear, in reference to one of your letters. It's not quite as easy as that—merely asking to be taken out of a combat zone. I assure you that 99.9/10ths of the boys in combat zones don't want to stay. Here in the Aid Station I can see for myself how many try to get back to rear echelons—and none do, unless they're wounded. The present set-up I'm in is as safe under the conditions as it's possible to be anywhere. You have no cause for alarm OK? I mean it sincerely.†

One of our group acquired a radio last night, and now we're trying to get it connected up. It certainly will help.

Received the Phila. *Record* Overseas edition—and was it a dis-

* Capt. Joseph R. Rich, of Liverpool, Ohio.
† Cf. Winston's letter of 14 January 1945!

appointment—8 pages of funnies, and they, too, stank from canned, selected news fit for G.I. consumption only. Keep it coming, though, it's *something* to read, at least.

You speak so much of Strasbourg. While I can't tell you exactly where we are—it's not Strasbourg. We're hoping and waiting for a Russian drive, and some help from the British.

28 December

Well, I just got something off my chest—a letter to the *Record* telling them what a lousy overseas edition they put out.

We try to pull some humor out of any situation and tonight we had a little fun.—Since the Captain is always losing his canteen cup we decided to play a trick. We took an empty box received by Doc from his wife, put in a well-wrapped canteen cup, 3 cans of C rations, a roll of toilet paper and 4 packs of cigarettes—a brand none of the boys will smoke. Poor guy, he was pleased at first, but soon realized it was a joke. However, he got as much fun out of it as we did—plus another canteen cup which he'll lose tomorrow.

29 December

You wonder what I'm doing at this moment? Well, for a little while things have been quiet, thank God, and the Captain appointed me Special Service Officer—while the title is really in fun, and given to the Regimental Officer in charge of all activities other than combat, food or clothing—there was a purpose in it, of course.

You know how much I like to make little improvements around the house—well, unconsciously I do the same around here and it's apparently noticed. So now when any improvement is needed, I'm called on to do it or make a suggestion. For instance, with periodicals coming in from all sources, I collect them and formed a little trading library so that all will get the opportunity to read each other's periodicals. When you mail packages, try to include a 25¢

paperback, something I'd be interested in. After I read it, it will be turned into the library.

Our outfit acquired a huge tub for bathing, similar to those our grandparents used for washing clothes. We heat up a room, and plenty of hot water—then go to it. Best of all, though, the Army does try to get us hot showers and changes of clothing as often as possible.

31 December

As Walter Winchell would say, "letteratorially" speaking, today turned out to be quite a day with 4 letters from you and a few others.

You ask about my duties. By this time you probably already know—but if you're still in question—I'm the Bn. Aid Station clerk. It's just the type of work I like and am trained for. I'm also called a technician—which means I help in dispensing medicines and care for sick boys who need attention. I have lots to learn, but know of no better place to learn F-A-S-T.

If you please—in the future you will address me as Private First Class. I have been "promoted." As to the injury—I assure you I'm okay. No scars—well, and happy as could be expected.

Glad the aspirin "cure" worked. Fundamentally, most of these "cold" medicines have an aspirin base. Colds are a problem, but like Doc says, with medication it takes 2 weeks to cure a cold—without medication, 14 days. I think he's right.

Tonight is New Year's Eve. Well—we'll make up for it next year. God bless and protect you all and give you courage until I return which I hope will be soon.

In part to keep additional American reinforcements from being shifted northward to aid in the U.S. Third Army's effort to seal off the German units which had moved into the Ardennes, the enemy forces along the U.S. Seventh Army front unleashed a savage counteroffensive on New Year's Day. Both the thinly spread 44th Division to the north of the 100th Division's sector and the 117th Cavalry to the south gave way before the onslaught, leaving the 100th Division in an exposed position. During the next several days repeated attempts were made to drive in the division's northern flank, held by the 397th Regiment, and the southern flank manned by the 399th, so as to cut off the division's escape route. The 2nd Battalion of the 398th was shifted to the flank of the 399th, and there was savage fighting. Reinforced by reserve units, however, the 100th Division held its ground, and during the ensuing ten days Germans and Americans repeatedly attacked and counterattacked. By 12 January the situation was sufficiently well in hand for the 2nd Battalion of the 398th to rejoin the remaining two battalions of the regiment. Afterward Lt. Gen. Jacob L. Devers, commander of the Sixth Army Group, commended the 100th for its performance, declaring that "inflicting great losses to strong elements of three enemy divisions, you have successfully protected an important sector in the Hardt Mountains."

2 January 1945

Yesterday, the first day of the New Year, the boys were more than a little quiet. I heard an American band play "Auld Lang Syne" and it was a little hard to take as it brought back memories of last New Year's Eve, when at the stroke of 12 we were kissing.

We had another one of those holiday dinners—turkey and trimmings—and it made me think back when I was home and read in the papers that "every American soldier was going to get a turkey dinner," while the civilians had trouble getting it. I wasn't convinced until our Xmas dinner, but now I'm sure that the Army does everything they can to make the soldier's life comfortable, though sometimes it's next to impossible.

Right now the ground is covered with snow and rather pleasant. The nights have been cold but the sun comes out in the afternoon and warms things up a bit. My cold is getting better.

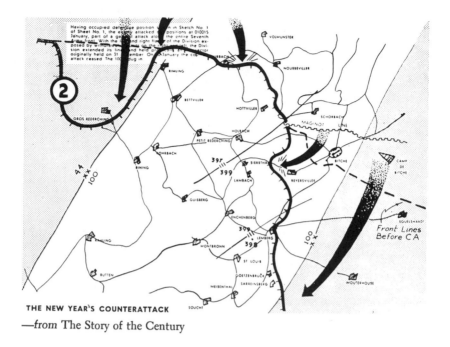

THE NEW YEAR'S COUNTERATTACK

—*from* The Story of the Century

Keep those letters coming—I'll try hard from this end. I love you all so much.

4 January

Our location remains the same. In my work today I drove a jeep. They're really great to get around in, especially on rough terrain.

The Europeans we've encountered are so backward—rarely have running water, and never any toilets in their homes. It's always a shed in the rear. Rarely do they have electricity or radio, and never a telephone. Of course, I'm speaking of small towns and cities.

Never underestimate American ingenuity. In this little country town we have telephones for inter-contact with our Bn. units, electricity which consists of a lamp (similar to car lights) connected to a battery of a truck radio—but we still use the back shed for a toilet.

Had a letter from Jim today. He's a lucky guy to be sent back to Division Hq. where he's clerking now.

5 January

Well, we've moved from our last home—the comfortable one—but what can you do.* We're in another house and the best I can say for it is that it is a roof over our heads. Your account of Bob and Norm coming in Xmas touched me deeply, and I felt a tear roll down my cheeks as I read it. Of course I'm not ashamed of your bursting into tears—in fact I'm proud of you and always will be.

I continue to enjoy my association with the Captain and the boys. My spirits are higher than you'd expect under these conditions. The Captain stands up for his men—come what may.

Still have snow. We wear rubber shoes and they keep the feet warm. I'm well, except for a cold which seems to recur often—probably due to the drafts I'm in all day. But it's not bad.

I ran into a fellow from West Chester, Pa., and we had a lot to talk about. He manages Montgomery Ward there. Another of our boys, a Staff Sgt., works for Sears Roebuck as an advertising man.† He draws these catalog pictures of girls, for instance, who look so good in brassieres and slips, etc. He says the actual picture is anything but enhancing, but after he touches them up, they look perfect.

5 January

Received two V-Mail letters at once and it was interesting to compare your own words about the war. In your first, you spoke

* One would never guess from this that the German counterattack was in full force, and that the 2nd Bn 398th Infantry had been moved to guard the now-exposed flank of the 399th on the southern edge of the salient.

† Staff Sgt. Samuel G. Cahoon, of Warren, New Jersey, who was later promoted to second lieutenant for outstanding service in combat. Cahoon was awarded the Bronze Star with Oak Leaf Cluster.

discouragingly about the war. You felt it wouldn't end until Spring. Then the next day when the German advance was completely squashed, you felt the war could end this winter. I'm the same way. It's an up and down see-saw, isn't it? Continue to give me your views as I know they're formed after listening to many commentators—and I'm far from informed about the whole front. I'm still restricted in what I say. I hope you're getting a little more news on the 7th Army front by now.

If people back home realized the importance of donating blood (through Red Cross), a lot more would be forthcoming. I've seen with my own eyes what blood plasma does for a wounded boy. If only the world could see a sick, injured boy hovering around death, then when blood plasma is administered, see color return to his face, see him smile with hope—more people would make it their duty to give blood. Today a boy came in in pretty bad shape, but by the time he left you wouldn't believe the improvement unless you saw it yourself. I felt so good to know that I might have been instrumental in an infinitesimal part of his revival. I'm always on hand to help the doctor.

10 January

Things are happening and we're busy. I may not be able to write as regularly as I'd like. I'm sure you get the picture.

We've been having a little radio trouble. However, our resourceful medics have procured telephone receiving equipment and a loudspeaker, and with a few ingenious machinations, most of our station personnel hear programs.

Our telephone set-up is great. The amazing thing about our organization, regardless if it's Bn., Regiment or Division, if all or any part moves—anywhere—a telephone hook-up is working within an hour after arriving at our destination. All the Companies, Medics, Headquarters are connected by wire. And it's really quite simple, too. I plan to make use of hook-ups throughout the house once I get back and equipment is available.

You ask me to describe the men I work with. In our outfit we have a physician (C.O.) who is Captain, as you know. We call him "Doc." Then we have a Lieutenant who takes care of the Administrative end. He's a tall, slim guy about 6' 4½" and was only attached to us recently. He saw service in Africa, Anzio, Italy and now France.* When relating his experiences he often says "beaucoup" soldiers, "beaucoup" jeeps, "beaucoup" this and that, meaning "much" in French. Now, everyone calls him "Beaucoup" since that's a perfect description of his height. He's a funny guy and does a lot for morale around here.

We're running into a lot of German-speaking people now—and with a little knowledge of Yiddish and German, I and the rest are gradually learning to understand them. A favorite expression of ours is "nix fushtay." And when they say something that may not be favorable, even though we know what they're saying, we smile and say, "Nix fushtay." This is exactly what they say, too, when they don't want to understand us.

14 January

Things have been a little rough. An artillery shell hit the Aid Station in one of the towns, killing four.† Thank God most of us are okay, but it's hard to get over such a tragedy, even though it's war and you have to be prepared for horrors like this. Many were hit by shrapnel, and they're on the mend. There is little more I can tell you of our activities. No specifics permitted.

The Russian advance has been real encouragement, and it may be the beginning of the end of our enemy.

Want to hear something funny? Right now the boys are talking about the fun they had at Ft. Bragg. It was pretty tough down there but now it seems like a country club in comparison.

Just took advantage of the hot water on the stove and took a sponge bath, and a pretty good one, too.

Mail and packages have not been coming through for about a

---

* First Lt. Anthony Scarpitta, of Parkville, Maryland.
† The aid station in question was the 2nd Battalion, 398th's, and Winston was at work inside it at the time.

week and for the first time I've really seen how much it means to all the boys. Especially under stress. When there's a delay as long as the present one, they show concern. They continually ask, "Has the mail come in? Have the packages come in?" Over and over.

You might like to know how we sleep. We use a sleeping bag, which with the extra insert is equivalent to 4 blankets. It zips up to the face and leaves a little opening around the mouth and nose about the size of a grapefruit in diameter. It's very warm and I like it. When zipped up we look like mummies.

We're always running into new experiences. Right now it seems we're treating more civilians than G.I.'s. These little towns have no doctors and when one shows up they besiege him. We get eggs, liquor and thanks in return. Today a 2-month-old baby was brought in. With no vitamins or cereals to prescribe, Doc hardly knew what to suggest. A change in diet would have helped the baby but all they have here is milk (for an infant). Anyway, we suggested feeding the baby water and sugar for a day or two. I gave the mother a couple of jars of baby desserts you sent over, but of course it's only a drop in a bucket, if that. You can't realize how helpless you feel in a situation like this.

The boys talk of visiting Paris which is some distance away. If the war did end abruptly, could you picture a few million G.I.'s with the same thought, converging on the city. Can you imagine the result?

Until later, Darling.

15 January

Today received so many lovely things from you—two letters, a V-Mail and another package which contained Schraft's chocolates, mixed nuts, etc. etc. and of course your very delicious nut-and-date cookies which you baked. They disappear faster than anything and the boys asked me to tell you how much they all enjoyed them. I'm requesting a repeat of both the cookies and nuts!

The situation here is relatively quiet and our civilian practise continues to flourish. Eggs and schnopps and "Opple Cookin'" come in as fast as we can eat it. "Opple Cookin'" is apple strudel.

Today we had creamed turkey. It was canned, but good, and it made me realize what a great job the cooks are doing. It's quite an order preparing and cooking food here, but even more trouble getting the chow up to the troops. They're doing as good a job as anyone in winning this war, and just as dangerous, too.

When we get a few free moments we play checkers. Anything to pass the time. I've been getting used to sleeping on the floor, and for the first time since I left the States, I've been sleeping better. The boys kid around, saying that when we do get home, we'll probably sleep on the floor for awhile. Oh yeah! I don't care what I sleep on—just bring me home!

The coin enclosed is a 10 pfennig piece, and since there are 50 to a mark, this is worth about 3 cents, plus.

The homes here, individually built, are typically Penna. Dutch, with stone walls about 2 feet wide, and similar to the farm house you see in West Chester County. The more I see of them, the more I love our little home. There's such a difference.

What's the latest on Mark?* Is he still in England? He's a lucky guy after all, and I hope he's still there.

I'm feeling well and you have no reason for alarm, due to my present status. I constantly think of you, love you and miss you and desperately long for the day we'll be together.

16 January

Today I was one of the lucky few to receive a letter from home. It seems you picked the right week to send V-Mail, as that seems to be the only mail coming through now. I enjoyed your letter immensely. Especially your account of Neil's safe home-coming from Washington with all his Christmas gifts—and David's thrill at seeing him. I love them so much—and their mother, too.

* Tec 5 Mark Winston, Keith's older brother.

I had a bath in a nearby town—saw a picture—all under Army supervision. I had already seen the movie *Tampico*. I disliked it before and on second viewing it was even worse. What a movie house! It was so cold we about froze, and only one reel shown at a time by an inexperienced operator. Certainly not like the State or Boyd— but I do appreciate the Army trying to help—and the boys do, too. With it all, I'd go back to see another movie when its shown.

With the snow on the ground I often think of Neilly and his sled—whether or not he's using it. And wondering if he takes his little brother for rides. Speaking of sleds, the kids all have them down here, and the streets are crowded with them. Being hilly country, it's fine sledding. The sleds are all wood, including the rudders.

Have had that "balloon" feeling the last few days caused by my over-anxiety to get home. I feel that something big should break soon—with the Russians on 3 sides and the English and Americans here on the Western Front.

Sent another little package off today, including the tree we used this past Christmas. I hope Neilly will enjoy them. God bless you all. Until later.

On 16 January 1945, American forces from above and below the Ardennes pocket met at Houffalize, and the German Bulge offensive was over, with the battle line now restored to its location on 15 December. Although the 100th Division did not know it at the time, its drive through the Maginot positions to threaten Bitche, and its subsequent stubborn defense against German counterattacks, had contributed to the German failure, for after the end of the war General von Mellenthin, commander of the 19th German Army, declared in a report that the 100th Division's threat to take Bitche had forced retention of the 11th Panzer and 25th Panzer Grenadier divisions in that area after they had been scheduled to move northward and take part in the Ardennes offensive. Following restoration of the American front, on 20 January the 100th Division was moved into positions along the Sarreinsberg-Goetzenbruck-Lemberg line, and for the next several weeks there was constant *shelling and local engagements. Meanwhile, at Supreme Headquarters Allied Expeditionary Forces, plans were being made for the drive across the Rhine and into the heart of Germany. Despite the opposition of Twelfth Army Group commander Gen. Omar Bradley and the heads of the several American armies, SHAEF commander Gen. Dwight D. Eisenhower had decided that the main thrust would be made from the north under the direction of British Field Marshal Bernard L. Montgomery, with the American Third and Fifth armies undertaking a secondary drive to the south of the Ruhr Valley. The U.S. Seventh Army and the French First Army would make only limited advances, serving in effect as an anchoring hinge upon which the Allied invasion of Germany would pivot. As we shall see, however, matters did not work out exactly as planned.*

17 January

Darling, all seems to be temporarily "quiet on the western front" and now I've come to the full realization of what that can mean. We have moved on to another town, consequently, another house.

The Russians news is exciting and I hope it continues.* It may be the turning point.

Today was mail-less but I have no right to complain. I'm hoping for some tomorrow as you know how it brightens my days, and what it means.—Today I received the lousy *Record*. It keeps you in a vacuum with all the other canned, pre-digested news.

We got Southern fried chicken today, and again I can't help but marvel at the great job these cooks are doing—getting these meals up to the boys in the foxholes under the most difficult and perilous conditions. Sometimes it's absolutely impossible, but when it is, they're there.

---

* The Soviet Union's winter offensive had gotten under way by mid-January. Russian armies were driving northward to the Baltic Sea to isolate East Prussia from the Reich, establishing beachheads across the Oder River in southern Poland, and advancing steadily toward Berlin. At the forthcoming Yalta Conference Joseph Stalin would claim that the Soviet advances had in effect helped extricate the Allies from their difficulties in the Ardennes, though in point of fact the American lines had been all but restored to their pre-Bulge positions before the Soviet offensive had begun.

18 January

Today you came through for me again—the first airmail in a long time, and numbered 120.—Glad you got out to see *Laura* though I'm sorry you missed the chance to see *Since You Went Away*—a story of a wife (whose husband is overseas) with two children, who lives from day to day for news and mail. It moved me deeply since it almost duplicates our situation.

Dear, I'm not interested in Eisenhower's carefully worded Communiques. That's all I get here—canned, carefully worded write-ups by the G.I.'s. I'm only interested in something of civilian origin, something that gives the public viewpoint. I'm sick of G.I. news— it's not only old but so poorly presented; I'm just aching to hear from the free press. It's like a craving now.

19 January

Suddenly we got "busy" and this is the first chance I grabbed to write. It has been snowing continuously. Last night, not only was it snowy, but pitch black. So dark, you couldn't see your hand in front of you. Literally.

Doc asked me to cross the street—where the Sgt. is staying—to pick up some supplies. Well, I tried and tried but it was so black outside, despite the snow, I couldn't find the house—not to mention slipping on the ice and walking headlong into a manure pile. (I'll tell you more about manure piles later.) When I came back empty-handed the boys laughed. So another guy tried—one who said it was a cinch—and he too returned with no results. So, smugly confident, the Captain said, "I'll go." And the four of us bet him 200 francs that he couldn't find the place either in half an hour, even though it was just across the street.

Well, for twenty minutes he was out there trying with no better results. But luck was with the doctor, for suddenly a gigantic flare (lights used by troops) lit up the sky brilliantly for about 3 minutes—and looking out the door we saw Doc running like the devil to that house. He found it, but we tell him he had to pull "rank" to accomplish his mission, by calling the line troops to furnish a flare. It cost each of us 50 francs but we got some fun out of it.

About the manure piles. Over here a civilian's wealth is measured by the height of his manure pile, which is kept in front (*not back*) of his house. Almost like a status symbol. And it stinks like hell— not to mention its ugly, offensive appearance. If it smells badly now in the dead of winter, you can imagine the stench in warm weather. I hope I'll be far away by then (meaning home). Chickens climb up the pile all day long, picking and pecking. Barns are part of the house and it's a familiar sight to see barnyard animals living in the cellar—right below the kitchen and living room. We've spent many a night in their company! Along with the rest of the household.

Also, in front of the house is a big pump. Never a toilet inside. Existence is the only thing these villagers strive for. Beauty or convenience never enter the picture, and is of no consequence whatsoever.

Today, four of our Air Corpsmen "took to the silk" when they ran into plane trouble. Everything turned out OK and lots of the boys ripped up the parachutes for souvenirs. The "chute" is silk. I've been a little souvenir conscious lately, knowing we have a growing boy who'd get a thrill out of things from this part of the world. Picked up a few more coins and will enclose a couple each day.

The cooks are really spoiling us. Chicken again today (roast). With all my love.

21 January

Finally, the mail is coming through and everyone, including me, is happy.—My morale is high since the news is so encouraging. Speaking of "encouraging"—that's a pass-word around here. It started when things looked pretty dismal, and finally when some good news trickled in, I said, very seriously and very slowly—"That's encouraging." Apparently, the words "took" and now every time we hear bits of good news we all say, "That's encouraging."

Now that the radio is working I get a wave of homesickness when I hear real American music. A complete hush falls over the group, "eating" up every note. Darling, America is so wonderful, we're going to enjoy and appreciate it even more.

Gen. Eisenhower has ruled our troops are not to fraternize with the German people, as they're just as much the enemy as the troops. This part of France is definitely pro-German, and it's shown clearly on the expressions of the civilians. Almost every family has a son or husband in the Nazi army. Very often they're hostile and resistant about accommodating us. But typical of Americans, we treat them with a decent amount of consideration, unlike the bestial Nazi, or our ally, the Russian.

22 January

Am a mixture of hope and anxiety as we've heard (unofficially) one of Germany's big Eastern centers has fallen to the Russians.

Speaking of the Medics and the Aid Station—where we're located, etc., and the questions you keep asking—all I can say is please don't listen to anyone unless it's an Infantryman who has seen combat. In the first place, every outfit—Engineers, Quartermaster, Transportation Corps, etc.—the inactive troops in the States or England, have Medics attached to them. The Infantry, however, takes the Medics right into combat with them. If it's right on the front, the Medics are close behind. Therefore, we being an Infantry group, and in combat, are always close by. I'm sure you're not being kidded. While there's no reason for alarm—not until this war is over, and all danger removed, will I be completely safe. Right now I'm in a somewhat better position than being on a litter team. However, if you're within 25 miles from the front you're subject to airplane attack. Now that I've told you everything I hope it answers your questions—unconsoling as it may be.

After another move we're in a big hotel in a rather nice village and the people seem a little more pleasant. Our set-up is far from ideal but under the circumstances we're satisfied.

Now, Dearest, forget all about my C.O. He'd like to know how to get home himself. If you only knew how things worked over here, and if you could only see how many boys really bad off are required to carry on, you would not mention this. Of course I realize the spirit in which you want to help, but just resign yourself to the fact that I will not get home till it's over—"over here."

26 January

Last night we received what we call PX rations and I'm involved with my "Special Service" problems this morning. The rations contain beer, cigars, candy for each boy and my job is to distribute the items and collect the money—about 25 francs each.

Again I enjoyed your account summary. Write about it often. I'll say as we do here. Whenever something interesting happens during the day, someone says, "Another paragraph"—meaning he'll have something new to talk about when he writes home. (We both know how hard it is at times to fill a letter.) Well, that will give you another paragraph. Me, too, ha, ha.

We're getting more snow but it's amazing how well our boys do under these conditions. It's been lots worse in the States so we have no complaints on that score.

Right now we're listening to Berlin Sally on the radio—the girl who plays American records and tears up the Allies as German propaganda. We all get a kick out of it.

We got Sunkist oranges today—and delicious, too. A little change and much appreciated. They do try hard to give us the best.

You wonder why my cold lingers. You must realize, Honey, that although we live under cover a good deal of the time, the doors are open constantly, with boys coming in and out of the Station all day. Many times I rush out on errands—or a quick move in a freezing jeep, etc. But it was never anything serious—just a hanging-on cold. You know, living conditions here aren't even a reasonable facsimile of home! I laughed at David's eating an apple and typing. I could just picture him. I see he's already becoming a radio addict—the sweet one.

The column by [David] Lawrence on Unconditional Surrender was very good and echoed the feelings of most of us. Keep clipping items of interest, we all enjoy them here.

28 January

It's Sunday but you wouldn't know it unless someone told you. You'll get a kick out of this. One of the Medics decided he'd like to attend Jewish services—but since there's no Jewish Chaplain he conducted the services himself. I was there with 15 others. The Catholic Chaplain supplied us with Jewish prayer books, and this young Medic did an excellent job.* There was humor in it, too. This fellow was so determined to have a good number show up, he kept looking out the window to see if any more were coming. He watched as one boy from a foxhole walked right past (the poor guy couldn't find the place) and he says, "That son of a bitch." The guy finally came in.

It was very moving to see these boys, all standing, and praying and singing, in full Army regalia—their rifles right with them. I was proud of my Faith.

At long last our Bn. was visited by the Red Cross. Two girls handed out doughnuts and coffee to the boys. It was wonderful to see American women and it made most of us homesick.

I can't say, however, that the Red Cross is doing all it should, or claims that it does. In the first place, they're always way, way back behind the lines. Sure, they do a good job for the rear echelon boys—the guys in offices and Quartermaster depots and occupational jobs in the rear—where there's no fighting or danger. But where it means the most, where our boys are really sacrificing their lives, always in danger from every description of artillery and mortar fire—where they're in dismal discomfort and in a semi-state of shock, you just don't know the Red Cross exists.†

What can they do? Lots. Unless you're lucky, you find it very difficult getting writing paper and envelopes. The boys in the fox-holes eat up magazines and periodicals, but they trickle in one at a time, and often see nothing for weeks. To keep from going batty they even read the contents on the labels of their K-rations package.

---

* One of Winston's fellow soldiers writes that the medic may have been Tec 5 Abraham Halberg, of Bronx, N.Y. The Catholic priest was Capt. Michael J. Buckley, of Brooklyn.

† This complaint about the American Red Cross's activities in the European Theater of Operations, whatever its validity, was frequently echoed by combat veterans.

This for something to read. Many a trip I've taken to the closest cities to get these supplies, especially writing paper and envelopes, and paid for them out of my own pocket. This should be the service of the Red Cross. Today, for the first time since we went into combat, they came up to the front. Now, that's not such a hot record, is it? The boys appreciated it, but I'm sure they'd be tickled seeing a Red Cross representative, perhaps once a week, offering these little services the Army cannot be expected to handle; there are innumerable ways of helping. And I say they are not doing the job the folks back home think they're doing for the G.I. up front. I'm not saying they do nothing, but I do say that where it is needed most— they're badly lacking.

Today, no mail from you, but a letter from Rose. She speaks of Luna's brother in France. I can say he is right near me, and at one time could have met him—although at that time I didn't know about him. His Division is rated as one of the best, and we feel very good that it is near us.*

Things look so good, Darling. The reports of the Russian advance are really exciting. Today, Prague, the Czech city, has been shelled. Koenigsberg is in a precarious state. The Oder River has been crossed. Montgomery reports clear sailing—and the Russian advance, if anything, is stronger now than at any other time.

30 January

We're back again in that hotel I wrote you about—where we were quite comfortable. Hope we stay a few days. But it doesn't seem to work that way!

It's tough on you, I know, but I get such a kick out of picturing little David opening up bureau drawers and emptying them on the floor. I was telling "Beaucoup" about it. He has an 18-month-old daughter and we both laughed together.

* Winston did not know it, but Lt. Monty Ereza, 157th Infantry, had been killed on 18 January 1945 during a counterattack at Reyersviller, Alsace. He had been wounded three times during the war, and was awarded the Medal of Valor posthumously. His sister, Luna Ereza Diamond, was a friend of Mrs. Winston's sister, Rose.

The packages have been coming in and they're super. Everything is delicious—nuts, chocolates, mixed dried fruit, fudge—everything.

The news continues good. By the time this letter reaches you, the Russians may be in Berlin.* It's not improbable.

31 January

We moved again and I'm feeling fine after a good supper with a family in whose house I'm staying. Guess what we had? Rabbit— and it tastes like chicken, and looks like it. Also fried potatoes and apple strudel. They raise rabbits in their back yards just for eating. Doc, "Beaucoup" and I were invited (we three sleep in the same room in this house.) We enjoyed the hospitality "tres beaucoup."

I can't speak French, but I do follow a conversation pretty well, and manage to make myself understood. Often I find myself mixing my "command" of German with that of French—i.e., "tres goot." The natives laugh since they speak both languages.

The news continues good—and something should happen soon— we all feel it in our bones. Doc's guess is Feb. 15, mine March 1. We're betting 8 to 1 on our dates which were picked before the Russian offensive.

Doc suggested I go back to the rear areas for a two-day rest. A change occasionally is a big help. I'll get a bath, a change of clothes, see a movie and maybe get my watch fixed. Will probably leave in 2 or 3 days.

Was interested in the *Upper Darby News* account, listing names of the "Century Division" area boys. How they got it I don't know but enjoyed reading it.

---

* Not until 25 April 1945 did the advancing Soviet armies surround Berlin. More than a week earlier, units of the U.S. Ninth Army had crossed the Elbe River, and sought permission to make a dash to the German capital. General Eisenhower, however, declined to order the move, on the grounds that Berlin lay within the agreed-upon Soviet zone of occupation, and that to expend what might well be many thousands of American casualties in pursuit of a purely political objective would be unfair to the troops concerned. Prime Minister Winston Churchill and the British dissented strongly. Eisenhower's decision, which was supported by U.S. Chief of Staff Gen. George C. Marshall and Twelfth Army Group Commanding Gen. Omar N. Bradley, would touch off a lengthy post-war controversy.

Our Division is known as the "Show-Off" Division of the Nation. That is, we were called upon in the States for parades, bond rallies, holidays (before I got in) and are well known. We've really done an excellent job in combat, too. Many of the boys in the Division were former ASTP (Army School Training Program) boys who required exceptional I.Q.'s to become a member. Then when it was disbanded, they were put into the Infantry—the 100th.

The guys seem to dig up ways of getting a little fun in. Last night it started with a snowball fight between a guard and 3 or 4 kids, and finally ended up with a good part of the civilian population fighting the soldiers—snowballs, of course—and everybody had a good time.

2 February

Do you notice how regular the mail comes to me? In fact, so regular that if I don't hear one day, I miss your letter even though I might have received two the previous day. I have no complaints!

Your error about Moscow being taken by the Russians reminded me of a standing joke around here. When anyone asks how far the Russians are to Berlin, we tell them. This happens all day since we have the only radio in the Battalion.

Sometimes, before they ask us, we say, "Did you hear the news? The Germans are in Berlin." They stand open-mouthed until they realize the Germans are in Berlin. ("another paragraph")

Just to get away from the Aid Station for awhile I went to Regt. Hq. today and it did my heart good to get a real warm welcome from the Major and Regt. Captain, who were genuinely friendly. Until recently I was just another guy to them, but it changed quickly due to something that happened not too long ago, and my C.O. telling them about it.*

---

* It has been impossible to identify with certainty the reference here. Sarah Winston declares that her husband made no allusion to it after the war. One of Winston's associates, however, writes that it involved some nasty anti-Semitic remarks made in Winston's presence by several patients at the battalion aid station. The men in question apparently did not realize that he was Jewish. Winston obviously informed them otherwise. His superior, Capt. Joseph R. Rich, who was also Jewish, was

The newspapers suspect a "big 3 meeting." It may be on now.*

Peace is not impossible by the time you receive this letter, and if such a wonderful thing happened, don't begin looking for me a week or two later. It could be a number of months, even six, but the first and biggest obstacle would be over.

If you get your hands on a good map showing Germany with both fronts, would you please send it? We're much in need of it to follow the Russian advance, as well as our own. These little maps with the Eisenhower Communiques are as clear as the communiques—and that means fuzzy—nothing.

4 February

Today I'm away from my group taking a 2-day "rest." Doc is rotating all of us back to rest camps, not only to clean up and see a couple of shows, but to get away from those damn weird mortars the boys call "screaming meemies." They sure can shake you up when they go shooting by.

Since noon I've eaten a hearty luncheon, sat in on a musical jam session, saw a movie, took a bath and changed clothes, and then treated to a "risque" stage show put on by G.I.'s. They go all out to make you comfortable here, and with the friendly, quiet atmosphere—what do you think it's doing to your husband? You're right, I'm homesick.

Doc and I get along very well. Last night we were speaking and he expressed more than a little concern about trying to figure out a way to bring a certain litter-bearer into the Aid Station. I told him if it would help I'd gladly step out, and he said, "Shut up. You're the only indispensable man around here." It was good to know he appreciates my efforts.

Even in the Rest Camp I was surprised to receive a letter from

---

involved as well. Had Winston wanted to press formal charges, he could have done so; his unwillingness to allow the incident to become a matter requiring official action was reported by Rich to Maj. Arthur E. Pollock and Capt. Jacob Schott. Another of Winston's fellow medics, who does not himself recall the incident, remarks, "That would be like Winston—too nice to press charges."

* President Roosevelt, Prime Minister Churchill, and Chief of State Stalin met at Yalta, in the Crimea, 4–10 February.

you, and from my big boy, Neil. You speak about my "elevation" to P/F/C "status."

Incidentally, I wouldn't wear the stripe unless it was compulsory. Over here, no one wears stripes or bars, except the privates. We call them "shower promotions." You see, when we take showers, we throw all our dirty clothes in, and pick up fresh ones. Quite often some private picks up a clean shirt formerly worn by a Sgt.— stripes and all—and in fun we call him a Sgt. When someone congratulates him on the promotion, he tells them he received a "shower promotion."

You asked me to describe the exact function of the Aid Station. First let me tell you how evacuation works: A boy gets hurt on the line. Within a minute or less a telephone message is sent back to our forward Aid Station, a distance of 300 to 1000 yds. from the front where a Sgt. and 4 litter-bearers are always on hand. They rush right up to the line with a litter.

During this time, the Company in which the casualty is a member, has their Aid-man administering first-aid on the spot—usually consisting of stopping the bleeding with Sulfanilamide powder externally, bandaging and giving wound pills internally. By that time, another litter team is there and carries the casualty to the nearest point where a jeep can travel—anywhere from 25 to 3000 yards, depending on conditions. The injured boy is then rushed to the Aid Station, one to three miles behind the line. Here the physician removes the first-aid bandage, makes a proper diagnosis and applies a more permanent bandage, administers blood plasma if needed, and in severe cases, gives morphine; makes the patient comfortable, warm, gives coffee, etc. Whereupon he's rushed back to a point known as Clearing Company pretty far in the rear—this time by a comfortable ambulance which stands ready for action at the Aid Station's door. Now—here, if the wound requires it, he's given emergency operation or attention. This place is well-staffed and well-equipped. Then the casualty is taken by ambulance to an Evacuation hospital further back where first-class attention is administered.

If the case is one whereby the wound or casualty is so severe and he won't get better very soon, he's shipped back even further to a General Hospital, and eventually back to the States.

At the Battalion Aid Station
—*drawing by Al Vidmar*

Reason for the continual moves? One of room. As the patient warrants a further move back, he leaves space for another boy, and needed room is of the essence.

The Aid Station has no beds. Its job is the most important—to evacuate the wounded boy from place of incident to the rear, after essential treatment is administered to save his life. The well-equipped rear stations get the soldier and handle him with the skill that is possible only in a quiet hospital.

So you see, the Aid Station is equipped only with essentials. As each boy comes in (sometimes a half-dozen at once) I help with necessary details—proper bandages, blood plasma, fill out tag, giving a brief history of the boy and his diagnosis, and what has been done for him. As each echelon does something more, it's added to the card which is then tied to the buttonhole in the boy's coat, so that pertinent information stays right with him. This, then, is the procedure with a front-line casualty.

Much of our work, too, has to do with ailments such as colds, flu, foot trouble, trench foot, etc. We treat them and they usually return to the line.

Well, does that give you a fair picture? (No typewriter in it, or bed-pans for that matter.)

This is my second day at the Rest Camp and I'll probably go back today. It was OK but now I think I'll go back to the front to get a rest! I found it pretty hard to sleep on a cot. Your living habits become more and more primitive at the front and you have to learn civilized habits all over again—I'm referring mainly to sleeping, which we do on floors at the Station, as you know.

Luna's brother, Monty, is nearby but I haven't been able to see him.

Am still hoping for an abrupt end before the month is out. It's funny—if funny is the word—how both of us live from month to month hoping for an end to it all. I believe we do this to keep ourselves going, for eventually end, it must. It appears, however, you'll have to plant the garden, though I may get to cultivate it—and surely eat it. OK? I always seem to miss out on the asparagus, though.

8 February

Am now back with the Section and happy about it after the "Rest" Camp. This town is about the nicest around here. Very agreeable is the lack of manure piles. And how they stank!

Did I tell you about the trip to Paris one of our group gets every ten days? We put all the names in a hat, and draw. So far one guy has gone and returned with many interesting souvenirs. I'm getting anxious to go.

We have a package problem around here—outgoing more than incoming. We make up a package of souvenirs and the like, and on the way back they're opened 2 or 3 times for inspection. Many items are stolen from each box by these G.I. inspectors—it's getting to be quite a racket. It's pretty paltry but the mail situation is so tremendous it's impossible to stop it. Well, that's the least of our problems, I guess.

I'm doing better with my French and when civilians don't talk too fast I understand them. I'm beginning to like the language more and more.

If this war doesn't end soon I think I'll explode. It will seem like a dream when I get home, and as I said before, it will require a little time to adjust to peacetime living. The boys think they'll hit the ground, as we do during incoming artillery, when they hear a loud noise (back home).

9 February

Today an order came down from the top, to clean (tidy) all areas where the boys are staying. The whole town was policed up— even the civilians helped and the improvement is amazing. It's been said of G.I.'s that you could follow them throughout France, merely by following the line of C-ration cans—and that seems to be true.

With the warm spell, all the snow disappeared and with the sun shining and everything so calm, you forget there's a war going on— only to be suddenly shaken into reality by a loud artillery blast.

The Section is divided into groups quartered in different homes. They all get comfortable—one fashion or another. I happened to walk into a house today at noon, where a group of litter bearers set themselves up—to see a beautifully set table for four. They had soup in big bowls, tea, bread and butter, French fries and dessert. You get a kick out of seeing rough and ready G.I.'s fixing up a meal with such a pleasant home touch.

The consensus among the G.I.'s (Don't know why there's controversy about the term G.I. I think it hits the spot—as everyone
else does in our group, without exception) is to let Joe Stalin say
the word as to the future of Germany. That goes for me, too.

11 February

Sent you a cablegram last week—and another today as a Valen-
tine greeting. You'll probably receive this letter before getting either
one of them. The older boys have a standing joke around here: "If
you want to write a few words—for a lot of money—and get poor
service—send a cablegram."

You speak about cleaning the house, and it reminds me of the
way the natives clean around here. You see, the homes are stone
and the steps and hallways are stone. Well, every day, Sundays
included, the people scrub their hallway and steps—and—without
fail—it's tracked up 5 minutes later by the chronic mud around. I
always feel sorry to see these people work so hard, and even before
the stone is dry, in walk a bunch of G.I.'s to track it up again.

Our outfit acquired a mobile 110-volt electric generator, suitable
for moving around. I don't know if I like the idea too well, as it
makes the same racket your Delco generator made in Andover—and
it clack-clacks all the time as we don't have storage batteries to
charge up.

We had another service today. Our "congregation" wasn't so
good because conditions are such that it was extremely difficult for
the boys to get down from the line—but still good enough.

Today we decided to get one of these European radios with 3
wave-lengths, and dials that give us, not the name of the station,
but the city. It's intriguing to read on the dial cities we hear and
read about—Frankfurt, Cologne, Berlin, Antwerp, etc. So I teamed
up with a boy who speaks French and we went from house to
house like door-to-door salesmen, asking civilians if they'd like to
sell or exchange their radio for food and cigarettes. We gave up
after trying 15 houses; in all cases they refused to part with their
sets though they're of no use to them now.

Last night we heard a Russian speak (in English) from Moscow on the internal German situation. Every word was encouraging—to the point he expected the war to be over any day now. Doc called him the Russian "Gabriel Heatter."* But it seems he had a solid basis from which to speak.

Received the *Record* today—a new and interesting sheet. I'm finally satisfied. Possibly my complaint—and 1000 others did the trick.

One of the civilian patients who came to the Aid Station was a pregnant woman almost ready to give birth. Doc briefed me on a few pointers and I was all ready to assist him. "Fate" intervened as we were ordered to move before the woman gave birth—but "we" did give her a few examinations, and I'll be prepared for the next if it should happen.

15 February

No mail today, but a delicious package with everything I like in it, including the Sears catalog—all of which was welcome.

My work keeps me busy throughout the day. Nothing spectacular in the news these last few days—but we've learned that before a big push or offensive there seems to be an apparent lull. It means preparation and more preparation so nothing will fail. Even the seemingly minor thing of keeping the boys in cigarettes each day, especially while on the offensive is almost as important as bullets—and that requires transportation, men, gas, etc.

So many boys who come through our Station receive the Purple Heart, and their major concern is that the folks back home not hear of it. They'll eventually hear about it, but it's better when it comes from the wounded soldier himself. I'm glad Jeff's wound was only slight. Believe me, his kind are the real heroes in this war—make no mistake about that. I know.

The news of the 1500-plane raid over Tokyo was indeed encour-

---

* Gabriel Heatter was a popular radio news commentator known for his optimism; frequently his broadcasts began with "There's good news tonight!"

aging. Remember, the European conflict is only part of the war, and Tokyo is a big obstacle.

Again we heard German propaganda in English knocking hell out of the Allies. You'd get a kick out of listening. It shows the real character of the German mind. On the one side of their mouth they're reviling the terrible American and British raids on the poor refugees leaving Berlin with "all their earthly belongings"— and on the other side they're boasting how thorough their robots have been in devastating London.—Just this minute heard 2000 bombers are over Berlin. It can't be long now.

We hear the boys are making fine progress over Japan.* It sure makes me happy as it seemed that side of the war was being treated like a step-child. The more extended that part becomes, the longer we'll be in the Army.

Darling, tonight as I sit here, many boys have stumbled in from the front line for some medical aid—"minor" reasons—stomach upsets, colds, foot trouble, etc. They're muddy and dirty and aching all over, and pathetically happy to be in under "real" light, where it's warm and comfortable, and away from where talking above a whisper could mean enemy rifleshot or a mortar sent screaming in their direction. They come at night; they can't get out of foxholes during the day for fear of being spotted. It tears me up to see them trudge back—and they do, even in pain because there are no replacements and the line has to be held. They know a buddy is depending on them.

If you knew what a lift your packages give these boys, I know you'd be mighty happy. I fix hot bouillon, tuna salad and anything else I can lay my hands on to prepare a nice little spread. It's a bit of a change from their usual Ration fare.

Not only do they experience the horror of battle and noise—but also something just as deadly—and that's monotony—which is something terrible when you're holing up all the time.

Maybe I've told you this before, but these are the boys our country should be grateful for. They're nothing short of heroes.

* American forces had landed on Luzon in the Philippines on 9 January, and by mid-February the U.S. Sixth Army was closing in on Manila. American B-29 bombers based on Saipan were staging raids on Tokyo.

They're supposed to get one "hot" meal a day, which is cold by the time they get it—always after dark—when they can't be seen. Imagine having an appetite under those conditions. No wonder they come in so much with stomach ailments.

Darling, when you read and hear about the wonderful gains our army is making, keep in mind it just didn't happen—that many guys gave a lot of blood, even lives, to gain that objective. Don't forget that—even when the newspapers say "our losses were negligible."

The boys were talking about getting a Bingo game. Could you pick one up? Games of that order could be enjoyed collectively when the boys have some time on their hands. This is my "dept." you know, as "Special Service" man.—Will close now as the mail is being censored.

21 February

As you see by the above date, we've been busy day and night and couldn't find time to write.

Over here we look upon that idea of "bringing the wives over" as a lot of baloney. Dear, we're on duty 24 hours a day—we travel regularly—and we get no leaves. Nor do we desire to have our wives see the conditions under which we live—to say nothing of the danger they'd be in. Some guy must have been thinking of some General friend back in England when he suggested such a crazy idea.

I'm enclosing a picture taken of me Jan. 10. The background shows Nazi prisoners captured a few houses away being interrogated immediately across from our Aid Station.—Also, the "Cross of Lorraine" is enclosed. It's the symbol of Free French, and it is worn by everyone in some form or another over here.

My French is improving steadily; the irony is that much of the language we hear now is German, which strikes me as terribly harsh and difficult, in contrast to French, a beautiful language.

MORNING—before mail censoring.

It's 9 A.M. and I've done all my early work—and do feel good after shaving. In this town I get up about 7:30 and eat breakfast.

Then I come down to the Aid Station, clean up all my book work, clean up personally—and help anyone requiring aid throughout the day. That's the way things are going in this town. It can change tomorrow.

Just noticed out in the Village Square a man ringing a bell, and all the villagers are walking towards him. He's the Town Crier and brings the latest news, rules, etc. It looks like something out of medieval times and fascinating to watch.

These Medics are really going "mad." To let off steam, the boys play football games in the "square." Another outlet is our water fights—and the whole village has been joining in the horseplay. The Medics fill their little syringes we use for shots, with water, hide behind an open window and squirt the civilians as they pass by. The villagers get a kick out of it, too, and now they're retaliating by throwing water from a second-floor window—and then a loud, laughing scream is heard. Some fun, eh? But it keeps the boys from going batty.

We've been eating local bread lately—and since the baker ran short of his flour ration he's been using ersatz flour stored in his basement—and boy, is it lousy. We can't stomach it.

Just got busy, Darling. Until later.

23 February

Last night "Beaucoup"* and I were discussing our homes, our families, our plans, our hopes. He's a nice guy—tall, suave, personable and a good mixer—the kind of guy who's always drinking your liquor and eating your food and making you like it.

The children, and adults too are vitamin and mineral starved. Three out of 4 require false teeth, get outbreaks and sores which are direct results of this lack. Did you get my letter requesting multi-vitamins? If not, I suggest you send me a supply regularly. Some I'll use and some I'll share with people in a bad way. Over here the greens are canned and overcooked and poorly prepared, virtually killing all vitamins.

* Lt. Anthony Scarpitta.

23 February   *Evening*

Soon after writing you I received 6 letters—all sweet and lovely. I zealously tore open each envelope and piled up the letters in numerical order—then started reading—for one-half hour straight! It was wonderful, Darling. I ate up every word.

Your reading *Black Beauty* to Neil pleased me very much. I recall how much I enjoyed that story when I was small.

I can understand George's angry remark that "when he gets home and hears people talk, etc."* People back home or behind Bn. Hq. over here just don't have the vaguest idea about war. It's just plain Hell. Primarily, I'm speaking of the soldier in the dugout. They're in these lousy holes for weeks at a time and they accept with a kind of deadened sense what is expected of them. They come into the Station with tonsilitis, chest pains, fever, deep coughs. Many just stay there in their misery and don't come in unless in really bad shape. One boy with a hacking cough came in only because he was afraid his coughing would alert the enemy.

And I can tell you now that the soldier over here *does* have a resentment toward the boys who are not. Nor does the fact that they have jobs to go back to make any difference.

26 February

Today was a lucky one. I won the drawing entitling me to leave for Paris March 2, and I assure you I'm looking forward to it. Have seven cartons of cigarettes which I plan to use for trinkets for you and the boys. Will be there 3 days and the Army provides the best hotel conveniences.

I did something today which was hazardous but sometimes it's necessary. Doc asked me to ride up to the front with him. We probably were not farther away than 100 yards from the Krauts, and I got a peculiar kick out of it. Of course we didn't go up there for the thrill of it—we went because of a real need. If it weren't for

* Sgt. George Horner, of the 83rd Infantry Division, a neighbor of the Winstons in Pennsylvania. Horner was wounded while serving as chief of a gun section.

my little family, I'll admit I'd be up there on my own accord more often—as there are lots of ways to help out on the line.

As each day goes by there's a better and better feeling among our group. We have a smooth, efficient team and really enjoy working together. The officers are great guys.

Last night the hotel proprietor (Station quarters) baked 3 great big "offul coogans" (apple pies), served coffee and we sang songs to complete a pleasant evening.

Tonight we had a chicken dinner mit cranberries. For the last few days we've been eating better than the soldiers in the States. Don't mean meals—which are mediocre—but from packages received, and you'll probably get a kick out of this—from the kitchens. It's this way—we being the Medics, inspect kitchens often and come back with plenty of juices, bread, jellies and other goodies. Doc says he weighs more now than he ever did. Remember, Dear, most of what we get goes to the boys that come down from the line—and nothing gives us greater satisfaction.

The news outside Cologne is "encouraging," especially the manpower shortage of the Jerries along the Siegfried Line. It's funny but the civilians, even without radio, learn the news quicker than we do. Yesterday the owner of the place came rushing in, "Did you hear the news? Egypt declared war against Germany." Even our soldiers with radios didn't know.

Darling, as my "Special Service assistant" I'm putting in an order for beaucoup de envelopes. Okay?

28 February

Today I treat myself to a shower—preparing for my trip to Paris. I'll continue to write each day while there. Doc asked me to look up Jules Grad—a fraternity brother of his, and a reporter for *Stars & Stripes*. He went into great detail telling me what a fine man he was, and how much of a gentleman he is—"Just like you, Keith," he said. Thought it might please you.

The fine weather continues. And football continues, and "sprechin wasser" on the civilians continues. We delight in hearing them say "nix sprechin"—but every chance they get they douse us plenty. This is not my kind of "sport" but the boys shoot off steam and since it's harmless and fun for all I go along in spirit.

I'm making a list—which grows bigger and bigger—of things the boys want from Paris and I'll try to oblige. We get a complete new outfit and it will feel good dressing like a garrison soldier for a change. I'll try to have a picture taken to send you.

Just got a chance to go to Division Hdqs. and thought I'd take it and maybe see Jim.

Two hours later—just returned. Saw Jim whom I completely surprised. Jim looked fine. He told me two of our former hutmates, Artie and Marty, both a part of the 106th Division, were caught in von Rundstedt's counter-offensive and are missing in action. It hit pretty hard as they were both close friends of mine. I pray to God they're well.

1 March

It's hard to realize Spring is creeping up on us and we're still here. Doc's prediction and mine were all wet it seems.

We saw a show "Sons of Bitche" (should clue you on our whereabouts) put on by boys in our Regiment. It's hilarious and has had 10 repeat performances and still going strong.

Tomorrow I'll be spending a day at the Rest Camp in preparation for the trip, and the little bonanza of mail I received from you this evening really set me up.

2 March

Here I am at the Rest Camp—outfitted in a complete new set of clothes and tomorrow we'll be on our way.

I laughed and laughed picturing David munching apples all day. Without a doubt he takes after his Dad on that score.

When they say Medics don't get as much pay as Infantrymen,

they mean Medics don't get Combat Infantry pay.* There was a loud racket when some brass hats made front-line Medics turn in their combat badges. If it were for the Medic's own security, well that was one thing but it should have been replaced with another significant emblem. Anyway, when they took the badges away there was a bigger howl from the Infantrymen than the Medics, arguing that regiment clerks wear combat badges and they take it away from a Medic—and as one G.I. put it, only hours before he's hit by mortar fire.—There was a lot of talk before election time about giving Medics in combat equal pay—but so far—no soap.

I was touched by Neil's reaction to my offering the jars of baby food. Darling, it's such an insurmountable problem, forget about sending me anything for the children as the problem is too great to tackle. However, you might enclose bottles of Vi-Penta from time to time so I can offer it when a real need arises. (The pity of it all, they all need it.) But some even worse than others. I had a similar thought in the beginning, but after seeing how many little ones in just one town—and realizing the necessity for following through for results—it's a losing battle—even though it gets to you.

4 March

I can't write you where I am (by now you know) but am finding the City a very gay and refreshing relief. Just returned from the Folies, and already reserved a seat for a sight-seeing tour tomorrow morning.—Have a private room in a hotel—and clean sheets—isn't that great? Times like this I miss you more than ever. Up front, my mind is so active with work and responsibility—but now with time on my hands our being separated really hits me.

Today I found out something about Luna's brother, Monty's outfit. He was caught in the counter-offensive not far from us over the New Year. I spoke with an officer in his Regiment and he tells me he's pretty sure he's "visiting" Berlin, but has no way of being

* The ruling that front-line medics were not to receive combat pay was highly unpopular among infantrymen in particular. A later ruling reversed the decision. See p. 293.

certain. It's difficult to write about these things as they're strictly censored. I hope none of the above is cut.

We're treated wonderfully—meals mit tablecloth and waitress—nice? An orchestra all day long—and Cokes. Cokes for 1¢ a glass, and a PX where I plan to buy you sumpthin'. They have an elegant department store—like Wanamaker's or Gimbels—right across the street. But—the prices—they're outrageous.

You know what happens here on the streets? Prostitutes walk right up to you and solicit business. I wouldn't believe it unless I saw it—and I did. It's disgusting, but many of the boys accept the "service."

I won't be getting your mail for a few days and will miss it. I couldn't write much about my relations with Doc when on the line (censorship, etc.) but they're on the friendliest of terms. He confides in me and often asks my advice—and tells me if "so and so" moved out (transferred or otherwise) he'd make me his Staff Sgt. As things stand, rank means so little here. But even were I looking for something like this, a good man can be held down by the Table of Organization in an outfit. And in the case of a new man, you can't judge him by his rank. Anyway, his attitude makes life so much more tolerable under the conditions and I appreciate it.

6 March

[Cablegram]
MY DARLING I AM HAVING A HOLIDAY IN A WONDERFUL CITY BUT MISSING YOUR COMPANIONSHIP MORE THAN YOU CAN EVER KNOW. ALL MY HEART.

8 March

Well, here I am back at the old stand—with the boys—after leaving Paris which was hard to do. It's a great city where the American soldier is appreciated and shown a good time (for a slight handling charge 10 times higher than American prices). The people are enthusiastic and really seem to like the boys—who, on the whole, do the U.S. uniform proud.

When I say prices here are terrific—it's not just to take the soldier over, but inflation is so bad everything is priced way out of proportion. E.g.: a plain sweater, the equivalent of $32. in American money, a simple dress $75. and I could go on and on. Black marketeering is rampant and the chief source for cigarettes, chocolate, soap which go for unheard-of prices. One boy had an ordinary dinner in a mediocre restaurant with a girl—spent $36. and says he was still hungry.

However, Parisians are typically French, very economical and self-reliant and look none the worse for it. In fact they look quite well.

I did get a few insignificant gifts—terribly high and not worth the price. But they do have souvenir value.

Just finished lunch made by Doc, Beaucoup and me which included my soups—1 pack noodle, pea and onion. Doc mixed it all together and the Lt. and I had to admit it was first rate. Then cocoa, bread and butter—and to top it off home-made jelly of Doc's. Doc and I get the packages, and the Lt. raids the kitchens. Our trio is some combination!

Had a letter from Harry.* Did I tell you he was hit? Not too seriously but bad enough. I carried him (with litter) off the "hill." There were so many horrible casualties that day, he had to lay there until we took care of the others. He was such a damn good sport about it. Not until later did we learn that his injury was more serious than we first thought and I felt mighty sick about it. I value his friendship as I've always found him to be intelligent and good company. Remember I was his "purser" on board ship?

More about Paree: The city is truly beautiful, often reminding me of Washington because of its wide, handsome thoroughfares and imposing buildings. You'd hardly know it has seen its share of war. All the architecture is influenced in some degree by the Louis or Napoleon whom they revere.

Napoleon's tomb in itself is quite a story. The tremendous ivory

* Harry Fienman.

casket was laid to rest in a huge room, and people view it from a landing above—thus compelling them to bow their heads as they view the great "conqueror." While holding Paris, the Germans, I heard, refrained from marring this edifice, even added the caskets of Napoleon's son and brother. However, every statue honoring great minds and progressives like Voltaire, Victor Hugo, Shakespeare was destroyed or confiscated. Anything showing Fascist leanings they let stand untouched.

While I was in Paris Doc delivered a baby boy—and is he proud. In return for his service he requested the child be named Joseph, after him, and in return, he (Doc) would send a gift each year to his namesake. Today a luscious cake baked by these folks was sent down to Doc—and on it was painstakingly printed "Viva Joseph." I saw the healthy looking baby and his parents who can't seem to do enough for Doc. They call him Docteur Joseph. I'm sorry I missed it after all my "training." Generally, deliveries are performed by midwives, but the people are thrilled when they can get a "real live doctor."

11 March

Today was mail-less, but so it was for everyone, and who am I to complain? A little while ago I read a copy of *Fortune* magazine and its advertisements really made me homesick—and sick of this mess.

We're finally leaving the hotel—and I hate to very much. We're going for what they call a "rest"—meaning we Medics are really going to have it rough since everyone in the Bn. gets typhus shots, examinations and the like, which will keep us damn busy. I got to like this town very much—and the people seemed to feel the same way about us. And again I say, c'est la guerre.

I find I'm able to carry on a conversation in French, however limited, and I've found the best way to learn is to talk to the natives—though a fast-talker still gives me a little trouble.

Something else about the Parisian "low-life." These prostitutes, licensed by law, make a point of hanging around the Red Cross

Clubs where soldiers live, and when one passes by, they say, "heelo beeby—zig zig?" Which evidently is their method of plying their trade. And the American soldier (maybe 40%) usually looks her over, either passes her by for a better looker, or stops and says, "Combien?" After dickering for a good price, he's taken to a hotel. Solicitation by these rather pathetic girls happened everywhere I went. It is commonplace in Paree. No embarrassment—hard to believe, but true.

I got a big kick out of distributing candy to the kids. I opened a package of caramels and gave them to a bunch of kids hanging around. They jumped up and down in glee.

The war seems to drag and drag, with the Germans hanging on regardless of the odds against them. All the civilians are sick of war; they've seen their homes demolished, plundered, their families broken up and their sons forced into the Nazi army.

Well, Darling, that's about it for now. All my love.

12 March

Well, today we're in our new place where we're supposed to "rest," ha ha. But I do have a swell deal. I am again staying with Doc and Beaucoup. This time we have three rooms and 3 beds—a radio, electricity, and a magnificent, soothing waterfall right outside our bedroom windows—very luxurious, not to mention conducive to good sleeping. However, the Aid Station is quite a distance away and I, being more or less the liaison man between the Aid Station and Doc, will probably be running around quite a bit, but I don't mind too much.

Haven't had any mail from you in about 3 or 4 days, and not too much for the past two weeks, but I understand airmail is a little slower now. Do continue with airmail, by all means, despite government propaganda to the contrary.

Continued, morning of March 13th. It's springy out and wonderfully sunny and warm, though still muddy. Manure piles are high in this town, and last night while playing football almost ran into a pile full force.

We're enjoying our evening snacks, though stocks are becoming depleted. My latest requests: tuna, mayonnaise, beaucoup cheese spreads, Pabstett cheese, and something new, canned tongue. Thank you, Dearest, for going to so much trouble without complaint. You can't know how much it is appreciated.

Lost my fountain pen yesterday and was "heart-broken." It wrote so smoothly I became attached to it, but don't send any replacement as I'll pick one up around here. How is my little David? I'm eager to hear new stories about him, and by all means, my big son, Neil, too. Take care of yourself, and please let me know everything when you write.

6. Attack, Pursuit

Bitche, Hardt Mountains, the Rhine, Heilbronn, toward Stuttgart

March-May 1945

The 71st Division was moving in to relieve the 100th Division, and the 2nd Battalion of the 398th Infantry had already departed for ten days of rest at Sarre-Union, when on 13 March orders arrived that changed everything. Seven days earlier, on 7 March, units of the U.S. First Army, driving toward the Rhine River, had captured an intact bridge at Remagen and had thrown troops across the river. The Allied plan had been for Field Marshal Montgomery's forces to make the first crossing of the river, but now the U.S. First and Third armies were given orders to exploit the breakthrough, and American troops poured across the Rhine. A general advance was ordered, and the U.S. Seventh Army was instructed to move forward. In two days of heavy fighting the 100th Division captured the heavily fortified city of Bitche, and then drove 100 miles through the Hardt Mountains to the Rhine. By 26 March the division was in position near Ludwigshafen, awaiting construction of a pontoon bridge. On 31 May the crossing was made without opposition, and the 100th swung southward for a drive toward Bavaria. Four days later, on 4 April, the division began its attack on the strongly fortified industrial city of Heilbronn. The 398th Regiment, which had arrived at Bad Wimpfen, crossed the Neckar River, and against heavy opposition fought its way southward. Under heavy fire, and in the face of repeated counterattacks by German SS and Hitler Jugend units, the 398th crossed the Jagst River on 6 April, drove toward Heilbronn, and on 12 April forced its way across the Kocher River. Meanwhile the other regiments of the 100th Division had crossed the Neckar and were slugging their way through the city of Heilbronn.

15 March 1945

I didn't write last night—as once more we're on the go. Today was hectic and I'm bushed. By the time you get this letter you'll probably know a little more about my activities (from the papers). Send me clippings of news of our Division.

Received your fine package and I can tell you those date and nut cookies were delicious, and everyone who ate them remarked about them. They were even better than the first batch as they were still very fresh tasting, and not dried out like the earlier ones—which were still very good.

That swell deal—private room mit bed and bubbly waterfall outside ended fast—and I really miss it as it was the most restful place I've been in since leaving home. The people were especially nice. The mother was sick at heart; her son was forcibly drawn into the German army and she hated Hitler and the whole German cause. She was genuinely happy to have us around her, even though she spoke German and we couldn't understand each other too well. We see many people and by this time we've learned that the largest percentage are pro-Nazi, even though they try to act and talk otherwise—but we can quickly tell. In this case, we were sure she was OK.

There's little I can write you concerning our activities—but can tell you things are bouncing and I'm on my toes constantly. Until later, my Love.

16 March

Today was good to me; two precious letters from you, and how I needed them. Enjoyed the picture, and sketch of Neil by Junie. He looked so good in his outfit—like a real American boy and it makes his father real proud and pleased. And David—too sweet for words.

Glad to know you received the German souvenirs. You seemed to show little interest in them—not that I'm over-enthusiastic—but they're generally picked up under such interesting circumstances which I cannot reveal now, but will when I get home. Further, I'm sure Neil enjoys them. Just leading up to the fact that another box is in the making and will be off soon. Was glad you liked the wooden shoes, though.

It's been frenetic today with everyone jumping all over the place. Wish I could tell you why—perhaps you've already heard

Germany, March 1945
—drawing by Al Vidmar

through the papers. Anyway, the news photographers and movie-camera men are here in droves. Tomorrow we're at it again. No rest if the war is to end soon, and this time, it does look good.

We occupy a building once housed by a branch of the Nazi Youth Organization. Here I picked up many souvenirs and a couple of fifes—another musical instrument pour vous.

17 March

Another day—and still elated over yesterday's victory. It's somewhat quieter today. I walked into an old castle built in the 17th century, with a moat and a 6-foot depth of water surrounding it—like in medieval times—and dungeons, etc. It was taken over by the Jerries and used as an Observation Post since it commands a view of the area for miles around.

For the first time now people are getting out of their cellars, seeing sun and breathing fresh air again. They all look a little sick—pallid and wan.

The boys didn't forget St. Patrick's day, most of them wearing some visible signs of green.

Boy, Honey, the G.I.'s have taken over this town com-plete-ly, and the population has now quadrupled. Now that "activity" is heavier the meals have been extra good lately—and welcome. We don't eat all day long as we sometimes did before. There's no time, consequently have tremendous appetites at mealtime.

Have you heard where Mark is?* I'm anxious to know. Try to find out.—How are my two boys getting along with each other? Neil will be home on his Easter vacation by the time you get this letter.

19 March

We're again on the move—and last night wound up in the weirdest, ghost-like place I've seen around here. You wouldn't believe this but only 3 houses in the entire village were left with roofs or ceilings. We're lucky to have one of them even though the windows are smashed and parts of the building are about to cave in. Just glad to be under a roof.

At the beginning of the German offensive over four years ago, they evacuated all civilians and used this town (as they did many

---

* Tec 5 Mark Winston, Keith's older brother, was in the Army Corps of Engineers.

others) as a training ground in village fighting—artillery and bombing. Consequently, the entire village is demolished.—But leave it
to the G.I.'s. By this afternoon they've made themselves reasonably
comfortable. You've got to hand it to American boys—by and large
they're an ingenious lot.

About 7 A.M., in this forlorn, desolate village we heard a familiar
voice walking down the street, crying, "Habisy, habisy, habisy—
essen, essen, kim essen, you dumkuffs." It was our cook calling the
boys for chow in typical German village fashion—by way of a town
crier. It broke the boys up.

We injected typhus shots in most of the guys today and it had
us stepping.

No mail today but I did get package 17. Again your nut and date
cookies made a big hit—especially with me!

21 March

Yesterday I was sick and nauseous which lasted through the
night, and at Doc's orders I'm here at the Rest Center and feeling
almost normal again. As I was leaving, 3 rays of sunshine were
handed me and they couldn't have been timed better. In addition,
I heard from Mark who's now stationed in Belgium on Detached
Service from his Engineer's outfit, and suggests we get together in
Brussels if ever possible. It gave me a lift to hear from him after all
this time and I hope he keeps well and out of danger. Also a letter
from Harry who's always good for a few laughs. He's really a swell
guy. He writes, from a hospital in England, "Despite my sundry
ailments, I'll be back in Co. 1 kicking the Krauts around. Glad to
hear of your promotion. You can probably find good use for the
extra 'five' up there, like starting a fire with it. It may all be over
by June. Can you sweat it out?"

Here at the Rest Camp they try to do a good job. It serves as a
"stop-gap" between the front line and hospital. When a fellow
has a problem, like a severe headache, bad feet, upset stomach,
etc., instead of putting him in a hospital they send him here for a

couple of days and invariably it does the trick. They do their best to simulate a home atmosphere. Hung on the outside is a huge sign "HEROES HAVEN" and they really treat these boys coming in from the front as heroes. All day long they serve fruit juices, provide movies, radio, writing materials, magazines—and they're doing a great job. It's sponsored by the Medics. Each Regiment in our Division has one.

Your question—"Just what happens when the Aid Station occupies a home—do the civilians move out?"—Usually they take it for granted that 1, 2, 3 or more of their rooms will be requested, and they're prepared for it. In fact, they welcome it since wherever the U.S. soldier goes he leaves so much food, cigarettes, etc.—and over here money means nothing—zero—but commodities everything. Therefore they gladly double up to make room for the boys.

There have been cases (very few) where civilians have sabotaged—like cutting communication wires, causing the whole town to be evacuated—but rarely in France. However, in Germany the picture will be completely different. The U.S. soldier is forbidden to fraternize, or even talk to a German.

Don't worry about what you write in your letters as no one but me sees them—even if they did we have nothing to hide—and *nothing* is personal over here.

The picture you enclosed of our house brought on more than a bit of nostalgia—a fancy word for homesickness. You have no idea what that little structure, so far away, means to me.

About Maurice Chevalier. He proved to the authorities that he sang for the Nazis under force, and is now accepted by the Free French. He's singing for the Stage Door canteen now.

Paris certainly is a gay city and I'd like to spend a couple of weeks with you—with plenty of moolah. But I'd forfeit any vacation—anywhere—for a chance to get home.

Doc just came over for a shower and is on his way back to the front. I was going to return with him but he suggested I stay another night. It will give me a chance to answer a few letters and visit a friend.

Think I'll take a walk in the warm sunshine—probably in Jim's direction—where I'll get the latest. He works in the news section. I'll close now, Darling.

22 March   *France*

Well—all good things must come to an end and I'm back in harness with the outfit.—Things are moving fast, as you must be aware from the papers. I'll probably be unable to write where I am after today. Reply to this dated letter when you write—comprende?

Hope you're clipping all news items concerning the 100th, or 397, 398, 399 Infantry—all members of this Division. Doc just showed me clippings about his Bronze Star award published in the Cincinnati newspapers. If anyone deserves it, he does. He's been at his post through everything since the war (for us) started—with no complaints.

As we're "going places" I won't get much time to write but will do my best.

Darling, we're rolling now—really rolling. Don't worry as a few more days like this and my chances of getting home sooner will be greater.

LATER: I'm sure you can guess where we are now. But in case you can't—I probably can get away with saying that when we reached this "sacred soil"—everyone stopped—and every troop, in ceremonious style, urinated.

This morning we saw scores of haggard Russians walking toward our rear—prisoners the Nazis had used as slaves and left behind when the Krauts retreated. Darling, when I saw their faces—their smiles of joy, their revived hope—and American food in their hands, it brought tears to my eyes for I knew I was seeing first-hand just what we're fighting for—the right to be free—to go unmolested, to have freedom from oppressive tyranny—something these poor souls hadn't known for years.

It was one of the most heart-rending scenes I've encountered, and I've seen plenty. Among this group were many women, aged beyond their years. To see their faces when they saw us is an indescribable experience. I saw many a "hardened" soldier with tears streaming down their eyes. A terrible world we're living in, isn't it.

There isn't much I have to say—or rather, am able to say. Just be assured that everything looks good.

What I've seen of the land here is beautiful but it's all dimmed by these bestial circumstances. If only these people had concentrated on their beautiful country instead of trying to destroy the world. But it all backfired like a boomerang and they've destroyed themselves in the attempt.

If we soldiers have anything to say about it—and we will—this is the last war Germany will start.

24 March

We're still rolling and with a few more bridgeheads over the Rhine, I can't see how the momentum can be stopped.

For the first time I saw what our Air Force can really do and I take back every mean word I've ever said about them. It was our first opportunity to see the effectiveness of the last 3 or 4 years of bombing. The Nazis withheld the news, but we saw enough.

In one section we saw miles of German vehicles, tanks and supply dumps, horses and wagons virtually end to end—and everything completely demolished. Despite what is heard from German sources, make no mistake about it, they're suffering and suffering acutely. Their towns and cities have been shelled, even more so, bombed, and nothing is much worse than bombing. It undermines and shatters morale, not to mention the country and materials. And they're showing it in more ways than one. Throughout the towns we've gone through, white flags of surrender hang from every window.

One of our German-speaking boys constantly hears the people bemoaning their state. They know the war is lost and they ask each other, "Why doesn't Hitler quit?"

We don't say a word to the German people. They seem to be dazed. Many smile, but we don't know what lurks behind the smile and we look straight through them. Others are outwardly bitter and treat us as usurpers, intruders.

If a G.I. is caught fraternizing, he is fined. Many amusing incidents turn up—like when a pretty girl walks past, a G.I. (with tongue hanging out) will say, "Here, Doc, here's my fine."

Had a letter from Henry (who married a girl after a week's courtship). He was wounded several months ago and his injury became infected. He had a rough time of it but now he's in pretty decent shape. In case you're interested in the outcome of my advice to the "lovelorn," everything is patched up between them, and from what he writes things are looking up. He's still recuperating in a hospital in England, however.*

Your suggestion of a vacation would be heaven. I'll leave it all up to you. Darling, if the continuity of my letters seems bad, it's because I'm up and down and on the go—and so many things are happening. I snatch minutes here and there to finish a letter.

24 March

Another day—and situated in another house. You once questioned our procedure regarding the people when we take over a house for our Aid Station. In France, where we cooperated with the civilians it was one thing, but it's different here. They're ordered to leave the house altogether—and we have in many instances—as we did today—insisted all villagers leave town. On the surface this may sound merciless, dear, but you haven't the slightest idea how these people hate and despise us and would not miss an opportunity to sabotage us—as other troops have experienced in the past—so to protect our boys from added dangers we're compelled to resort to this. It's a temporary measure, and believe me, when we move on we don't leave the house in shambles as the Krauts did to every house they occupied. As a last gesture, they made sure they smashed everything worth smashing if they couldn't take it along. Not an ounce of compassion in their lousy souls— they followed orders like robots, usually going it one better. On the other hand, our boys while no angels, have feeling for people, and their homes are little the worse for being occupied—except for a few small "liberated" items to send home as souvenirs.

If you have any human feeling in your heart you don't like to put people out of their homes—but it ceases to be a personal matter but one of security for our boys.

* Pfc. Henry Black, of Springfield, Massachusetts.

The news is better than good but those dumkuffs still don't give up—we can't understand it. Apparently we have to do the job 100% which will mean more unnecessary casualties, enemy and civilians, big cities demolished, and worse yet, losses and casualties of our own.

25 March

Is it possible that one year ago today I left home for the Army? This year, with its heartaches and pain, has made a big change in our lives and when we're together again we'll appreciate life even more. Over here you see how precarious it can be from day to day. And you learn to take nothing for granted.

Today is Sunday—and beautiful. While awaiting orders we're resting in this little town in a modern 6-room house—definitely for a better-than-average incomed family. I'm in the back, sitting up against a fruit tree, writing. There's so much here to remind me of home—the little garden, dwarf fruit trees and a large open field in the back.—There are chickens and we get fresh eggs. A strawberry patch, too.

War is such a peculiar phenomenon. As I write this letter I can hear the city—close by—being bombed. I can see our planes overhead on their way to this city. And I can see the enemy flak pouring on them, trying to down our planes. If I watch closely, I can see the smoke rising as our planes lay their "eggs." Yet here we are just a short distance away, relaxing, waiting for the Air Force to soften this city so our force can go in and take it. God, war is weird.

The enclosed copy of *Stars & Stripes* is significant. Am not permitted to send you any portion, so am sending the whole sheet. One picture will probably give you the story. Much has happened since but you'll know where I was at that date. And we're all very proud of it.

Enclosed also is a pin which Hitler issues to Mamas who produce babies for the Fatherland. No matter if they're married or not—he just wants babies for future cannon fodder—and for this they get medals.

The boys are having a field day—eating fresh eggs and plenty of chicken. If only they weren't such lousy cooks.

It's hard to believe we're in Germany. It's more like America than any place I've seen. Generally speaking the people are healthy looking, dress well and certainly live well.

We expect the Russians to strike a finishing blow on Berlin any day now. The radio announced that Washington expects the war to be over within two weeks. Oh, God, hurry that day.

In a letter you wrote a few weeks ago, you told me to have my gas mask with me at all times. Your wording was exactly the way our Colonel ordered it—and everyone got a kick out of the similarity of your "order." We realize that gas could be used any minute and always have our gas masks with us, Dear. However, I doubt if they'll resort to it as their own people will suffer, since the war now is right smack in the big German cities and heavily populated.

26 March

Today, two great letters from you, Sweetheart. The weather continues warm—and the airplanes continue to come out in tremendous numbers. We spotted about 500 Fortresses and it was a big, beautiful sight. The news is better than good and any hour we could hear of a complete rout. We're still awaiting orders.

Re: Red Cross. My complaint is that they put emphasis on rear echelon area and very little on the combat man. We're not looking for girls and doughnuts, but many other little vital things where the Red Cross could fill the bill. But always some excuse, "We don't do that—it comes under Army" and a hundred other excuses—the biggest one—"no shipping space." It seems there's plenty of shipping space for the stuff they bring up to the rear echelons. I just burn over it, so much so that in the future will recommend to my friends they do not support the Red Cross.

27 March

Again two very nice letters. I'm sorry, Dear, but something in one annoyed me so much I can't help but get it off my chest. I wrote you that the Red Cross is not doing the job for the combat boys, and then I get a letter from you telling me you contributed $5.00 to this organization. The way I feel now it will be the last money they ever receive from us—and whenever a Red Cross campaign is under way I'll take the occasion to send a check to another charity. Consider yourself bawled out! I burn, because I see it as a glamor outfit—basking in the glory of being "overseas" and "doing a fine job" to the rear echelons where it's safe—and reason enough why those boys don't need priority over a front-line boy.

As far as looting goes, I'm beginning to see that the Americans are just as bad as the others. However, you can't be critical of line boys since they've gone through hell—sniped at—faced death 1000 times because of these louses, and they hate them with all the venom a human being can muster up. It's one thing reading about the rotten tactics of the Nazis, but getting wounded, seeing your foxhole mate killed beside you or seeing a wounded boy helpless on his back being shot at again. This does things to you.

And so often our boys who've been sniped at by a lousy Nazi all day—missing death a dozen times—will see him come forward—after he's shot all his ammunition—yelling "Komerad" (I surrender). Do you blame our boys who fight clean for not stopping at anything—and in this instance, looting is minor. I've been right on the line enough times to see the fighting tactics of both sides, and let me tell you, Honey, it's like day and night. I don't go for looting but I can understand it. I've been there, Charlie.

The thought of the folks back home making big plans for V-E Day provoked me, when boys over here are still giving their blood, and plenty of it. Even though the reports already have the war won, remember, until V-E Day we're sweating out enemy artillery fire that goes with war. [Censored sentence.] Until the final second of victory, the boys are *in* there. Until then, there's no reason for celebration.

It's hard to believe we're in Germany except for the fact people are under constant surveillance and not permitted near troops who occupy their homes.

I hope I wasn't too harsh with my comments, Darling—they were not directed at you—but I hate to see the Red Cross taking credit for work they *don't* do—the vital job everybody thinks they do. That's my primary beef.

28 March

Am in much better spirits, Dear, especially since I hold before me two very sweet letters. Also *Time* and *U.S. Business News.*

We all had a touch of homesickness today. You see, "Beaucoup," who has been overseas 24 months, was notified he's getting a 30-day furlough to the States—the lucky guy. He sure deserves it; he's been through Africa, Italy, Anzio, etc. But I'll admit it's hit us all since there's little chance of a furlough for most of us.

Something funny happened tonight. One of the fellows from a line outfit, who often spends the evening here, kept up a steady stream of cussing. The poor guys have plenty of reason to spout steam—I guess it helps them to keep their sanity. Anyway, I kept kidding him—how it hurt my ears, etc.—Well, do you remember my telling you that Doc calls me Reverend occasionally? Anyway, he did this time, and the boy, who suddenly became quiet, asked the fellows if I were a real Reverend. And with sober faces they all said, "Yes." So, very sheepishly he apologized to me for his foul language. He wondered why I wasn't a chaplain, and the boys told him I preferred being a plain soldier!

Today, Passover—and right here in Germany 1000 Jewish boys attended service—a solemn, inspiring observance—with a real Passover supper—matzos and all—sponsored by our Corps. I wasn't able to attend, but heard all about it and regret missing it.

We're moving at a good clip although we're still awaiting orders for a rest, as our Division broke the record for being on line longer than any other outfit—141 days straight. The boys are quite proud of our record—but also very worn.

29 March

The Division band was down today and relieved tensions with a good concert. I could listen to them all day. Marlene Dietrich and Bobby Breen are visiting soldiers nearby. It's surprising how little desire I have for movies and shows now, unlike my training days. Only good semi-classical music satisfies me at this time.

"Beaucoup" acquired 45 bottles of the best champagne and 30 bottles of cognac, equivalent of $1000. value. You see, the Nazis stole the finest from the French and we got it through military channels. Our boys, the Medics, drink sensibly and don't go on binges.

We're still in this town near the front where our troops are mopping up a good-sized German city very much in the news.* Over the radio came the news of the false armistice reported in the States. I can imagine the reaction on hearing of peace, and then to hear it was only an error in reporting.

I must tell you about one of our group, Max, a German refugee. Up until recently we've been calling him Mox. Now, it's Wilhelm, to confuse the Germans. I may have mentioned him to you before. You can imagine how he despises Germans and wastes no opportunity to show it. Everyone here understands his state of mind in Germany and we're behind him all the way.

He's a pleasant guy and likes to cook. Each day he picks up a few chickens which he prepares with a gourmet's touch—wine and all. In his last letter to his wife he writes, "Eight chickens were AWOL, probably missing in action."

His home in Germany is 40 miles from here and he's desperately hoping to find his parents (he's Jewish).† We're all hoping we get near this town so he can make the effort—if they're still alive. Everybody knows each other's business in a little town and he says

---

* Ludwigshafen.
† Pfc. Max Haas, a native of Beerfelden, was a resident of New York City when he joined the 100th Division. Although there had been rumors of mass deportations of Jews, not until the war was over did full realization of what had happened take place. More than six million Jews, Slavs, Gypsies, and other "undesirables" were murdered in the infamous Nazi death camps at Buchenwald, Dachau, Auschwitz, and elsewhere.

—drawing by Marius N. Trinque, from The Story of the Century

that the first person he knows who tells him they don't know of his parents' whereabouts, he will kill. I doubt if he would. He's no killer type, but everyone here understands his despair.

30 March

Beaucoup left to go to the States and it's been a day of depression. I gave him our phone number. Hope he calls you from Baltimore and tells you what I'm unable to. When he left, we sang "Auld Lang Syne" and it took will power to keep the tears back, as the significance of his departure hit me pretty hard.

Champagne was served, and a toast offered for a quick end to the

war. Also, today, Beaucoup and Doc were officially awarded the
Bronze Star, and I took pictures of the ceremony. They were both
thrilled and rightfully so as they deserved them.

Still awaiting orders and expect a change soon. The word continues good, and again I repeat, any hour could bring the real news.

We listen to the German reports over the radio and since Mox
talks German we enjoy getting their version—which is a continua-
tion of fantastic lies.

Sometimes the American propaganda station broadcasts to the
Germans in their language and gives the true picture. This morning
he was talking in perfect German, when all of a sudden he says in
English, "Excuse me,"—then "oh, my"—then continued quickly,
"On shultish" (excuse me). He got his languages mixed and we all
had a good laugh.

I miss you all so much, Darling. It just hurts to think of you at
times—and now is one. Neil, I crave to see. I'm looking at his picture now and it tears at me to be away from him—not to guide him
as he grows up. I know you're trying to do a capable job, and it's a
consolation to me.

There was a picture story in "This Week" about a G.I. returning
with a mangled hand—and about his adjustment. There will be
thousands, perhaps hundreds of thousands, going through the same
experience—and probably worse.

1 April

We've left our old location and are presently comfortably quartered in a small bungalow, but will be moving again today.

Again I saw what our Air Force has been doing these last few
years. Dear, you read and hear of so much devastation in Germany
now—but I have seen big cities—very big cities whose main areas
are reduced to a pile of rubble—all bricks and stones. We saw a
tremendous bridge (comprende?) knocked apart.* It's like a dream

* Between Ludwigshafen and Mannheim, across the Rhine.

looking at all this especially when you see so many things directly connected to Hitler—huge swastikas on the remains of an airport and big buildings. It's hard to believe the things you read about are actual—but they are actual.

Ate up every word of your account of David—when you had to wake him five minutes after he fell asleep—and how sweet and unaffected he was by it all. I could just picture his every action.

Since the previous paragraph we have moved again, and again comfortably situated for the night. We're now in a different time zone and turn our watches ahead one hour. Hope soon to be turning them back—on our way home!

These towns we enter are newly Nazi-army freed villages, although the civilians, I assure you, are still Germans, and our orders are very strict—to be always on guard, never to walk alone, and the stress is on fine or imprisonment if we fraternize. The boys are holding fast to these rulings—and the Germans, knowing we enter as conquerors—not liberators as was the case in France—look on us with hate and loathing.

2 April

Four juicy, sweet letters—and I'm a happy man. Heard from Jim, too, and learned that Artie is a PW. Bad as it is it gave me a lift as I feared he was killed. If I hear the same about Marty I'd be thrilled. Marty was my tentmate in bivouac if you remember. I thought the world of him—a really fine guy. It may sound peculiar that I'm happy to hear about anyone being a PW which is pretty bad—but at least there's a thread of hope. Death is pretty final.

We visited an old city—close by—famous for its University and romanticized by Sigmund Romberg's beautiful music—and also fc. its castle which is world renowned.* It's truly one of the lovelier cities, and enjoyed roaming around the streets. If this gets by the censors I'm sure you'll recognize the city.

* In its advance on Heilbronn the 398th Regiment passed through the city of Heidelberg.

4 April

On the "go" again. "On the go" means we'll be together again that much sooner. We're situated in a little village but ready to go again at any moment.

Why in hell doesn't someone come forth who could accept a peace? We now know that mad-man Hitler doesn't dare tell the Nazis to lay down their arms. He'd sooner see the country leveled, and he cares even less for the populace. Right now the only thing that matters is his own hide which isn't worth a plugged nickel. And no one knows it better than he. But in the meantime our own boys suffer needlessly.*

Speaking of our forward march, and the mail. When we move, the A.P.O. moves, too. Thus, with all the little delays, I say the mail service is super, and the boys who make it possible deserve no small amount of credit.

Got a card from Lou—a form mentioning his purchase of a $5.00 share of "Red Cross" and dedicating it to me. How lucky can a guy get! Now, if it were the Salvation Army. . . .

Soft, beautiful music always succeeds in making us a little home-sick and we're getting a lot of it tonight. As we listened, one guy said, "It sure makes me homesick."—Another guy—"Chuck," a real rough and tough soldier from Arkansas sitting beside him (who can't read or write—the only one I know of in our Division—but innately intelligent, and with a heart of gold)—spoke up loudly, "Oh? What in hell reason do you have to be homesick? We got enough grub to eat, we got a pad to sleep on, we're healthy and we're living."

For awhile no one spoke, and then I looked over to this rough and tough "illiterate" whose teary eyes met mine, and he blurted, "So I am crying—a guy can get homesick *once in awhile.*" We all burst out laughing. And he did, too.

---

* The 100th Division was encountering fierce resistance as it moved across the Neckar River to assault Heilbronn.

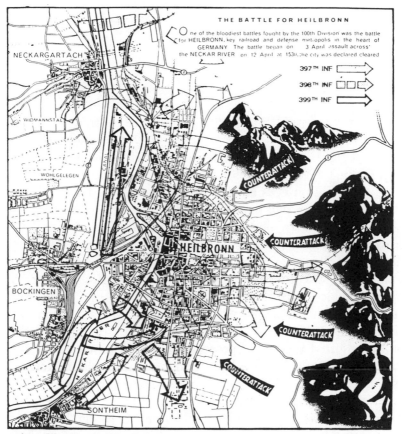

THE BATTLE FOR HEILBRONN

One of the bloodiest battles fought by the 100th Division was the battle for HEILBRONN, key railroad and defense metropolis in the heart of GERMANY. The battle began on 3 April, assault across the NECKAR RIVER on 12 April. At 1530, the city was declared cleared

397TH INF
398TH INF
399TH INF

—from The Story of the Century

5 April

We just moved again. Am a little tired but do want to get a few lines off to you. Was pleased and happy to get two letters from you today which as usual were genuine morale-boosters.

It's April 5 and the war continues. Perhaps the Pope's appeal might give Hitler the alibi he needs to ask the army to put down their arms. This devastation is senseless. Darling, I assure you the war is still on and our boys are still meeting hard resistance, and the casualties continue. I hope and pray the people back home realize it. Don't be deluded by optimistic newspaper accounts. Of course gains are being made—but not for nothing. If people only knew what is happening while the "good news" is being headlined.

8 April

What better way of being greeted on a dismal morning than with a bright, 4-page letter from my sweetest one. It certainly did start the day off right. As you see by the above date, I missed a couple of days writing so you must know things have been hopping.

Yes—our Division does have a newspaper but the latest ruling is that we're not permitted to send it back home. It's called the *Century Sentinel*, is pretty good and comes out twice a month.

An appalling sight throughout the villages we travel, is to see so many men and women with "P" or "R" on a patch sewn to their clothes. They're Poles and Russians who work as slaves for the German people—another example of their bestiality. Each community, according to size or political advantage, has an allotment of these "slaves." One village, say, about the size of Westgate would be allotted 100 and disposed of at the discretion of the Burgermeister (mayor). Some of these people, we hear, have "found a home" and seem reasonably contented in these small towns where they have food to eat and a place to put their heads at night.

Others are migrating in tremendous numbers to the rear where they're placed in camps for eventual disposition to their homeland.

German civilians, in direct contrast to the French we've seen, are very healthy, proving they've been eating well and living under conditions comparable to Americans. They've been stealing food and labor and about everything else from their conquered nations. Here, everyone has electrical appliances—radios, irons, stoves, sewing machines, even electric razors. You see, they haven't been "deprived."

Something occurred today that brought the war even closer, and made me realize even more why Americans have no right to be softhearted (a fact which the German mentality relies on) or to forget that because of these Nazis many American boys are dead

—drawing by Marius N. Trinque, from The Story of the Century

or maimed for life: A wounded Nazi was brought in (as many are during the day) and given aid—the best possible—and I don't begrudge that. But just as we'd finished dressing his wounds two wounded G.I.'s walked in—and both—as they met the Nazi's eyes, said, "That's the bastard."

And then they spilled the story. This same Nazi kept sniping at their whole platoon as they went by, wounding them and three others. And as they waited for treatment—imagine—they had to wait (not many minutes, though) until the Jerry was finished being treated. And the incredible part—one Medic who spoke German questioned him in such a friendly way, "Are you married? Any children? Where do you live—how old?" etc. etc. Well, I burned to see this pleasant discourse carried on while our own G.I.'s waited for attention—and waiting until the rat who shot them was treated first.

Could you imagine this being reversed? Well, I blew up—and told this Medic and all the others that their function is not that of a welcoming committee and in the future will refrain from uttering a word to the enemy. All questioning can and will be done by the interrogators. I assure you this Medic, or any other, will still treat the wounded enemy well—but that's where it will end.

This Medic was merely acting like many others not within gun-shot range—or likely to be targets. Some of them don't seem to know what it's all about and forget that the enemy is not their friend—and would do them in the first chance they got.

On the lighter side—I've been telling Doc, when my packages arrive I'll have plenty of mayonnaise (a favorite item around here) —in fact, I figured I'd have at least 4 jars before the month is out. He said I wouldn't and insisted on betting $5.00 I wouldn't. Sounds silly but this went on over a period of a day. Now I'm sweating out packages for mayonnaise. If it has been put in all the packages your letters say they were, I'm in for sure. The money means nothing— the satisfaction—plenty! These foolish little things help lighten a day.

9 April

Well, Darling, today I hit the jackpot. Four of the sweetest let-ters any man could hope for—and 4 packages, plus a Bingo game from my big boy, Neil. And everything delicious including the stuffed dates you made. And I'm $5.00 richer, as each package con-tained a jar of mayonnaise! Wait till Doc hears this.—And Neil, everytime the boys play Bingo, we'll think of you.

Neil's delight at receiving the German helmet and souvenirs sure pleased me. The boys are really picking things up. Their biggest charge is getting hold of German guns and arms—but unless one would be handed to me, I have no desire for it.

For the first night in a week we're enjoying the radio. It's amaz-

ing to think that with the front line only 200 yards away we're enjoying news and music from the States!

A few days ago I viewed one of the most graphic and exciting
sights I've ever seen. From an observation post I witnessed a battle. I could see our doughboys creeping and crawling and lying
low—and off in the distance I could see the Nazis firing and rushing
for cover when our mortars went off. Then I could see one of our
Companies trying to outflank the Jerries—and then one of our men
fall as he was hit. In very short order our litter-bearers were out
there picking him up. At this point the battle was getting hotter
and it was necessary for me to come down and get over to the Aid
Station to attend the casualties. If only I had a moving picture
camera! Rarely can you see a battlefield, showing the enemy at the
same time. A war photographer would have had a real scoop. To
allay your concern, I assure you I was up there a very short time—
and would not go up again.

The news is still good but a little too slow. We're presently getting equipment on the other side of the Rhine (can't tell you
which side) for a tremendous last push, coordinated with the
Russians.

10 April

Today was mail-less but I have no reason to kick except that this
war is lasting longer than it should—and the Krauts are stiffening
their resistance—and I'm still here—and you're still there.

Just had lunch—Pabst cheese melted on Melba toast, soup, cocoa
and cookies. Very good. Your packages are put to a lot of good,
Darling, and we do appreciate these extra delicacies.

We're now listening to the Lucky Strike Hit Parade re-broad-
cast. Over here we have a special Allied radio hook-up—with broad-
casting stations in Paris, London and other large cities, so the reception is extremely good, although those damn Nazis try to disrupt
by cutting in on the same wave-length, making noise, or having an
orchestra playing loudly, or a speaker babbling just to make listening inaudible. Despite their efforts, our stations are so strong we al-

ways hear what we want. And lately, they've been reducing their nuisance value to a minimum as they realize they're not interfering too much with our reception.

One guy the "doughboy" loves is "Muldoon at the Front." It's a cartoon series by Bill Mauldin which appears regularly in *Stars & Stripes*, portraying the front-line Infantryman in his daily chores and problems. It never fails to hit home as he brings humor into the most desperate of situations. The guys break up when they read him; he captures every mood, gripe, feeling with such accuracy every G.I. can identify with it.

Mauldin is a Sgt. who used to be a front-line soldier with the 45th Division—but after he finally got a break with the Division newspaper, *Stars & Stripes* took him on (because his fame spread)—and now over 100 newspapers in the U.S. syndicate his cartoons. However, despite the lift the G.I. Joe gets from reading him, the bigwigs (Generals) are using their influence in keeping him out of *Stars & Stripes* because they're the targets of many hilarious slams. General Patton is strongly against some of his stuff. You might think he'd be above it. Tonight I notice Mauldin didn't appear and our group really miss him. We hope it's temporary. He certainly has captured the true inner feelings of the G.I.

A large German PW camp filled with many of our boys from the 106th Division captured over the New Year, was freed by the Allies in their drive. I pray Marty L. and Artie K. were among them.

11 April

Another day, another move, another house, another village. These towns are picturesque—always on the side of a little river or stream—often with hilly terrain or mountains looming in the background. These "innocent" little rivers invariably present a big obstacle. As the Nazis are pushed back they blow up the bridge behind them, leaving us with the problem of crossing.

Where the situation warrants, a bridge is immediately put up. In some areas, blasting by the engineers at strategic points diverts

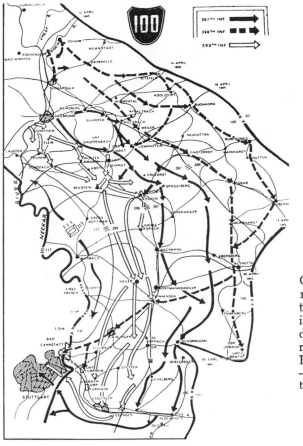

Operations of the 100th Division after the fall of Heilbronn in April 1945. The dotted lines show the route of the 398th Regiment.
—from The Story of the Century

the water, making it shallow enough for vehicles to cross right through. In other instances, to get to a village immediately across the river, it's necessary to move 15 miles or more up on the same side of the bank, cross on a pontoon bridge, and 15 miles down on the other end of the bank.

You can see that with problems like these a Battalion Aid-Man is deeply concerned with evacuation—how to carry a man who's been hit back to the next rear echelon. Being Americans, with typical American ingenuity we've solved it. We string a cable across the river and evacuate by row boat—using the cable as a guide. Always waiting on the other side is an ambulance with two drivers and 4 litter-bearers. So far the evacuation has worked beautifully and we're proud of our record.*

I had my first chance in a long time to exercise a little of my French. These Frenchmen (former slaves of the Nazis) had the same harrowing stories to tell. As you know we're not permitted to speak to Germans, under penalty, and the rule is strictly adhered to.

Honey, you should have been here to see the look on Doc's face when I confronted him with 4 jars of mayonnaise! He said not a word, but pulled out a $5. bill from his pocket, smiled and walked away.

After nine days of fierce resistance, Heilbronn fell to the 100th Division on 13 April 1945. From there the division raced southward to seal off the city of Stuttgart, which was under attack by the French First Army. By now German resistance everywhere was crumbling, but pockets of diehard defenders remained. The 398th Infantry was on the left—eastern—flank of the division's motorized advance. On 23 April the 100th Division linked up with the French Third Algerian Infantry at the Bad Cannstatt–Stuttgart bridge, sealing off the Stuttgart area, and the 100th was pulled out of the line after 170 days of front-line service.

13 April

The day was one of intense interest. Doc and I visited the German civilian hospital here and were surprised to find no doctor, little or no medicine and only 5 nurses doing everything. Doc asked to be shown the worst cases and as we went through the halls,

---

* What Winston does not point out is that while in the rowboat, and while loading the wounded onto the ambulance, the medics on the east bank of the rivers were under direct fire from German artillery. So fierce was the shelling that during part of the operation the 100th Division headquarters called on the 163rd Chemical Smoke Generator Company, a black outfit (the American armed forces were still segregated racially during World War II), to lay smokescreens over the river crossings.

everyone glared at us—probably fearing an order to be moved out. We then entered a private room occupied by a mother and child, both of whom had been hit by shrapnel. The mother screamed bloody murder as the bandages were removed for Doc's observation. An infection had set in and Doc ordered an operation. So both she and her daughter are to be removed to a G.I. hospital.

While this was going on, an elderly woman came over to me, and in perfect English asked a number of questions. (She came in each day to help the nurses.) She said, "This country was so beautiful, and then *he* came to power and half the people were never for him. They are beasts, I tell you, beasts!" Her eyes filled with tears and she walked down the hall a few feet, turned around and cried out hysterically, "Beasts, Beasts!"

We've heard so often that the older generation never condoned the present regime, yet we find many that did.

The woman (who was to be moved to a hospital) spoke a few words of English. She was studying medicine in Estonia before the Russians captured it. Her husband was killed and she was evacuated to this place with her daughter.

War—casualties—heartbreak—each a story of its own. Nearly every home in France and Russia, England, America—even Germany—has a story, a tragic story because of a few power-crazy creatures.

The weather continues warm. We're wearing summer underwear now. Took a ride across the river on a row boat. Incidentally, we have an outboard motor on one of our boats, expediting more rapidly the transfer of patients.

With the exception of a few nights when artillery was heavy I sleep soundly and look forward to bed and rest each night. Except for my homesickness, I am well and doing fine. How are Neil and David? Much of my day is in constant thought of them and you.

14 April

Last night, dead tired, we reached our destination at 2 A.M., only to hear that one of our boys was wounded. Since I was on the first vehicle I was called on to bring him back—and no time to spare. I led a group out—well over a mile—and we carried the boy all the way back. He weighed over 200 pounds and he seemed to get heavier with each step. Finally got in bed at 5 A.M. and awakened at 8:30 for another move. So-o-o I'm pretty bushed as I write you this lunch time.

Since the above we moved to another town. In my "travels" I've found all the villages we enter "kapoot"—ruined. It got to me when I saw the ruins of French villages—and boy, what ruins! But I don't feel that way in Germany, as this didn't have to happen. Hitler's following was pretty strong, there's no denying. Only in defeat do they talk through the other side of their mouths.

It's surprising, though, to see plenty of cows and chickens and no immediate food shortage around, and as I've said before, everyone looks pretty healthy.

I've just come up from a dark, damp cellar where we treated a German soldier who deserted a week ago when wounded. There were a dozen mattresses on the floor where people lay in fear of our bombers and artillery—and in terror of our soldiers.

As the Germans leave these villages they tell the civilians the Americans will beat and rape them, destroy and steal, and loot everything they see. As these are their tactics they expect the same of Americans.—At first, when they saw us coming down they were terror-stricken, but after the first few minutes you see the relief all over their faces. All we heard was "denk a shein," "denk a shein"— thank you, thank you.

My Darling, this minute I have just learned of our President's death.* I am shocked and dazed at the terrible news. May God bless his soul. He was our friend. The world will suffer.

16 April

The mail hasn't caught up with us the last few days as we've been on the run, but we're promised mail tomorrow so I'm hoping.

* Pres. Franklin Delano Roosevelt died suddenly at Warm Springs, Georgia, on 12 April 1945.

"Business" was booming in the Aid Station last night. We got a call to pick up a wounded G.I., and when the jeep returned, it carried one wounded Jerry, one wounded Frenchman, one G.I., an injured civilian and a pregnant woman. That was rather a unique haul.

Doc examined the woman with instructions to notify him when she got regular pains. Well, about 11 P.M. she called, but it still wasn't time. Then 2 A.M. another call and Doc and I flew over only to see it was false labor. We were up practically the whole night. Doc gave her another examination and said, by the position of the baby's head, she wasn't due for another few days.

But now we've moved and the poor woman will have to find a midwife or an experienced mother—as there are no doctors.

The war is supposed to be over but these fanatics we're meeting don't know anything about it. It just adds up to more soldiers wounded and killed—including our own. Destruction is everywhere. A large city we recently took was unqualifiedly—except for a hospital—just a series of piles of stone and rubble. Even here our boys had to fight from shamble to shamble to clear the city. Small "pockets" (back home they speak of these as inconsequential—nothing) often keep a Regiment busy for days—with many deaths resulting.

Darling, I'm getting accounts of the President's death—its significance, the reactions of the men all around. We feel that we've personally suffered a loss. I can't tell you how much all this has saddened us.

Patton and the British 9th have made fine infiltrations and things look very good. Haven't heard much from the Pacific theatre, but hope for a more sensible attitude from the Japs when all doubt of our victory here is removed.

Lately we've been eating "feel hier"—many eggs. We're not permitted to fraternize as you know but asking "Haben zee hier" gets us more results than "casing" chicken coops as was our first practise. Fresh eggs are a definite treat.

17 April

It's about noon and our march still continues. Not as fast as the newspapers will have you believe, however. It's still tough and rough. I'm well but very tired due to rushing around and moving constantly. Haven't taken a bath for weeks and I do feel cruddy and filthy from traveling on these dirty roads almost continually.

Our outfit acquired a new member. A real small puppy—and the boys have really become attached to her. They bedecked her in a gay-colored muzzle of coral-like material and the shade is a good contrast to her jet black body. We've put a Red Cross band around her to make it "official."

Since the above we've made another move. I had a picture taken of me beside a tank, and on my left a still-smoldering building burned to the ground. I get little joy out of such sights, but assure you the Americans don't shell aimlessly. There's always a sound militaristic reason.

18 April

We expect to take a few days breather, beginning tomorrow, at which time we'll get a bath, clean clothes and a relief from the immediate front. I sure hope something official, as to peace, is declared while we're in this position.

Doc left for Paris today, the lucky guy, but he really needed the rest—his first since we went into combat.

Today we continued easterly and are completely bushed after so many days of "moving." The war still keeps going even though those crazy fanatics don't refer anymore to an Eastern or Western front—just one front. I'm sick and tired of the whole lousy thing.

Every town we enter is in bad shape and houses are still smoldering. Dead cattle are strewn all over the countryside. Electricity is kapoot, no running water—a pump far from the house.

Had a letter from Harry today. He's getting a good deal in England. He's pretty well recovered and was appointed an instructor in physical training. He's surely qualified, and after what he's been through, certainly deserves it.

The boys seem to be pistol-crazy—I mean picking up small pistols whenever they can. The German Luger is the most popular and sought after—so much so, that when one is found the owner is besieged with offers of trade or sale. They'll pay as much as $100.

The other day one of the Companies captured a town, and in true G.I. fashion had to "inspect" the bank. They helped themselves to a few "samples." Quite a few in fact. These guys have been through hell and they have no qualms about anything they "liberate." I don't think they knew the money could be turned in for the present value (10¢ a mark) or they'd probably have emptied it completely. War brings out the worst; I despise everything about it.

Dearest, I apologize for the tone of my letter. I'm just not in a writing frame of mind. Perhaps a few letters from you tomorrow will help. Anyway, always know you're ever in my mind and are my constant inspiration.

20 April

Now that I'm resting and feeling better I'll admit that the last couple of weeks have really been a drain—what with our 5 A.M. calls and quick moves and right up there where the action is hot— sometimes up all night tending the wounded. But now that we're in [censored] behind the front in a beautiful little city, in a lovely home—and me in a private room—it sure helps morale. I invited two of our group to share this luxury.

Yesterday 4 lovely letters from you, but for the first time I was so played out my mind didn't function on them. But now, Darling, my mind is so much more at ease and I feel well—absolutely no reason for alarm. Our "breather" is due to be over about 4 days after Mark's birthday. The fact mail wasn't keeping up with us didn't help my condition last week, either.

This place we're in is a bright little home with surroundings not unlike ours. A large field adjoins the house—and plenty of shade. The young people living here (the husband's in the army) couldn't bear to leave. On one occasion I went down into the cellar and saw the young mother with an infant in her arms crying her heart out. If these people could realize our putting them out is only temporary and means that the war will be over that much sooner, it might help. To put it mildly, they're all war-weary and you have to have a heart of stone not to feel some compassion.

My activity on the line this week has been an unforgettable experience I'd never want to go through again. But I did get a first-hand view of how the war in Germany is being fought, how well our organization clicked—and the major concern shown our men which resulted in fewer casualties.

Enjoyed the Camp Blanding newsletter. See if you can learn anything about Marty or Arthur. They're on my mind a lot and I pray for their well-being.

The weather is perfect. Took a sunbath today, had a bath and clean clothes and am beginning to feel human again.

21 April

Though we changed quarters—in the same town—today has been one of complete relaxation. Again a nice private room. Incidentally, this town has electricity and we make good use of it.

While fixing up things in this house I found I'd picked up a book from the other house by error and went back to return it. I found the mother, daughter and grand-daughter working in the garden. They seemed quite upset. They said the cellar door was open but the rest of the house was locked and they wanted the keys. I told them I'd see what I could do.

Of course, it only takes a few seconds to tell you this. But it took a half-hour—3 dictionaries—and finally 2 neighbors who could speak a few words of English to help out. While a second "translator" was being rushed to the scene, the mother was telling me in language I couldn't understand—but understood enough to know that her "mon" was "drind" in the Atlantic "wasser." War is weird and makes no sense. Here, I'm feeling sorry for a family put out of their home—and minutes later they're telling me their "mon" was probably shooting torpedoes at us—sinking ships, etc.

Today in the Aid Station I began to feel that old familiar queasiness in the pit of my stomach. The radio was playing soft, beautiful music, the sun was shining, the windows opened to let the warm breeze in—and it seemed like a little touch of home. It always affects me the same way.

The Russians are 4 miles outside of Berlin—and all armies are moving smoothly.

We're getting 3 meals daily now. This A.M. fried eggs—sunny side up, tomato juice, hot cereal, coffee. It's funny, but fried eggs will get me up when nothing else will. This evening, roast chicken. The cooks are doing a wonderful job.

22 April

We're through with our "breather." Today we moved again and now located in the most beautiful home I've ever been in—like the Main Line [Philadelphia] homes that run for about $50,000. A tremendous terrace in the rear, magnificent flowers in bloom, and overlooking it all are breathtaking mountains. We're thrilled with the set-up and hope it lasts a few days. Our activity remains the same as previously explained in letters.

This home is owned by two doctors. Beaucoup rooms, many lamps, extra radios, and right now I'm sitting comfortably at a desk with a bright light on and a radio nearby. The enclosed literature, found in their home, proves they're A-1 Nazis, so putting them out doesn't keep us from losing sleep.

23 April

Another bonanza today! Six letters and a package from you. Thank you, Darling.

We're still at this mansion living the life of luxury. While the news is encouraging, you know, Honey, I'm arriving at the point where I will not figure on an end to this mess until the official announcement comes through. Again, remember "pockets" is just newspaper jargon—it's still war and men are dying wiping out these "pockets." It's hard to keep from resenting over-optimism from outside sources when men are still coming into the Aid Station badly maimed and wounded.

Got quite a kick out of your contributing "practically the contents of the closets" for the needy in Europe. I assure you it's needed—terribly needed. The French are poverty stricken and can use everything they get.

I think we're able to say that we were in Ludwigshafen and Mannheim—cities across the Rhine. The first city is the home of I. G. Farben Co.—the firm that was connected with those cartels in the U.S. These cities are heaps of rocks and ruins—no exaggeration. Mannheim was once a beautiful city with its grand hotels and city parks and circles—you should see it now.

I can say now that we were in Heidelberg—the only German city still standing. It's a lovely place, filled with history and tradition. The University is truly beautiful. The people appear to be rather intellectual, far above the average German we've seen. Details I can't give you, but crossing the Rhine was interesting and exciting. Until later, my Darling.

24 April

Two wonderful letters today, and a package that contained everything that I desire.

You wonder about my disposition when the war ends. For both our sakes and peace of mind don't be too optimistic about an early discharge. The end of war doesn't automatically mean I'm on my way home. Remember, I'm just a number as far as the Army is concerned—with so many points—and my marital status mean nothing. They have millions of individuals to deal with—each with a good story why he should be released early. I pray I'm lucky, and assure you that I have a head and a mouth and can use both when the time or occasion demands—if I have a leg to stand on. It hurts me to write this but I prefer being reasonably realistic—and would like you to feel the same.

Just heard something on the radio apropos to the previous paragraph—"Look for the Silver Lining," and sung beautifully—only to make me terribly blue. But we *will* look for the silver lining—OK?

The boys are making themselves at home here to the point of wearing pajamas they find in bureau drawers—and playing ping-pong on the terrace. Good things don't last long around here and we'll soon be on the move we're told.

25 April

The music goes round and round—another day, another move, another house, another town. I can't elaborate but things have been going pretty well the last week or so and we hope it will continue.

This part of the country is fascinating. We've driven over areas so high you could look down and see as many as 25 villages—all quaint and picturesque with their red roofs hitting against the sun, in pleasant contrast to the green of the countryside and blue of the sky. It's really quite beautiful.

It's easy to be fooled by these people. Yesterday, the owner of the house came over. He's a physician, too, and in perfect English, with beaucoup de flattery thrown in, asked to enter his house "for a few items." Now, if we hadn't already seen his pictures with a swastika on his arm, smiling broadly in the midst of a dozen S.S. troops, we might (we Americans by European standards are naive) have succumbed and permitted his entrance. But we didn't. We run into this every day but we absolutely refused entrance.

Incidentally, the Germans have tremendous concrete air raid shelters—many private—others public, built like subway stations, and every house is equipped with black-out curtains. You can see why non-fraternization is so necessary.

26 April

We're located in still another house. Doc just returned from Paris, seems rested and in a better frame of mind.

Our Aid Station is located in a large apartment house. Every couple of guys has a two-room apartment, but have to share their bathroom and kitchen with two other guys—mighty inconvenient, isn't it! Doc and I share the same apartment. We all have radios, and beds with clean linen. There might be a good chance we'll be here awhile, and we're looking forward to clean clothes and hot baths.

The radio tells us Bremen is taken—Berlin almost taken—and the Italian patriots taken over in Northern Italy. All looks "encouraging." And now we hear Goebbels resigned—and Mussolini is running out.* Sounds good, Sweetheart.

Today's movements took me again through this beautiful land. I usually ride in the ambulance but Doc asked me to ride with him in the jeep. (Vision isn't too good in the ambulance.) The scenery is indescribably breathtaking—but I'd trade it all for South Street if it meant being with you.

Just saw Doc outfitted in "his" nightgown and it broke me up. I might even get into one myself tonight. They're so generously provided by the owners along with clean towels "just for you fine Americans"—nice of our enemies, don't you think?

Remember Mox? (Max Haas) the Jewish refugee boy who had relatives over here? Today we heard a rending, pitiful story. He was finally able to visit his home town, and when he got to his old house, the occupants told him his parents had been sent to Lublin concentration camp 3 years ago—and you know what that means— wholesale slaughter. The poor guy. You should have seen him when he came back. His eyes were red and swollen, his face wet with tears. No one or nothing could console him.

---

* The port of Bremen surrendered to the Canadian First Army on 28 April. The final Allied offensive in Italy had gotten under way 9 April, and German resistance soon crumbled. Benito Mussolini, his mistress, and other high-ranking Italian officials were captured by Italian partisans at Nesso on 26 April, and on 28 April they were executed. Joseph Goebbels stuck by Hitler to the last; the day following Hitler's death on 30 April, Goebbels murdered his six children with injections of poison, then had himself and his wife shot to death by an SS orderly.

The boys were tripping over one another trying to make him feel a little better. What can you say to a boy with a tragedy so decimating as his. No one could find the right words. Even Chuck, the "rough" G.I. from Arkansas, who's never at a loss for words. Then he stuttered, his voice husky with emotion, "God damn, Mox, I'll git me a rifle and go out pussonly and pick off a few Krauts. Them lousy, heartless sonofabitches." He was dead serious, and even Mox smiled through his tears.

We're still in our apartment and hope the comfort continues. (It's easy to take.) News continues good, with the Russians and Americans finally making contact, Berlin 3/4ths taken, Mussolini captured and our army only a short distance from Munich—Germany's last stronghold. After it is captured Eisenhower will declare the European part of the war over.

You might get a bounce out of this. As you know, I take full charge of the Aid Station—records, details, what have you—even to prescribing for the "not too sick" boys—everything except the actual responsibility for the wounded.

Well, this morning I was busy as usual when the Sgt. walked over to me. He said, "Keith, now you take off and let the others do something." I appreciated his concern, but you know me—I don't like to depend on others, so I continued working. Shortly after that Doc came down from our apartment and said, "For the next two days you're not to do one thing around here—just sleep, eat and take it easy—you do more than your share." I started to say, "But,"—and he stopped me short. "Keith—that's an order." So now everyone is treating me like a guest—or a long-lost uncle. I assure you I don't do that much, but it's a good feeling to know it's appreciated.

Helen Gahagan Douglas hit it on the nose with her retort to that Congressman who said the war was already over. You recall she said, "The war isn't over until my husband is returned to me." And I'm sure that's the way every other woman feels about it.

28 April

Today has been one of restfulness. We saw a movie, Judy Garland in *Meet Me in St. Louis*, and it was beautiful. Not the story so much, which I couldn't follow as I arrived half an hour late and the vitaphone was lousy—but just to see an American setting, with American songs and Americans was a real treat.

Himmler, the radio tells us, offered his historic acceptance of unconditional surrender—but only to us and the English. It did my heart good to know we'd do nothing without Russia.* Unquestionably, we are and should be a trio never to be divided. I assure you the boys on the front line will always fight for this combination—particularly U.S. and Russia. Oh, boy, do the Germans fear them. You can't begin to imagine the hatred and fear the little German—the average German—has of the Russian. Why? First, the Russians wiped out hordes of them, 2nd, the Germans, having used Russians as slaves, fear reprisals—3rd, though German propaganda has been going all out to cover up the atrocities perpetrated upon thousands and thousands of poor, innocent Russian civilians, everyone knows their attempts at white-washing is a lot of claptrap and won't do the Nazis one little bit of good.†

The boys are getting closer to Munich, the Bavarian capital, where peace riots are reported. Any day, Darling.

Still in our apartment and contented. Doc and I fixed a nice lunch—from packages. Campbell's vegetable soup, tuna salad, melba toast, butter cocoa, candy. Now that we're not in direct combat, 3 heavy G.I. meals are a bit much.—We picked up clean clothes today; combat soldiers don't get pressed clothes—just clean ones. They throw our pants, shirts, etc. in a washing machine—dry them—and we grab whatever size looks right. However, with plenty of

---

* Heinrich Himmler, chief of Hitler's SS and Gestapo, did approach Count Bernadotte, head of the Swedish Red Cross, in late April, with a view toward surrendering all German forces in the West to General Eisenhower, but his offer was spurned. After the German surrender Himmler was captured near Hamburg on 20 May, but promptly committed suicide by biting into a concealed vial of poison.

† Pfc. Winston's hopes for continuing U.S.-Soviet cooperation, like those of the American high command and most of the American people, would soon be dashed. Indeed, by late April of 1945 the Soviets were already showing signs of their unwillingness to live up to the guarantees of free elections in the occupied countries of eastern Europe that had been given at Yalta.

Vol. III
No. 82

Century 🛡️💯 *Sentinel*

Saturday
April 28. 1945

Stuttgart Encircled by 100th In Sensational Sweep to South

CONGRATULATIONS, GENERAL! Brig. Gen. Andrew C. Tychsen, Assistant Commanding General of the 100th, receives congratulations on promotion from Maj. Gen. Withers A. Burress, commanding general.
Photo by Pfc Johnson, 100 th Signal Co.

More Truth Than Poetry

Most descriptive report on the lightning tactics of the 100th during the encirclement of Stuttgart was the cryptic message sent by Lt. Col. John M. King, 397th 1st Bn. commander, to Regimental Hq, in response to a query as to his outfit's progress. His to-the-point message read:

"Krauts and mines cleared to ditches!"

Throwing the German Command's defensive time schedule entirely out of gear, the Century Division, in a sensational sweep to the south and southeast this week completed the encirclement of Stuttgart, one of southern Germany's largest and most important industrial cities, broke the back of Nazi resistance in the area and captured 3,218 prisoners in two action-packed days.

Loss of Stuttgart, which had a pre-war population of 493,000, proved a mighty costly setback to the Nazi's hopeless cause. The tremendous number of prisoners "bagged" testified to the speed, power and deceptiveness of the Division's south-ward surge. On several occasions, the advance was so rapid that bridges across the Murr River at Murrhardt were seized before the retreating Nazis had a chance to blow them.

The main bridge at Murrhardt was knocked out, but a railroad bridge and a secondary span were still intact as doughboys of the 398th's 1st Bn. dashed across and slashed on to Fautspach shortly before midnight on April 19.

Nazi defenders everywhere were caught napping by the 100th's fast-moving columns. In many places, Kraut units fled into the woods as motorized columns pushed through. They returned shortly however, to carry out delaying raids, ambushes and attempts to harry movement in every possible way.

The 399th, operating on the division's right flank, ran into particularly rough going. Rugged mountain terrain through which they pressed the attack offered Nazi defenders excellent positions and they fought savagely to stem the tide. The 399th's 3rd Bn. bore the brunt of heavy resistance from Nebelwerfers, artillery and stoutly defended road blocks.

The most astounding factor about the 100th's drive is the total
(Continued on Page 4.)

HURRY-UP JOB. Blown bridge at Backnang didn't hold up Century Division's speedy pursuit of fleeing Nazis long. Engineers of Co. A made it passable by throwing in filler material, while more durable steel treadway was being constructed elsewhere on Murr River.

Lt. Gen. Falls to 100th In Eszlingen Hospital

Lt. Gen. Vernard von Claer, commander of Nazi defenses on the southern end of the Western front and the highest-ranking German officer to fall into the hands of the Century Division was discovered and "captured" this week during a routine check of a hospital near Stuttgart.

Von Claer, who had been reported in command of German defenses at Heilbronn during the division's bitter nine-day battle for that bastion, was a patient in a Nazi military hospital in Eszlingen when Maj. David Klickstein, Division Dental Officer, came upon him.

Maj. Klickstein was interrogating German patients in a ward. At one bed, he addressed an older man and asked, in German, for his name and rank.

"Von Claer, Lieutenant General," shot back the patient in perfect English.

Asked what was wrong with him, the German general replied:

"Your Air Corps gave me a flesh wound in the thigh."

During the past year, General Von Claer appeared to have been charged with organizing anti-tank defenses throughout Germany.

Col. Tychsen Wins Promotion to Rank Of Brig. General

It's Brig. Gen. Andrew C. Tychsen now! The Assistant Commanding General of the Century Division, who has served in that capacity on the Division's General Staff since last December, received official notification of his promotion from the rank of colonel last week.

General Tychsen has served with the 100th since its activation at Fort Jackson, S. C., on Nov. 15, 1942 at which time he took over command of the 399th Infantry Regiment.

He led the Powder Horn boys throughout the period of training at Forts Jackson and Bragg, on maneuvers in Tennessee, and through their Baptism of Fire in the Vosges Mountains campaign in November and early December.

When Brig. Gen. Maurice L. Miller left the 100th last December, General Tychsen was called from the 399th to take over as ACG.

Task Force Riley Leapfrogs 19 Kilometers in Two Days

With infantrymen and tanks leapfrogging each other, closely supported by artillery and planes, Task Force Riley, consisting of doughs of the 2nd Bn, 399 th Inf, and tanks of the 10th Armored Div. and 781st Tank Bn. swept forward from Pfedelbach to Ob Rot. crushing all Nazi resistance on the way. Easy Co. riflemen led the way throughout on the right with F & G Co's alternating on the left side of the road.

NAZIS' UNDOING. What goes up must come down - and civilians of one town in Century steamroller's path tear down one of numerous roadblocks erected by enemy to delay our pursuit.

Colonels Rat on One Another; Both Wind Up in PW Cage

A Nazi lieutenant colonel squealed on a Nazi full colonel and the full colonel ratted on the lieutenant colonel, and thereby lies the tale of how the 397th Inf. took prisoner the highest ranking German officers taken by the Century Div. up to that time.

After the 3rd Bn of the 397th had moved into Bachnang, a handsome, nattily dressed civilian came over to an MP and gave himself up. Taken to IPW headquarters and interviewed by Lt. Harry Klaar of Portland, Oregon, he produced documents to show he was formerly a Lt. Col., the chief of staff of the 20th Airborne Div., stationed in Italy, and had been discharged from the Wehrmacht for having knowledge of the July 20th, 1944 plot to assassinate Hitler.

"Have you picked up the full colonel living next door to me?" Upon hearing this the Lieutenant, accompanied by T/3 Max Silberman of Cleveland, Ohio, 397th interrogator, and a Sentinel reporter, dashed off and found the full colonel in civilian clothes, hiding out in a gorgeous home overlooking the city.

The colonel claimed he was a regimental commander on convalescent furlough after being

wounded five times on the Russian front. He had been ordered to report to his unit but was unable to find them in their mad retreat before the Red Armies and returned home,—sick and tired of war—as he put it. After being told he would have to be taken in to undergo the regular PW formalities, he also inquired:

"Have you picked up the lieutenant colonel living next door to me?" Satisfied receiving an affirmative answer, he insisted on getting into his uniform, and, a few moments later, emerged dressed in full battle regalia, sporting four medals on his chest,—the Ritter Kreuz (equivalent to our Legion of Merit), the Iron Cross 1st Class (for bravery), the German Cross in Gold (Bronze Star equal) and the Gold Medal, indicating five wounds. The haughty Nazi officer proudly entered the jeep as the amused stares of doughs of the 397th and was driven away.

UNCONDITIONAL SURRENDER. Towns in path of Century blitz were quick to hoist flags indicating surrender.

60 German Soldiers Find Hospital a Poor Hideout

The Century Division's task Force Hoth, which drove recently through the towns east of the Neckar River, just south of Stuttgart, calculated the red cross-marked hospital was going to be stricly for the medics.

Instead, the 399th Infantrymen of Lt. Robert C. Hoth, Milwaukee, Wis., unearthed some 60 able-bodied German soldiers who had taken refuge in the building. There was not a single medical case there.

Apparently, German injured had been evacuated, and the healthy newcomers had drifted in with the surge of the American troops from the north and the French from the west of Stuttgart.

Covering a distance of 19 kilometers in two days against tough resistance, over hilly and heavily wooded terrain ideal for sniper concealment, the Task Force met with at least 20 road blocks, that were not only heavily mined and manned, but also came under zeroed-in Heinie artillery and

mortar fire. Mines were particularly troublesome, being of the non-metal type, hard to locate and skillfully booby-trapped.

Taking turns in moving out ahead, doughboys would go to work to pave the way for the tanks by clearing up all opposition when
(Continued on Page 4.)

Front page of 100th Division's newspaper, the Century Sentinel time and a pressing iron, our Aid Station boys have been pressing their clothes. Though it feels good we've been getting plenty of ribbing about looking like the suave garrison soldier—those back in the States who always look slick.

The enclosed snapshot was taken in the "quiet" little town where we spent last winter. Now I can tell you that this town was only a mile from the front line (a holding position) and casualties were carried in every day—and every night we anticipated a counterattack. It was the closest we were to the line for such a prolonged period. Doc took this picture and I think I look pretty healthy, don't you?

Today the Division band showed up and gave us a concert. Doc was up in our apartment playing along with them on his cornet. In the middle of the piece "On Wisconsin" they stopped suddenly. And Doc, from the 2nd floor apartment—leaning out the window—continued to play on as a soloist. (He played it often when his alma mater, Ohio, played Wisconsin in football.) Well, he got a big ovation. It was good fun since everyone in the Battalion knows him well.

29 April

It's Sunday night but I'm not listening to Walter Winchell or Phil Baker or Fred Allen—as we did together. I'm just contenting myself with thoughts of you, and looking forward to the day when we'll always be together again. With all the good news coming in, how can it last many more days?

While looking over the wreckage of a railroad terminal, an English-speaking German came up to us and said, "You're looking at a once great rail terminal. One of the finest in Germany." And Doc said, "I like it very much the way it stands now. I assure you it looks much better than ever before." The German gave us a dirty look and walked away.

These French are hard to understand—many are real screwballs. While our army makes every effort to enforce this non-fraternization policy, the French—after all they've suffered at the hands of these beasts—not only fraternize, but make much of the German girls. I could tell you plenty but it would only be censored.

Just heard great news. Our troops have taken Munich and released 25,000 American prisoners!* How about that! 25,000 boys and their loved ones are reborn tonight.

Three of these poor fellows had supper at our C.P. They talked very little because they were gulping food like animals. It broke your heart to watch them. May God help us end this murder soon.

1 May

After 4 days of no mail—one letter finally came through tonight. Darling, don't be alarmed unless you know for sure I'm being shipped to CBI.† The news media can be terribly alarming and misleading. I'll not be convinced until I'm on my way there—so don't bother your pretty little head.

Incidentally, if or when I hear of an official order moving me— if I can, I'll telegram you thusly: CBI—Hello, Darling; the States— Hello, Sweetheart; Occupation—Hello, Dearest. Let's hope it's "Sweetheart."

Just heard Hitler is dead.‡ So what. Even if he's alive, he's dead now. I'm only interested in hearing one thing—"The war is over!"

I'm homesick and freely admit it, and the boys know how downcast I get when CBI is mentioned. In fact, they kid me about it. Tonight, just as I finished reading your letter, and feeling pretty low about the CBI news, "Junior," one of our young boys came rushing into the Aid Station yelling, "Where's Keith, where's Keith Winston," and reads his mother's letter telling him the same thing you heard.§

I had little to say and a few minutes later went to my room, lay down on my bed and read Stars & Stripes. Still feeling dismal, I

---

* Munich was occupied by the U.S. Seventh Army on 30 April.
† There were reports that various units now in Europe would be sent to the China-Burma-India theater of operations.
‡ Adolf Hitler killed himself with a pistol shot through the roof of his mouth in Berlin on 30 April 1945.
§ Tec 5 Howard F. Fontaine, of Escanaba, Michigan.

came across a poem about Roosevelt written by a G.I. It touched me so much a tear rolled down my cheek. Just at that moment, "Jr." walked in. Thinking the tears were over the CBI news—he ran right back to the Station telling them how it affected me. Now the boys are falling all over each other in their concern, knowing CBI would be tough for me to take in view of my little family.

Doc, who's concealed his homesickness up until now, finally broke down admitting it, and he's really taking it hard.—By the way, Doc said he is turning in my name for a decoration—the Bronze Star—for meritorious service throughout the last six months. You know, Honey, this might have turned me on at one time—but now all that excites me is a one-way trip to America—and fast.

3 May

The mail hasn't been too good—but today, 4 grand letters and 2 delicious packages. I'm glad we decided to number them so now I know what to expect in the way of back mail. So pleased you liked the Paris package containing the bracelet and watercolors.

We've been discussing the inequities of the Gov't. and Army—their unfair treatment of soldiers in so many respects. Once you're in the Army—you seem to lose your identity—there's a strict dictatorship. You don't have one little lousy word to say as to your disposition. If the Gov't. decides it's easier bookkeeping to keep the men in the Army (or any other service) to decrease drafting of new men, etc. it just means the stroke of a pen to affect millions of boys. Continuing to draft and replace men who should be discharged would mean more paper work, and "that just can't be."

This old line about "seasoned troops" is for the birds, I assure you. I know. After any Infantryman has been under a shell barrage—he's a seasoned troop. He knows enough; how to take cover—take precautions—always on the alert. With his excellent IRTC training, a 5- or 10-minute barrage creates a "seasoned" troop instantly. I see it first-hand.

About this non-fraternization policy of the Allies (apparently the French don't know about it). Any young unattached boy naturally wants to mingle with young girls—regardless of nationality. But as you know our policy doesn't permit it. The Germans, fully aware of this, employ all sorts of ruses and temptations—just for the satisfaction of seeing a G.I. succumb.

While our Bn. has a clear record, one of the battalions has had 12 cases of rape reported against them. Actually, we know there weren't 12 cases of rape—I doubt if there was one. Here are a couple of their tactics. They smile and flirt with the boys from their windows, leading them on. Once they get inside, they either let the boys use them for a price, and then report they were raped, or just report they were raped. Period.

The boys don't have a leg to stand on—they were committing the serious offense of fraternization. I doubt any will be convicted of rape, but they'll be heavily fined and it will go on their service record.

In one case a girl tapped on her window, giggled and motioned for the boy to come up. He did. In a few minutes the girl told him she wanted to go to the corner for some food and drink. She went to the corner—not for food and drink—but for an M.P., and the guy was fined $65.

The other day I heard about Gertrude Stein criticizing the Americans who visit Paris. "They don't let themselves go," she said, "are very serious, too much absorbed in the sights—not so much interested in women and drinking as soldiers ordinarily are." To which one American soldier replied, "Perhaps it's because we have another war to worry about after this." For once, it was said, Gertrude Stein had nothing to say.

4 May

Feeling well, living comfortably—with little or no artillery racket—ours or theirs. The war here is just about over—certainly is in Germany, and finishing up in Czech. and a few "pockets" in Austria. Just heard of Holland, Denmark's surrender—and now await Norway's, at which time Eisenhower will make his long-awaited announcement.

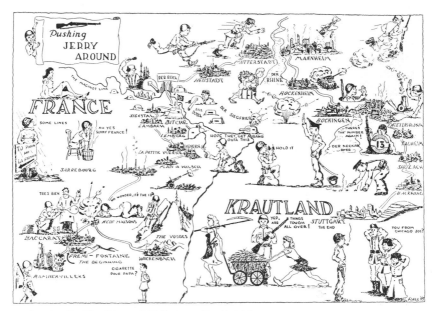

—drawing by Pfc. Howard Hall, from Combat Company
(Co. G, 399th Infantry Regiment, 1945)

This little town is typically beautiful of this section of Germany, and the homes are untouched by the Americans. Only the railroad terminal is kapoot.

One of our boys was asked to lecture on sex this morning. He said he couldn't because he had an appointment at the hospital for a Wasserman test. Ha, ha. Well, another "paragraph" anyway.

After the war is over there will be lots of interesting trips for the boys, like the Riviera, Nancy, Paris, Brussels, London, Strasbourg, whatever is left of Vienna, Naples, Switzerland, Rome—that is, if we're not shipped out too soon. If we are—I pray it's the States. If I'm able to telegraph, I will, and don't forget our code.

Since we've been in Germany the boys have never wanted for champagne, cognac or schnopps. Wine cellars are common in Europe (and the Nazis cleaned out most of them), especially Germany. They drink at all meals and for any occasion; the Army is finding huge warehouses that were filled for the benefit of the Nazis. However, the boys' drinking habits are well under control.

Whatever few casualties we get in the Station are not serious, and whenever we can we play plenty of softball and volley ball. It's both relaxing and invigorating.

5 May

I was delighted to receive a letter dated April 27—8 days service—pretty good, don't you think.

Today I've been doing a lot of running around in the jeep. You see, we must keep in close contact with the Companies in the Bn.—and each Company is strategically quartered in different sections of town. Since the regular drivers were "dubbing" and I know where each is quartered—and since I enjoy driving anyway—I was glad to do it. Then Doc asked me to drive him around to inspect the kitchens. Everyone passed inspection—and now the Medics have beaucoup de eggs, bread and butter, fruit salad and coffee. Comprendez-vous?

Something happened today to make us speculate as to our final disposition. In a day or two we're to be issued "Eisenhower" jackets,* and it might have some significance—we don't know. All the boys are conjecturing—some say it means occupation, others say CBI, still others, the States. We'll soon see.

Took a walk into town today (plenty of G.I.'s around for protection) and to my surprise found it was hardly touched, except for the railroad station. Now we can see why von Rundstedt claimed strategic bombing was the chief reason Germany was defeated.

Tomorrow is Sunday. All over Europe, war or no war, everyone dresses up in their "Sunday best." During the week, we saw so much black, in mourning for Hitler—and of course, a dead giveaway as to their true sentiments.

Lilacs are everywhere and the most beautiful I've seen. Many wreaths were made of them the day after Hitler's death was an-

---

* The Eisenhower jacket—so called because Gen. Dwight D. Eisenhower wore one throughout most of the campaign in Europe—differed from the customary Army dress tunic in that it was waist-length only and drawn in along the bottom, rather than extending below the waist with side pockets and, for officers, a belt. The jacket in question was not usually issued to troops in the continental U.S. until 1946.

nounced. So, you see, most of them did condone and adore the dirty dog. Occasionally you run into someone who seems sincere in his relief that he's dead, saying because of him Germany is ruined. But then again, many who backed him completely say that *now* after their homes are ruined—but if they weren't personally affected would probably mourn for him too and all he stands for.

The American flag is secured over Bitche by Captain Thomas H. Garahan, 2nd Battalion, 398th Infantry, March 1945.–*U.S. Army*

Captain Thomas Garahan being evacuated by medics after sustaining an injury during the 398th Infantry's attack at Jagstfeld during the Heilbronn fighting.—*Douglas Smyth*

Company E, 398th Infantry at Hohenstadt. Captain Thomas Garahan is at left, back to camera. Medic Tec 5 Joseph H. Wheeler is seated, between the two posts. Next to him, standing, with carbine, is Lt. Warren E. Haught.—*Douglas Smyth*

Civilians clearing a roadblock at Ludwigshafen, Germany, as 100th Division infantrymen move in to continue mopping-up operations. March 1945.— *U.S. Army*

Heavy shellfire sends troops of Co L, 398th Infantry, diving for cover behind trucks in Almhutte area of Germany, April 1945.—*U.S. Army*

Off-hours for the medics. Top, musical moment in Alsace. Capt. Joseph
Rich, with horn; Winston, left; Pfc Yves Fontenot standing behind Rich.
Below left, Winston and Staff Sgt Samuel G. Cahoon, near Stuttgart.
Right, Winston waving from atop captured German radar equipment.

Devastation: Heilbronn, April 1945.—*U.S. Army*

100th Division troops advance through ruins at Heilbronn, April 1945.—
U.S. Army

100th Division soldier looks out at Heilbronn from observation post, April 1945.—*U.S. Army*

After V-E Day. Above, Staff Sgt Pascal Pironti, left, and Keith Winston prepare to take a jeep jaunt. Below left, Winston, right, with Tec 4 Robert G. Emond, left, and Staff Sgt John Turner at the Opera House, Stuttgart. Right, celebrating Staff Sgt Samuel G. Cahoon's promotion to commissioned rank. Standing, left to right, are Tec 3 Douglas S. Smyth, Tec 4 Robert G. Emond, Tec 5 Abraham Kaplan, Staff Sgt Pascal Pironti; seated, left to right, Winston, Lt Cahoon, Tec 4 Harold S. Horrigan.

Above, Keith Winston. Right, Lt Sam Cahoon, center, looks on as Winston and unidentified medic tend field stoves. Standing at left is unidentified infantryman. Below, Lt Cahoon, Winston.

7. Victory over Germany

Schorndorf, Waiblingen

May-August 1945

Berlin had surrendered to the Russians, and on 7 May 1945 the German High Command accepted the Allies' unconditional surrender terms. The documents were formally signed on 8 May, both at General Eisenhower's headquarters in Reims, France, and Russian headquarters in Berlin. Germany was to be divided into four zones of occupation, garrisoned by the United States, Great Britain, France and the Soviet Union. Soon after V-E Day American troops were shown a movie in which Generals Marshall and Eisenhower explained the workings of a system of separation from the service that would be based on points; depending upon how long a soldier had been in the Army, his age, marital status, the number of months overseas, combat experience, unit battle stars, medals and citations, each enlisted man would receive a certain number of points, and those with the highest totals would be discharged first. The movie explaining how the system would operate had been prepared long in advance; the GI audience could tell that, because Marshall and Eisenhower were shown wearing on their uniforms the four stars of a general rather than the cluster of five designating the General of the Army rank to which they had been promoted on 15 December 1944, by act of Congress.

The war with Japan, of course, was still far from over; American forces were locked in a deadly struggle with the Japanese defenders on Okinawa, which had been invaded on 1 April. Not until 22 June was the island declared secured. In preparation for the ultimate invasion of Japan itself, which was expected to be extremely costly in American lives, some units of the Army would have to be transferred from the European Theater of Operations to the Pacific. As could only be expected, the prospect of such a transfer did not appeal to most of the troops, who had already completed the winning of one war. The chief topic of GI conversation in Germany, therefore, had to do with points—and what they signified about the chances of going home permanently, being assigned to the Army of Occupation, or being shipped out to the Pacific.

7 May 1945

TODAY IS THE DAY WE'VE WAITED AND SWEATED FOR.

Yes, I'm very happy, but somehow I can't get too excited about it. Why? I'm still here—and you're still there—and miles and months between us.

Yes, honey, the war is over but the joy diminishes when I think of all the boys who've lost their lives in the struggle and are not here to enjoy the victory always uppermost in their minds.

And all the boys in terrible shape languishing in hospitals. Some of them better off dead. Basket cases. Physically and mentally.

And my sadness knowing that our President, instrumental in our victory, is not here to enjoy the results of his efforts—and not here to guide us on to complete victory, and hopefully, a lasting peace.

I know my spirits should be higher since we do have more to look forward to now, Darling. But I know you'd understand if you had seen all I have seen.

Here's the latest demobilization plan—can be changed hourly. First—300,000 men to be discharged according to points. Figure me out under that plan what with boys who've served 3, 4 or 5 years, with 1 to 3 years overseas duty. However, there's still a glimmer of hope. Of the 700,000 men to be discharged by age and dependents, I may stand a slim chance. But let's not expect too much—and hope and pray for an early reunion—and above all that I'm not shipped out of the States once I'm returned.

We walked and drove through the Bavarian mountains today. Nothing quite compares to the natural splendor here. Scattered like dabs of color throughout the mountains are summer retreats— nothing elaborate but they seem to enhance the magnificent background. How I wish you were here to enjoy this with me.

Today no mail, nor yesterday or the day before—but maybe tomorrow. I seem to live for the "tomorrows."

In a day or two we're due for our battle star. Many of the boys feel we were gypped as our outfit is given only one star for the battle of Germany, and we actually participated in the liberation of France. But I can assure you I'm far from worried about it. You know my feelings about stars. And one star I don't want—a So. Pacific star!

Front page of
Stars and Stripes,
6 May 1945

We're now located in the Western entrance of the Bavarian mountains, 60 or 70 miles from Munich.* I'd be happy if we stayed right here until we're to be shipped home.

I notice with disgust the return to G.I. regulations—compulsory saluting and all the small-time stuff I despise in the Army and ache to get away from. During combat all that nonsense is discarded, and it's even more unpalatable now that combat is over. Fortunately the Medics don't go in much for that. Now all I want is to get away from it all as soon as possible.

* The 398th Infantry Regiment was now stationed near Schorndorf.

8 May

The day was made considerably brighter with 3 rays of sunshine. There's nothing in this world I look forward to with greater enthusiasm, except you, of course.

While we've learned by intimation of our disposition, I can't say anything about it yet since there's still a war on—and nothing is definite till we get our classification forms completed telling us where we stand. So for the present be content I'm out of danger and much closer to home than before. These coming weeks will be tough on us, Honey, but keep busy as I plan to do—and before we realize it we'll be in each other's arms for good.

Our combat ribbons arrived and I'm enclosing mine. The "Merry-Go-Round" was sure revealing—and as Drew Pearson said, could be the seeds for World War III. I read with regret Pearson's colleague, Col. Bob Allen, lost his arm—but at least he was freed from the Nazi prison. America needs many more men like them—men who see the truth and are willing to expose it to the world, regardless of repercussions.

9 May

We had a parade today—not necessarily a victory parade, but a "dry run" practise in preparation for a Division parade next week. Six months of active combat didn't seem to take away any of the first-class soldiering our Division is famous for. They're OK.

I've heard many reports, maybe rumors, on the demobilization plans and still hang on to the hope I'll be home before the summer is out. However, everything depends on the progress of the Jap war.

The final defeat of Germany didn't seem to make a whole lot of difference here. The boys have no way of celebrating, no place to go and they're still in the same war set-up—no closer to home, and perhaps missing it a little more, especially in view of the jubilation, the celebrations back home and knowing they're not a part of it.

As for the civilians, they considered the war over when we took over this town. The only difference is that they don't have to run to their "bungas" (air shelters) and no more fear for their lives, or that their homes would be "kapoot" anymore.

Well, Dearest, tomorrow we move again—probably a little more permanent a setting than this one.

11 May

We try to keep busy with sports, hikes, jeep rides but they don't satisfy. And educational programs, which have been promised, are not due for 60 days.

Last night we filled out our "deployment" sheets which figured credit on the basis of (1) Service in the Army—(2) Overseas credit—(3) Battle decorations—(4) Dependents. Unfortunately I'm way below par on length of service and overseas credit and the only group where I stand a chance is Age and Dependency. As to decorations, I have the Purple Heart, German Campaign Star, and a Bronze Star pending.

Our present set-up is comfortable though we have no electricity. The people are typically German—although they insist as they all do everywhere—they never favored Hitler and his actions. I'm beginning to wonder where all his support came from.—Especially when driving through the countryside like Doc and I did today, we found scores of civilians, almost all females, at various well-planned points along the road—always near the top of a steep hill or a sharp curve, or a huge pothole or break in the road—or near a blown-up bridge hastily repaired. Their purpose? To wait for the big truck transports carrying German prisoners.

And they travel all day long every day to throw food and bottles of schnopps to the prisoners as the trucks pass by very, very slowly due to the aforementioned obstacles to driving. You can't blame them for sticking by their badly beaten boys, but their feelings for Hitler are very strong and what they tell us is without basis, we find out all the time. It's their way of placating the enemy to make their lives a little more comfortable.

12 May

Today started a little different. I told you about the German women with their baskets of food and drink, waiting at advantageous points to toss to Nazi prisoners as they're hauled back in big trucks. Well, it seems that many of these Nazis are getting more than their share to drink. This morning two of these guys were soused and jumped off the truck in an attempt to escape, whereupon our guards shot them. Both were in bad shape and we were called to go out and fix them up and then evacuate them. It served as a good example to others who might entertain the same ideas.

I'll be busy the next few days as we'll be giving physicals to all the Companies, so today I took advantage of the beautiful lake about 100 yards from the house and spent a couple of restful hours.

17 May

Now I'm able to tell you that we're located close to Stuttgart. Was in this same area on that "rest" when the war ended. I can tell you, too, it was our Division that was put in the 7th Army Reserve as the war was coming to an end. Reserve actually means "held" for emergency if the call arises—fortunately, it didn't. Our outfit, I may have told you, was on the front line for over 170 straight days, and that is a record for the 7th Army.

Speaking of whether or not my job is considered combat—you can bet your stars it is. Now that danger is over I can speak freely and tell you I consider myself a very lucky guy in not getting killed or hit. Rarely did a day pass that it couldn't have happened.

Our Medical Section of 32 men was by far the luckiest in the Division—even with that we lost two (killed) and at least six seriously injured, missing death by a hair.* At least 10 more were in-

---

* Two members of the 2nd Battalion, 398th Infantry Regiment medics, Tec 5 Ellis Medvin, of Rochester, N.Y., and Tec 4 Irving Hunger, of New York City, were killed in combat. Tec 4 Anthony Ranieri, of Brookline, Mass., was so badly wounded that he was evacuated back to the United States. Pfc. Orville M. Clark, Jr., of Pikesville, Ky., was severely wounded and did not return to combat. Other 2nd Battalion medics who were seriously wounded but who did return to the unit

jured to the extent of being evacuated to England. The two dead boys were good friends of mine, so you can imagine how I feel. One, in particular, Ellis, must have had a premonition something might happen as he gave me his brother's address two weeks before he was killed. He asked me to write him of the details should anything happen. I was pretty shaken up about it. I plan to write when I get home. I can't seem to get myself to do it now.*

As far as combat is concerned, Darling, unfortunately it means practically nothing—a battle star meaning only 5 points. It's appalling in view of the fact that a combat man risks his life every second of 24 hours. I have spoken to these men, and ten minutes later carried them into the Air Station on a litter as casualties. And almost six straight months of it. One's hair can and does turn gray.

Of course, all Medics are not combat men. However, if you're in the Infantry and attached to one of the Battalions, you're actually on the front line—no ifs, ands or buts. All battalions are made up of 32 Medics, and it's up to the Bn. Surgeon (Doc, in our case) to use these men to the best advantage. Eleven are Aid-men—the roughest and least glorified job in the Army. Ask any Infantryman and he'll tell you. He speaks of his Medic with reverence. Then there are 12 litter-bearers, of which I was one when fighting was toughest. When a guy got hit on the front line we went out and got him. We picked up a boy one day in German territory while our own Infantrymen kept shooting over our heads to keep the enemy down. That's just one instance.

Then there are two non-coms who take care of handling the men—two drivers, four technicians who stay in the Aid Station to care for the sick and wounded—and one clerk.

If an emergency arises your position means nothing. If it calls for 5 litter teams immediately, Doc and I will go up and haul. He and I were doing it one day with no facilities at all.

After a guy gets hit he must be evacuated to a "collecting com-

---

included Pfc. Michael Annicchiarico, Jersey City, N.J.; Pfc. Ralph J. Barb, Jr., Pittsburgh, Pa.; Pfc. Henry Black, Springfield, Mass.; Pfc. Henry F. DeForge, Hartford, Conn.; Tec 5 Fred B. Hart, Titusville, N.J.; Tec 4 Harold S. Horrigan, Bronx, N.Y.; Tec 5 Paul J. Kutzman, Brooklyn, N.Y.; Tec 4 Willie J. Mullens, Calcasieu, La.; and Pfc. Bruno Ghingo, Astoria, Long Island, N.Y.

* After the war, Winston did write to Ellis Medvin's brother, who in turn thanked him for his letter.

pany" made up of about 100 Medics in the Regiment. These Medics who sometimes run into hazardous duty, are not combat men actually, but are given that distinction. From that point the casualties are sent to a "clearing company" of the entire Division and there are upwards of 100 Medics in that situation. They see no action at all. Then to a Field hospital, Evacuation hospital, General hospital—all strictly rear echelon.

Yet for all the danger and risk to our lives—5 points are added to our score. Any guy on the front should receive no less than 5 points *per month* of combat credit. People back home don't have the slightest conception what combat means—not the slightest. They may think they know, but until they've been running for cover with airplanes strafing them, with 88's screaming over their heads— they just don't know. There are so many instances I can tell you about—things that make me shudder as I think of them.

This new house we're in is most pleasant. It belongs to a German officer discharged because of an injury. He's been around and took a shine to me but I politely avoid him. His wife is the type who tries to use her sex to get what she wants but isn't getting to first base with our crew, who know she's after cigarettes and other commodities. They won't be around again after today.

Right now we're giving physicals throughout the Battalion. Our job now, in essence, is just to remain around the Aid Station in case a sick boy shows up—or an emergency—auto accident or the like. As personnel is sent back to the States, less men will be used in a Station.

Darling, not much more to say. I am well—lonesome—and just about fed up. My mind is far from clear—so many things happening. Right now I feel I want to go home and get in our bed and sleep, sleep, sleep (with you in my arms)—where it's quiet and no G.I.'s around. I want to get into a hot tub of water and just lie there for hours and get these lousy O.D.'s off me and never see them again—and become a civilian where I'm equal with everyone and don't have to salute and say "sir" to some slimy Lt. who got in the OCS when they were begging for officers.—I love and miss you.

19 May

I'm settled in a cool, quiet spot overlooking the water, and an ideal place to write my dear little wife whom I love with all my heart. Have you heard that before?

We're all finished with the physicals, inspections, injections and the like. I take charge of almost everything, and since Doc depends on me completely I don't like to let him down. But sometimes in hot weather as we've been having, and our constant moving, I get pretty bushed. It's times like this I get solace in getting away from the Aid Station for a few hours, where I can answer your wonderful letter that gave me my lift for the day.

Heard an interesting story. One of our Companies was guarding a town some miles from Bn. Hq. We took this same town a month ago but we kept on moving, taking one town after another. But while stationed there the Company occupied a number of homes and took reasonably good care of them.

A few days ago, this same Company was assigned to return to that town, same houses. Having no idea who'd be occupying their homes, the owners loaded their wagons with household goods, radios, mattresses, etc. During the loading a few of our boys came up to one house to wait around until it was finished. However, when the civilians recognized the same bunch who'd been there 5 weeks earlier—without a word, they unloaded their possessions and returned them to the house. They were confident these guys would leave their house in decent condition as they had before.—It is not our idea to impress them—far from it—but evidently we did in our non-fraternizing, civil way, characteristic of most Americans.

20 May

Last night Doc, I and Sam (Staff Sgt.) went for a ride, and on our way back ran into a couple of Poles. They took us to a German "Gasthaus" (beer tavern). Over here these places are frequented by families, though it was empty due to the late hour. Wine, bologna and pumpernickel were served. We all ate with "goot appeteete" as the atmosphere was quaint and pleasant.

The Poles kept talking about their "wonderful" army (which went kapoot in 6 weeks) and their horrible experiences as labor prisoners for six years. They were so happy to meet Americans, they talked and talked and talked. Their stories were the same we'd been hearing about Nazi terrorism and atrocities from many others.

I'll admit that by going to the Gasthaus we didn't follow strictly to the non-fraternization policy, but then it wasn't so terribly bad and it was a change we all needed.

This letter is the first uncensored one I've written overseas, and now I can tell you that Doc rarely, if ever, checked my letters. And because the responsibility was put square on my shoulders I was probably more cautious than necessary.

We're in a typical German "Stadt" called Steinheim, about 20 miles north of Stuttgart, and 20 miles south of Heilbronn.

One of our soldiers burned at a remark a young German girl made to him. In broken English she said, "Was it fair for your planes to ruin our beautiful land?" The soldier quietly explained that our planes only hit targets of military significance, and further, he added, he wished she could have gone through France like he had and seen with her own eyes the devastation her people had unloaded on that country. She was taken aback with that and all she could say was "Oh."—These people know only one side. They have absolutely no idea what their army did to the Allies—only what we did to them, and of course, their cause is right, and ours wrong, naturally. No German likes to entertain the thought that they brought on their own destruction.

Darling, this war—any war—is Hell. It tears families apart; absence is such a strain. We're fortunate in having a solid basis in our marriage and in our little family, but I have seen so much heartache along these lines—so many "Dear John" letters—so many guys falling apart—it's a terribly disheartening sight. And guys over here attaching themselves to one women after another because of long separations and sheer desperation.

We're probably considered occupation troops until a disposition is made. That may be one month or six months—and either way—

East or West. But we'll try to take it as it comes, and face one problem at a time. Yes, Dearest?

21 May

This afternoon I took a couple of blankets and went into a field nearby and fell fast asleep. And this evening, though a steady drizzle, I took a long walk in the rain trying to shake off this gnawing feeling that seems to be constantly with me.

Doc was telling me again today how homesick he is now that he has so much time to think, but I don't think anyone could be more homesick than I.

Got a kick out of Neilly's comeback when his friend, Joey wanted to "buy" David for $10—that he wouldn't take all the money in the world for him. The dear little guy—I'm so proud of him.

Today the roads are filled with freed German prisoners. What the actual reason is I don't know. They were a sad, beaten crew— expressionless, worn out, filthy—but many of our boys have been in worse condition under their ruthlessness. Perhaps they were physically unfit and the Army felt it better to release them. Whatever the reason, they were on their way home.

The ETO has decided to feed us all the surplus stew and spam and hash they've stored up here, and I'm not looking forward to that kind of chow. Your packages will mean even more now.

22 May

In your letter today you ask about the current situation on points. As of now the frozen figure is 55. When I get my Bronze Star it will be good for 5 more. How quick medals take on importance!— I agree with you that the whole thing is a farce. I think it would be fair to institute two categories. One on the point basis, and another on the age-dependency basis, dismissing a smaller but substantial number.

Another thing—these lousy combat ribbons should not count. The Air Medal is handed out like a prize in a Cracker Jack box while the Infantryman gets no such opportunity. Remember, 9 out of 10 heroes never get a medal—and why should a Purple Heart count 5 points when another guy who's had shells fall around him, but never got hit, receive less credit. He may not be struck physically by a bullet but his mental state is stricken, often for life. In the Army they have to see blood before you're considered a "hero."

Now that fighting is over our Division is "occupying"—meaning systematic guard duty. The Aid Station is always a necessity to a battalion though we're not too busy. Also, with the war over, the quality of food has deteriorated, nor do the boys get as many cigarettes. And with the constant inactivity, they want to smoke more than ever.

24 May

Today was lucky for your husband. He got four letters that raised his morale beaucoup de points.

Heinrich Himmler committed suicide. Other good news? I got 5 more points today. Our Division was awarded another battle star for our drive toward the Rhine. So now I have 60 points.

Stuttgart is a large city—about 300,000 people in normal times. Now it's literally flat.

Heard over the radio that the whole First Army is on their way home already. If there are facilities for a full army of 75,000 to 100,000 all at once, shipping is not as bad as we're led to believe.

Doc broke the ice and received the first package either of us has had in a couple of weeks. The food box is as bare as Mother Hubbard's cupboard. Some of mine should be trickling in now.

Played volley-ball tonight. We beat one of the line company teams and tackle another tomorrow night.

Today Doc, Sam and I took a jeep ride and stopped at one of these old, old "Gausthofs," a rustic tavern built in 1614 (its age is nothing spectacular around here). The proprietors—an old couple—were very cordial and we made arrangements to return later

for a dinner of "puffstake mit kadufles"—beeksteak, onions, potatoes and salad. We're not exactly permitted to eat off the Germans, but bartering is now OK. As you know, the G.I. meals have
been lousy lately and we grabbed at the chance for something more
palatable.

You're probably alarmed and feel we're taking unnecessary risks,
but you know I wouldn't be trying to get myself into trouble. I'm
constantly on the alert, usually carry a little pistol in my pocket in
case we run into difficulty, and we always carry them when we go
out walking. We're very much aware of possible danger.

This meal is due for 9 P.M. and it's about that now so will stop
until I get back.

Later—Well, Darling, here I am after a steak which ranked only
2nd to ours (at their best) with delicious French fried potatoes.
We enjoyed this more than anything we've eaten in the ETO, and
we set another date for Sunday. The charge—11½ German marks—
the equivalent of about $3.50 for all three dinners.

The asparagus sounds yummy. Glad you're getting a yield. We'll
fertilize it well when I get back. Over here there's so, so, so much
farmland and each family cultivates a few acres. Riding along the
road you see women working the soil—usually mothers and daugh-
ters. Often a baby carriage under the shade of a tree, or two or
three kids playing around while the adults work. It reminds me of
our garden—only about 100 times as big. Everything is done by
hand—no horses or machines, and the farms are well cared for, with
very good results. They don't know much about commercial ferti-
lizers—only manure, and they use that beaucoup.

26 May

I'm writing you sitting in the shade of a magnificent old tree,
and the scene stretched out before me is one that Van Gogh must
have used in painting his farm picture. It's almost an exact replica.
It's so restful and my thoughts "wing" homeward to you.

Apparently, the war in Europe is still not over. Yesterday a boy
came into our Aid Station all battered up. He'd been disarming

civilians and picked up an arm similar to a bazooka which exploded in his hand. He was "lucky" at that—losing a hand, and severe powder burns on his face. He could have been killed.

The boys are still getting furloughs—Paris, Brussels, Riviera, England. Our section gets 4 a month, and my second turn has still to come up. Actually, I don't have a great desire to visit these places as there's so much traveling involved and most of it by truck, which is not my idea of a holiday. Besides, the cost is terrific. My trip to Paris set me back $75. and nothing much to show for it. Now the boys don't have extra cigarettes to defray the cost—they don't even get enough for themselves. Each pack is counted closely now—but in all fairness no man on the line can complain about the liberal treatment they got while the fighting was on.

27 May

Today is Sunday—the day I miss my little family the most. Your letter arrived in 5 days—the best ever.

Your desires are the same as mine in many ways, in reference to my eventual disposition. *Disposition.* That word really hits me. Sounds like something distasteful—to be disposed of for expediency's sake.—But to get back to what I was saying. Foremost, I fear the Pacific, 2nd, I want a discharge—if that's not forthcoming, I'd settle for an assignment near home. However, I think I prefer this occupation instead of an assignment on the West Coast and a strict training schedule. I detest going back to garrison life after what we've been through. Here it's informal, and changing back to Army discipline would be rough. But your desires and mine mean nothing to the Army, so we'll sweat it out and see what happens.

Just had lunch—Sunday dinner—which was OK. Roast beef, wax beans, stewed tomatoes, cake. I brought a big platter over and had the Company kitchen fill it up for 3, then carried it back to the house where we—Doc, Sam and I—had a nice Sunday spread in the dining room.

29 May

There seems to be no let-up on monotony. So far no arrangements have been made for organized educational programs or trips, and things are terribly static and boring. When I get in these moods I go off alone somewhere, and when I return usually feel better. Like tonight—and as I walked along I came on a huge cherry tree dripping with luscious black cherries and I gorged myself on them.

You have no personal life in the Army. As I'm typing this letter, unbeknown to me, this young kid in our group ("Junior," who we like very much), has been standing over my shoulder reading every word I write.* He loves to eat, and when I wrote about the cherry tree, he asked me where it was. I broke up when I realized what he was doing. Some guys complain when I write in longhand, because they don't understand my writing!

There's a new set-up on the cigarette and candy deal. Every week, in bulk, we receive 7 packs of cigarettes (5¢ a pack), 3 bars of candy (4¢ a bar), and a 4¢ pack of gum—totaling 51¢. By the way, I never did get that $30. I loaned that fellow, nor expect to. The guy owes everyone in the Bn.—I didn't know about that. C'est la vie!

The road continues to be jammed with German soldiers returning home and it gives me the most peculiar sensation. They're dressed in military outfits with full field pack, and as you see them off in the distance your first inclination is to duck for cover. A month ago, a scene like this would have meant trouble. Now I hear these guys have been released to help in fields and other places where they're needed.

I miss out on a hike the group takes each morning. Handling sick call—which always seems to be in the morning—I lose the opportunity to join them. These hikes, unlike the long, grueling marches in the States, are enjoyable and invigorating. They walk through beautiful wooded areas at a comfortable gait, talking—and best of all—no formation. But don't feel sorry for me. I get all the exercise I want playing ball—and my own private hikes.

* Tec 5 Howard F. Fontaine.

30 May

You'd never know it is Decoration Day around here. It's no different than any other day.—For something to do Doc and the boys tried to play a trick on me—in fun. They got a card from the P.O., the type used when guys leave the ETO for the States—a change of address card. They put my name on it and threw it in with the mail. Of course I suspected the joke, but didn't let on. Anything to keep up morale!

Enclosed is my citation for the Purple Heart.*

Today it rained a good bit but not enough to call off a baseball game.—No news yet on the "disposition" front. The Yanks seem to be doing well over Tokyo—and the French, as usual, are gumming up the works. Over here the boys are somewhat disgusted with the French who seem to be more cantankerous than dependable.

The boys threw a little party tonight—whiskey, wine, cake, coffee. The wine is terribly watered down, not like the stuff at home, more like cider. We've been eating "feel de" cherries; they're very good and plentiful, too. We pick them right off the trees almost anywhere.

3 June

One of the boys with 102 points was wondering what was holding up his transfer to the States. Since this info was at the Division area, 50 miles away, I drove him over in the jeep. What countryside! I can't stop raving about the natural beauty of this country. After all, you can't hate a country—only the people in it.

---

* The citation reads in part: "During this lengthy period of combat operations against the enemy, PFC Keith Winston, medical technician, displayed rare courage, technical skill and a devotion to duty in carrying out his daily duties. Participating in the bitter campaign for the Vosges Mountains in Alsace Lorraine, penetration of the Maginot defenses near the fortress of Bitche, and the push into Germany proper, PFC Winston risked his life on unnumberable occasions so that wounded soldiers could be given the proper attention. On November 8, 44, Winston, when trying to rescue a wounded soldier in a mine field, was wounded himself."

You can see hills and valleys coursing all through the country-side, and at many points in the mountains you can see for miles and miles—scores of little towns, conspicuous with their red roofs—all breathtaking and awesome. On Sundays, the roads are crowded with natives in their Sunday best—and all through the week these same people work in the "felda."

In a couple of days we're moving again, this time to a village called Waiblingen, still in the vicinity of Stuttgart. They issued us completely new equipment—shoes, overseas caps, and painted our helmets and haversack, and now shelter-halves. Gradually, the rest will come. We did get Eisenhower jackets which all leads to specu-lation that we'll probably be back before David's birthday.

Latest rumor: We get a 3-week training course on something—don't know exactly what—and also that the CG (Commanding General) already has our camp in the States earmarked. He comes from Richmond, Va., so I hope he gets a camp near Washington.

Dear, in case you're still not convinced about the inequities exist-ing in the point system, here's a classic example: I read that 34,000 casualties came from the 3rd Division. You don't realize what that means. There are 5 to 7000 front-linesmen in a Division and, of course, they're the casualties. In other words, men in that Divi-sion—the front-line soldiers—have changed between 5 and 7 times—which is staggering. Then you hear of an artillery outfit with only one casualty in ten months of combat—and this from their own ack-ack. This is not hearsay, this is fact—from the boys themselves. They're also called combat boys and get the same battle star credit for combat as the doughboy who sleeps in a wet foxhole risking his life every second.

How I want to get out of this lousy army. I've been taking stock of myself lately and while I find the Army still hasn't affected me too much, I want to get out before it does. Getting kicked around by some of these young officers still wet behind the ears—just out of college—and others who got in early when there was an acute shortage—really gets to me. So many take advantage of their rank. They think they're being saluted or respected, when it is only their bar—and that's compulsory. After being in combat like I've been, and being close to Doc and Beaucoup, I know these guys (not necessarily Doc or Beaucoup) as a group are no better than the average enlisted man, but they act like the ground they walk on is sacred—and that the Lord gave them their commission.—There are exceptions.

Imagine! They have a toilet for officers, and a toilet for enlisted men. Right here in Germany!

My association with the men has been good and we all get along very well. It's a good feeling to know that everywhere in the Battalion I have friends—officers and enlisted men, and chiefly because of the manner they're treated in the Aid Station. I'll admit to taking credit for the friendly, personal system we have down here—it was far from good before I took over.

Darling, again I read your poem and it touches me very much. I have a feeling we'll be seeing each other before too long.

5 June

Two more letters which spill over with your love and devotion. They're a great comfort to me. The pictures of David are great—he's always smiling, that sweet one.

The enclosed pictures I took recently. The huge mechanism I'm standing on, supposed to be the largest radar machine in the world, was German.—Those flowers I'm looking at are poppies—the largest I've ever seen. The other fellow in one of the pictures is Sam, our former Sgt. and now Lt.—earned for his wonderful work on the battlefield. The other three are typical farm scenes.

Through an unofficial but reliable source, we learned today we definitely will *not* be occupational troops and should be heading for the States in a month or two. That may be good or bad. We'll have to wait and see.

Tomorrow is moving day—to Waiblingen, the town I told you about.

We haven't been doing so good on food lately—our chief diet, canned ration foods. Occasionally some fresh meat. This morning dry cereal and powdered milk, also a novelty. Your packages sure save the day.

7 June   *Waiblingen*

Now we're in Waiblingen, a beautiful city not far from Schorndorf where I was stationed when the war ended. In about two weeks
we'll move on to Schorndorf to receive some SOP (Standard Op-
erational Procedure) training—stuff only needed in garrison life,
not to win wars. All this damn theory is only given in garrison, but
in real combat little or none is used. It really nauseates and this is
no exaggeration.

This house we're quartered in is tops. The owner manufactures
dining trays that roll on wheels—I guess you call them tea wagons.
Each man has a room and wash-stand if not a toilet. OK, isn't it!
The set-up is really "prima." Hot water, a washing machine, big
beds, gardens, cherry trees mit "feel" cherries. And we're high up
in the mountains overlooking a magnificent view of the village.

Rumor persists that we'll be on our way home before the summer's end. But this army is so full of surprises and disappointments
I won't believe anything till I'm home—not before.

By appointment I went over to the owner's factory today and
picked up a few things—3 tea wagons, 4 sewing cabinets—something you don't see in the States. I know you'll like them. They
have lots of trays which I plan to buy, too, when I return again.
Mostly Chinese red and black in color and quite effective. Perhaps
I seem foolish making a fuss about these things, but you have no
idea how I crave going into a store and buying—as you rarely get
that thrill around here, as there's nothing to buy.

Right now, Darling, I'm out on the terrace with a radio beside
me. Nobody on the "Main Line" is living in more luxury.

After suffering through 7 months of war here I think I'm dreaming when I see some of the things that go on now. The towns are
full of German soldiers still in uniform, and as I said in an earlier
letter, my first reaction is to run for cover. How many times during
combat I'd see them in the distance and always a dread feeling of
fear came over me, as invariably fire followed in our direction. Now
we brush against them, right on the street when walking, or when
they're working around their homes, always in uniform, and it gives
me a slightly sick feeling. Almost all look tired, worn out, unkempt,

haggard and definitely harmless. Some of the horror stories we now hear of the bombing during the air offensive, give further evidence how vile a traitor Hitler was to his own people.

Being a soldier, I can see the need to lead a battalion or regiment or army into an almost hopeless cause for tactical advantages gained in another sector—but to prolong a lost, hopeless war in which thousands and millions of his own people are in literal agony both from fear and bombings, that mad creature and his henchmen could not have been human.

10 June

The boys visited Munich today. I didn't go as I'm convinced that every big city in Germany is just a pile of rocks. And that was the story the boys returned with. They did see one of the German prison camps—one of the most notorious 7 miles out of Munich—and the prisoners, members of French, Polish and Russian armies, are still there in a deplorable state. An American hospital, now part of the camp, is caring for these poor victims in the best way possible. And all this the result of a madman who drew unbelievable support from his people.

Sometimes I think I'm dreaming, as I told you yesterday, when I witness all the bizarre things in the span of a day. Well, I'm not alone. I just finished reading "G.I. Diary" in the Sunday *Stars & Stripes*, and it points up vividly what happens in a day around here. Most of the guys are thinking and feeling the same things.

Know what I had yesterday? Ice-cream! And for the first time since leaving the States. Our kitchens don't have the facilities to make it, but the civilians do, and since we supply the ingredients, we've gotten together and the results are OK even with powdered milk. I need not tell you how popular it is.

11 June

Today is our anniversary. It hurts not to be with you on a special day like this but I hope this time next year we'll have a real celebration—just we two.

I was deeply upset to hear of Mutty Wasserman being killed in action. I liked the kid so much, and for the first time over here, in this cockeyed unnatural setting (probably due to "peacetime" circumstances) found a death affecting me emotionally. With so much death and casualties around at all times, I'd learned to adjust to these horrors; to dwell on each case could throw you into a fit of depression and you guard against this, otherwise your function would be nil. For a time this worried me, thinking the Army was dehumanizing me, making me insensible to tragedy and sorrow. But I realize now there wasn't time to dwell on it, with all the work and continual pressure of self-preservation—all of which was part of us 24 hours a day. War does strange things to people and makes them less than human at times. Now that my mind and outlook is returning to normal, news of the death of Mutty, a sweet innocent kid, is pretty unsettling.

Food continues 3rd rate and we can only blame it on the officials as the cooks do wonders even with those C rations, and always make an effort to do a little something special like baking a cake or pie; and beg, borrow, steal or buy with their own money lettuce, tomatoes, onions, etc. to make some part of the meal more palatable. I imagine, with this part of the war over, the officials are determined to use up the huge stores of B & C rations in the warehouses. But we do get first-hand information that the rear echelons are eating first-class food.

13 June

How is my little family today? I miss you all so. When I see how cruel and corroding war is, I swear that I shall always fight for peace—regardless of the price. Millions of homes broken up, families separated, men killed and maimed. I see so much of it and I shall never forget it.

Doc is leaving for two months of hospital practise and will return if we're still here.

We're getting ready for a parade Saturday. I don't know why—we're not showing off to anyone, and besides our marching is probably mediocre to the over-trained, goose-stepping Germans.

I often think of our cherry tree as I pick them here. They're in such abundance, I eat them faster than I can pluck them, and especially now with the lack of fruit, they're so refreshing.

Just got through double-timing and a bath and feel good. It's a good toner-upper, and Junior and I have decided to give it a go each evening.

We're injecting typhus shots again. Today we took care of two companies—tomorrow, the other three. I got mine and contrary to most of the boys who gripe about shots, I welcome them knowing they're safe-guards against disease. I get a kick out of some of these tough veterans—men who've seen battle, slept in swamps, and gone through Hell, who become scared as hell before a shot which actually is hardly felt.

We continue the life of luxury here. Last night we had a jam session. Our Dental Surgeon plays the piano well—Doc, the trumpet, another guy the violin and I joined them with the clarinet. We had quite a time and plan to try it again soon.

Ice-cream is served pretty regularly now. Chocolate yesterday, and comparable to any in the States. It's really delicious and each serving is about a pint. Some guys can't eat it all.

Speaking of can't eating—right beside the garbage cans where we throw our excess food, there's always a lot of people ready to grab it as it's thrown. It's pitiful to see, especially when kids are involved. There's an ambivalence of feeling around here. We still have a strong distaste for these people, our enemies—many still think their troubles stem directly from us. Yet, if you possess an ounce of compassion it's not easy to be around this sort of thing day after day and not be moved by it.

I'm rather tired with my work around here. Doc depends on me for everything—all clerical and administration details. He and the rest say they don't know what will happen to our Aid Station if I were to leave.

Today for the third time I've been offered a rating and refused it—this time technician 4th grade—equivalent to Sgt. The catch is I'd have to leave my organization to go to Regiment where I know I wouldn't be happy. All my heart, Dearest.

16 June

Am getting so sick of all this, especially after hearing that 86% of the U.S. people (who know nothing—zero—of the hell a soldier endures) want unconditional surrender with Japan. It's so easy to want all—when you give nothing.

Darling, you'll forgive me if I don't write you the details of the mine accident you asked me to. I'll have plenty of time to tell you later. I get sick at the thought of it. The main thing is that I was lucky to get away with a minor injury and suffer no after-effects now. The boy on the other side of the litter lost both his feet. Another blinded.

We're about finished with the typhus shots and that's a relief. How is David? I hope no German measles. German, no less!

Non-fraternization is a failure now that the war is over. Naturally there's a limit to fraternizing, but everyone does, from Generals on down. Already the Army sees the futility of it all but can't openly concede it.

Remember, I believe there's a limit, but people back home can't realize what it's all about just by reading the local newspaper. Without a reasonable fraternization rule, the boys could go crazy.

20 June

We just finished giving a farewell party for Doc who leaves for two months of hospital training in Epinal, France, as I told you.

Practically all the refreshments came from your packages and the boys really do go for it. I made a salad with lettuce, tuna, cheese, and the works—served nicely on a great big tray, and we had drinks along with it. Hard and soft.

Saturday we have our parade. An order has been issued compelling all civilians to come out and view it. Not so hot, is it? It smacks too much of Hitler and Fascism—but I'm just an unimportant enlisted man and therefore have no right to express an opinion.

Something getting very serious here is the rising venereal disease rate. Our Regiment came over here without one case and now it's pretty rampant. And most of it contracted since the cessation of combat—many from France, and I'm sure many from German frauleins. We're treating them and hope to cure it, but it bothers me to see the steady increase.

It appears to be another result of the non-fraternization rule, where a guy having trouble controlling his sexual drive will go off in some "corner" with a tramp, whereas his being able to fraternize openly might have ended up with a long walk with a girl, and his drive somewhat mollified. Remember, there's another side to this non-fraternization problem.—It hurts to see some of these boys—mostly kids—whom I've known from the first day of battle—come in with a "case." These same kids might not have frequented houses in Paris or Brussels if they were not so starved for want of being with someone other than a soldier.

Over here, supposedly "nice" women proposition soldiers openly. One guy tells me a so-called "respectable" woman asked him over to her house. He was a little leery at first, feeling it might be another set-up to get him into trouble. But he took the chance and went. She was in her forties and sex-starved. After that they met secretly many times—purely physical—no romance attached. When he'd come in she'd ask right off in German, "Habenzee guma?" (Do you have prophylactics?) And this is not an isolated case. It happens all the time we know. Most of them are promiscuous and will take on any guy that will have them. So you can see how easy the disease can start spreading. Many guys pursue these women from sheer boredom—just for some kind of human contact.

The latest "latrine rumor" has it that we'll be home by August

8th. Remember, it's only a rumor, and I'm beginning to think many are started just to keep up morale!

21 June

Back again to SOP. Two letters and very welcome after a couple of "dry" days. I'm happy to hear of Neil's interest in baseball, and now since 50% of the family (a possibility of 75%) is baseball wacky, I'm afraid you don't stand a chance, Dearest, so you'll just have to come along.

Sometimes I wonder if the Army is going to worm another year or two or three out of our lives. I'll fight with everything I have to get out of this damn aristocracy as soon as I hit the States. Once you lose your civilian status you're only a number; you don't quite realize it while it's happening.

I was offered another promotion this morning. I told the Lieutenant I'd only be interested in the Section Leader's job—otherwise I prefer remaining a first class private. But the present Section Leader, a fine gentleman, who has really seen the war as a 1st-class soldier, will probably hang on even though he's in Class D.* If he left—on his own volition—then I'd be interested in the job—it's Staff Sgt. However, since I'm called on to do everything an officer does, ratings mean little to me. And the "glory" of a title means nothing at all.

24 June

Today is Sunday, and again you came through. I love you, Darling for never letting me down.

Everything points to our heading toward the States soon. Our

---

* It is not clear to whom Winston is referring here, but several of his wartime associates report that the description could apply appropriately to either Tec 4 Pascal A. Pironti, of Newark, N.J.; Tec 3 Douglas S. Smyth, of New Bedford, Conn.; or Staff Sgt. Harold G. Davis, of Brooklyn, N.Y.

Division is now in Class 2B—meaning we're slated for the Pacific by way of the U.S. I'm certain Occupation is out.

As to my feelings about the Red Cross, they're very much unchanged. Remember, I contended they were OK in the rear, but up front, where it was vital the only thing furnished was excuses. All the front-line boys feel the same—and they're legion. Now, since the war is over we haven't seen or heard from them. They're great at writing letters, giving excuses and explanations.

Being in the Army is so difficult for men like me. Some of these kids have found "a home" in the Army, but I find it harder and harder to take being away from my family. If the Pacific struggle would end abruptly everything would work out. Darling, we're just going to find some way to make up for all this lost time.

27 June

Things are still moving in the same uninteresting, boring direction. I see where many Senators bear me out on this non-fraternization policy, calling it another "dry" law. It couldn't be better expressed.

You can't imagine how I felt today when 10 of our "D" personnel were transferred to the 36th Division—committed as an Occupational Force. It's not easy saying goodbye to a bunch of guys you've gone through Hell with. It happened throughout the Battalion and many tears where shed by these "hard" veterans—all great guys. Darling, there's so much good in everyone regardless of faults we all have, but in the larger picture seem so trivial. When you live with a group of guys there's apt to be irritations and annoyances, but when it comes to a showdown these are insignificant and the positive things are the important ones. And when suddenly they leave, you feel it. We were all a pretty dejected bunch.

We all ate something yesterday that upset our stomachs and we feel rather lousy today—apart from the above. We should snap out of it by morning.

You should see the rivalry in our kitchens. The five chief cooks in our Battalion are continually trying to outdo each other. They even post a menu in an attempt to lure the guys to come in and eat. Our chief cook goes out of his way to buy garden vegetables which he serves twice a day. And you should see the pride he takes in the imaginative combinations he concocts from C rations. I hear it's the same with the other cooks in the battalion. When there's a large turnout of boys they take personal pride in it for it's supposed to reflect their culinary skill. It's quite a game and we all get a kick out of it.

I'm glad I'm not attached to an Occupational Division. I think I'd go nuts.

29 June

My Bronze Star was finally awarded officially—by written order— and I know you'll be pleased. I'm pleased, too. It means 5 more points! And points are mighty precious these days. Enclosed is a copy of the citation.*

Want to hear a bit of typical Army snafu? Today I hitchhiked to Geislingen, 35 miles from Division Hdqs. to get an identification card—something every Medic was required to have, particularly in combat—but ironically couldn't get one at the time due to combat conditions! I got a hop right back. You see, my "thumbing" ability is helpful even here. Of course G.I. vehicles are the only ones on the road—so who could miss?

Did Luna ever hear from her brother? I couldn't tell you this before but I heard the story of the 45th Division before Luna wrote. Four hundred boys attacked up this big mountain—and only 100

---

* The citation reads: "Keith Winston, 33927775, Private First Class, Medical Detachment, 398th Infantry Regiment, for meritorious achievement in action during the period 6 November 1944 to 30 April 1945, in France and Germany. As a medical technician, Private Winston has performed his duties in an exemplary manner throughout this period of combat operations against the enemy. His technical skill and knowledge, coupled with his courage and an intense personal devotion to duty, have made his assistance invaluable. On many occasions, Private Winston, without regard for his own safety, crawled through intense enemy fire of all descriptions in order to give immediate attention to wounded comrades. As a result of his sincere and capable efforts, Private Winston has greatly contributed to the efficient performance of the Medical Detachment. Entered military service from Philadelphia, Pennsylvania."

came back. This occurred during the "Battle of the Bulge." We were out on the furthest tip—being the only Division whose lines didn't move during the counter-attack around the holidays. We were on the left of the 45th at the time. I pray he was one who returned.

4 July

Your letter came in and few letters could have been better timed on this extra lonely "holiday."

We hear by the radio the Japs are talking peace. Nothing official, but after what our bombers have done in a short time they must realize what another six months can do to their country. I've told you what bombing can do to a city, and a people's morale. You can't conceive what it means till you yourself are on the receiving end. It's the most fearful, terrifying, ghastly feeling—especially when you hear children wailing.

Again rumor. This time our Battalion is up for the Presidential citation. It's a unit award the boys are pulling for since there's quite an honor attached to it. We'd be given a blue ribbon to be worn on the right breast (other ribbons on the left)—but with all that "honor" no points are attached to it. We also hear the French are presenting the Division with the highest French unit citation—the croix de guerre—for our successful attack on Bitche—the first time in history this tremendous fortress was taken by force. I still feel the same about ribbons, but I'd wear every one of them if they'd mean points to get me home! They're good souvenirs, anyway.

6 July

It's midnight and I just finished a large can of tomato juice, had a bath and a busy evening. We got our cigarette rations tonight— mit candy and beer and it takes time to distribute them equally.

Now I've several cartons of cigarettes and patiently waiting for a nice trip where I can do a little trading.

Darling, it's very hard for me to write the following, but the facts must be faced. Our General (Burress) just returned from the States and advises that we'll probably not move until March. We're considered "Strategical Reserve" as you know, and we're here for anything (uprising, etc.) that might arise. He further stated we're not headed for the States until all 85 pointers and wounded, etc. and priority Divisions are shipped. Of course orders, plans and the like can be changed as conditions change in the Pacific, but I'll have to admit I'm very much upset about it, Darling. I feel the Jap war is coming to an end and I'd hate to be caught over here when it does.

We're doing our best to keep busy—built a nice darkroom for developing pictures. I've got to keep interested and occupied. It's late and everyone's asleep. You rarely have privacy and when you do, it's a treat. My heart is heavy—it will be hard holding out for so long a period, but we can't do anything about it except to continue writing each other each day, and make our love thrive on this separation. Others have stood the test over a longer stretch of time, and under more difficult hazards, and we will too, won't we, Sweetheart?—You know—things can always happen. Maybe the Jap war will end, maybe fathers will be sent home—lots of things can happen. They say it's blackest before dawn. Yeah, that's what they say. May God bless you and our little ones.

7 July

Did a bit of walking today, chiefly in the direction of one of the many little surrounding towns. These walks are a source of pleasure, not only for the exercise, but the scenery is so breathtaking it gives me a feeling of well-being. I ate some ripe pears right off a tree; there is so much here—apples, pears, apricots, grapes, currants. My mouth waters.

Sam and I are talking about a trip to Strasbourg, a large city in France (200,000) and about 125 miles away. There, perhaps, we could trade cigarettes to pick up a few souvenirs. We'll take pictures and make a day of it. You can't plan too much ahead as things change from day to day, but we'll try. The boys are heading for Nurnberg tomorrow, Sunday, in the truck but I prefer taking trips during the week and relaxing Sundays as we used to at home.

That Ripley "Believe It or Not" was quite a coincidence. The boy mentioned was treated in our Aid Station and I spoke with him as I filled out his evacuation card. He was hit in Lembach, France (not Germany, as stated), and was he "lucky" he was hit January 7th. Three days later his entire Company was wiped out—killed, wounded and captured. I once wrote you about that same Aid Station where an artillery shell hit the building, killing four people. It was one of the hottest places I was in throughout the campaign.

Again I say—disregard anything you hear—no matter what the source. Joe's officer-friend does *not* know any more than the next one. Even our General gets his orders from Corps, and they, from Army, and Army from Washington. It can go in any direction. We could leave tomorrow if the war gets tough—and conversely, if transportation eases up we could be home by October. The 45th Division is a good case in point. They were officially ordered to report to a P.O.E. for redeployment to the States—and today the order was rescinded—so there you are.

If I'm not collecting anything else I seem to be making it up in ribbons. Have 4 now—the Overseas with 2 stars—Good Conduct (you see I'm a good boy), Purple Heart and Bronze Star—and soon a "Victory" ribbon. Also earned is a Combat Medics Badge which will be presented with other Medics at a ceremony. Whoever thought I'd be taking time to talk about my ribbons—but I know Neil will enjoy them as souvenirs.

How is my little One—the German one—oy—I mean mit the measles. And the big guy mit the "cook-out"? How is my trailleader? How I miss you all.

9 July

Today's *Stars & Stripes* announced our Division will not be leaving this year, reiterating the General's announcement. We were hoping against hope and it was a real sock between the eyes. Especially since the Army has done nothing about keeping the boys occupied. No organized instruction in *anything;* even passes to the big cities have been cut since cessation of hostilities. Oh, yes, just imagine—boys with over 2 years of college are permitted to study in the Sorbonne or Oxford—that is, if you're lucky to be one of the 800 chosen in the 7th Army—a ratio of 1 to a thousand. Big Deal.

I'm trying to develop an outlet and the camera seems right at this time. But cameras are mighty hard to find. Sam, I and Mox drove to Stuttgart where 2 big camera factories are located. How about this kind of luck? Up until today the city was occupied by the French. Today we came in only to find the factories under heavy guard—and no one—not even Generals were permitted to enter, this being a 7th Army order. The whole damn ETO wants cameras so it doesn't look encouraging.

10 July

You can't win! Today two letters and a joy to me—in fact so much so they succeeded in making me blue—they pointed up our separation even more.—So David says "Da-Da" to my pictures. That's encouraging. What I wouldn't give to hear his "vocabulary" now.

You made a haul on tuna, didn't you, you sweet thing. Keep those packages coming—and for the benefit of the Llanerch P.O. I request tuna, cheese, jelly, etc. etc. You know, this request business is a lot of bunk.

Darling, when you find time could you pick up a flag about 3 x 5 feet? Our Aid Station has a nice flag pole but no flag. I'd feel so good seeing it wave right outside my bedroom window. We mustn't forget we're Americans—the best country on this earth. When you've gone through Hell and seen some of these other countries, you'd be able to appreciate my request. Besides, it symbolizes home to me.

Don't get too worried about our occupational status—it can change overnight.

15 July

Yesterday we traveled around until 10 P.M. and when I came "home" I found two of the dearest letters anyone could ask for.

Our day of travel was an eye-opener—interesting and frightening—something I wish everyone in the world could see, and then I don't believe there'd ever be another war. First, we saw Stuttgart again, and as you view it from top of a mountain (Stuttgart lies in a tremendous valley) it looks like a picture of Greek ruins. As you look at it you think you're dreaming—this just can't be true. The contrasts are weird—beautiful countryside and indescribable devastation. We drove until we came to Pforzheim, a village the size of Upper Darby, demolished—leveled.

Then to Heidelberg—quaint, picturesque—untouched by war (except for the bridges over the Neckar blown up by the Nazis)—its beauty incomparable. Heidelberg is nestled in a gigantic valley on either side of the Neckar River. We kept driving along the Neckar, through portions of the Black Forest, breathtaking in itself, with its many mountains and dense forest for as far as the eye can see.

Then finally to Beerfelden, the home of Mox. Even after all these years, everywhere Mox went crowds of people gathered for they all remembered him well. It was tough for him to go back again to this town where they dragged his parents off, but for some reason of his own, he seemed to want to. We had quite a time earlier, but all this was such deep trauma for Mox we came away feeling lousy. He was silent all the way back, and no one said a word as we were all feeling his despair.

I'm relieved you're accepting the fact I'll be here awhile—and as long as I have to, I'll make the best of it—taking courses (if and when), trips, going out on "quartering" parties or whatever else may present itself.

16 July

We've been doing a lot of clerical work lately and decided we need a typewriter. But getting one was a problem. However, as in former circumstances we advise the Military Gov't., and they procure. How? We don't ask. That AMG seems to be quite a racket—the boys in it get hold of anything and everything they want. You see—they're the "law," and Germans are the bribinest people you ever did see.

Today Sam was offered a Leica camera for a bicycle (which he doesn't possess). Since bicycles are easier to find than Leicas I made a deal with Sam—if I procure a bike—I'll get his old camera. Although it's ready to fall apart, it takes prime pictures. So now, "in my travels" I look for a bike, too. All this helps to keep me busy and interested.

One of your letters spoke chiefly of my delayed return home. Darling, being in the Army is tough—but being in the Army overseas is like having an incurable disease. Mutty is a good example of a boy who couldn't be sent home, even after being hit three times. Now he's dead. And he's just one in hundreds of thousands who take it on the chin needlessly.

Got myself a private room now, fixed it up real nice and tacked all your pictures on the wall pin-up fashion. Near my bed is a writing table with lamp, and I really enjoy the seclusion and luxury of my own room.

Just this minute heard that I get the next trip to France. Seven days at Dijon. A city about 150 miles from Paris—and I hope to be able to spend 5 of those 7 days in Paris (unofficially, of course) unless Dijon appeals to me. Don't know much about this city but a change of scene at this point won't hurt one little bit. I leave the 19th. It's times like this I long for you even more.

21 July   *Dijon, France*

My first day in Dijon and I did enjoy it. Was surprised how big and busy it is for a city of 100,000, reminding me a lot of Paris. It's now 11 P.M. and I've just returned from a G.I. nightclub where they served drinks, had orchestra and show. Many boys brought girls along and danced. After the show, I upped and went.

Besides reminding me of Paris, this town charges even higher prices—I didn't buy anything, nor do I expect to. I saw a belt painted with Parisian scenes and I just knew I was going to buy it for you—but, Darling, they wanted $8. for just one belt! Well, that set me thinking and I decided to make one if I can find the material. I already bought the paints here. Don't expect a good job, but I can try.—Lately, my interest has turned to paintings. It's surprising how few satisfy me, and while it's hard for me to explain why I don't like a certain picture—as I'm not a student of art—I know I don't like it. Purely subjective, I suppose, but I do enjoy spending time looking at them.

We're staying at a fine hotel and our meals are served by waitresses. I can't begin to tell you how wonderful it is to get your food served to you instead of thrown at you. Tablecloths make you feel a little more civilized, and certainly stimulates the gastric juices.

Tonight as I walked through the dark streets back to the hotel, I just ached for you—to hold your hand walking, as we so often do. These months wasted here are lost months. By no stretch of the imagination do I want to go to the Pacific, but at least if a war were on I might think I was making some contribution. But over here I feel I'm wasting valuable time away from my family. If you could see the wholesale waste of manpower, and the demoralizing effect it has on many of these guys, you'd know what I mean.

23 July   *Dijon*

Here I am still "sweating" out this "rest." Today I ate, slept, walked and went to a movie. Oh, yes—and since I was aching for excitement, took a trolley ride to the end of the line (10 min.). I bumped into one of my policy-holders—he's a mail clerk in the A.P.O. and a fine boy. I really enjoyed talking with him.

This hotel has a kapoot elevator, and walking up to the 6th floor about 6 times a day is beginning to get me down.

It's so dull around I thought I'd catch a ride over to the Swiss border (100 miles away) but just my luck no trucks or jeeps go that way.

Sometimes I get pretty down in the mouth—like today, with nothing to do and lots of time to think. There's absolutely no sense to war and one of my aims in life is to fight and fight for Peace. In war everyone suffers—victors as well as vanquished. A guy feels like a piece of flotsam and jetsam helplessly floating around in a vast vacuum they call the Army. His voice is *nothing*. If he does have something to say, he says it to his C.O. who must first approve it before he sends it on to *his* C.O.—then through one channel after another—and finally winds up back where he started right in the beginning. The organization is a closed dynasty. I want to get away from it for good—it's only a bad dismal memory from start to finish.

Please forgive me for going on like this, but this whole stinking situation gets me down—I just don't seem to have the patience or will to write, and often when I do it's with a heavy heart. You just don't know how much I miss you and the children. Perhaps when I get back to my little room in Waiblingen I'll do better. Again, please forgive this outburst.

24 July   *Dijon*

Well, I have one more day, I'm glad to say, and I'll be on the way back to my outfit where I can get some rest. Doing nothing is debilitating in any language. I do feel a little better today, however.

You'd be amused at the set-up in this town. First, they have a Red Cross Club which serves coffee and cake all day long for a slight charge—and what is extremely distasteful is that they have a separate dining room for officers. Can you imagine American contributions going for anything so anti-democratic? I took pictures of it so I could prove it to skeptic Americans when I return home.

Then they have an M.P. Battalion in town, who, with the help of M.P. funds hired a jazz band, a hotel lobby, some ham actors and put together a nightclub which pays for itself very well. Of course, profits stay with the Bn.

Realizing the crowds were too large for one nightclub, another Bn. got one together along similar lines—and it, too, is "going to town."—Then the 7th Army "Rest Center" decided the idea was so good they're running one, too, with business booming.

Now Special Service enters the picture. Their function, to provide G.I. transients with a place to eat while passing through (there are no French restaurants), so they turned up with a G.I. Joe's restaurant.—But all these set-ups are for boys who go in for drinking, night life and girls—and only during the evening. So that leaves me out, and as I said before, day activity is a great big zero.

25 July   *Dijon*

I'm packed and ready to ship out at 1:30 in the morning. You can see that time makes little difference in the Army. And the trains—don't ask!! It would make those G.I. complaints about redeployment to the West Coast look sick.

Just returned from the movies where I saw *My Reputation* with Barbara Stanwyck. It was a little different—revolving around a widow with 2 boys. Every time these two little boys—one was called Keith, too—were shown on the screen, I'd think of my two little guys and the tears would start rolling. I don't recommend your seeing this picture as it's a heart-breaker.

Coming back I ran into this fellow, Meade, the mail clerk, you remember. He's a swell guy and it felt great talking with someone from home. Then I packed, and started writing you.

An incident this afternoon gave me quite a laugh and a bit of embarrassment. The operetta, *Rosalind*, is in town for 3 days, and with nothing to do in the afternoons, the members of the cast walk around town. Well, in the Red Cross Club I ran into a few, and I spoke to one, a dancer, a cute kid about 20. In an effort to show appreciation, I said, "You (the cast) were great last night. I enjoyed it even more than when I saw professionals play it." To which she curtly replied, "Well, what do you think we are—amateurs?" So in trying to explain away my faux pas which clearly ruffled her, I said, "I mean better than when I paid $2.28 to see it." (I didn't mention the little fact that *that* amount was for the two of us.) So she says loftily, "Is *that* all you paid?" At which point I says to myself, "Keithie, boy, you'd better make an exit—and quick." And I did.

27 July   *Waiblingen*

Back again at my little desk, in the quiet of my room, surrounded by pictures of you and the kiddies, and just filled up with love for my little family. When I arrived I rushed over to a drawer where your letters would be—those arriving while I was away—and will admit to a bit of disappointment to find only 3. But no sooner than I picked them up, today's mail arrived with 5 more! Well, I sat down, made myself a little "book" and settled back comfortably to read. Just reading eight letters after a week's absence is a story in itself. One page has me giggling, the next has me holding back tears, the next has me disagreeing with you, and the next, agreeing—and throughout the letters you are happy, then sad, mad at Judy, then glad—disgusted with Neil, then ready to "eat him up." I've never enjoyed reading your letters more and I want you to know your devotion is something I'll never forget.

Not much to tell about my return except to say I was happy to get back and the boys were happy to have me back—and that was a good warm feeling.

Here's a scoop on something that happened here. I think those involved would prefer it out of the newspapers—but here it is and you can tell it to whom you wish—no military secret! Furthermore it's authentic. Now that I've told you that much you're probably thinking, "Oh, it must be big and important." But it really isn't.

Jack Benny, Ingrid Bergman and Larry Adler gave a performance for the 100th Division last night. However, the previous night, around midnight, they drove through our area (2nd Bn. 398th's) and were stopped by the guard to check on passengers, etc. He had no idea who was inside the vehicle. But they didn't stop as ordered, and acting within his rights he picked up his pistol and shot a bullet right through the back of the car. It zoomed through the luggage trunk and out the fender. (Fortunately, the guard used a pistol—an M-1 rifle would have been shot accurately and possibly killed a couple of the occupants.)—Well, when that happened they were pretty frightened, and stopped. Jack said, "I'm Jack Benny." The guard said, "I don't care who you are—you stop when ordered." Then Jack said, "You shot twice, didn't you."—The boy answered, "No, Sir, over here you only shoot once, and it has to count—otherwise I'd be on the other end of the bullet." Lucky for them it didn't count.

I can't vouch for the conversation, but that's how I heard it. And the rest is true. It caused a lot of excitement around since it happened in Waiblingen. (Benny and troupe played in Stuttgart.)

Good news is coming in from Japan; we're expecting Russia to declare war any day—and I think Japan wants peace before that day.* Maybe I'll be home before Christmas.

29 July

Today is Sunday and I'm here alone in this big house (Aid Station). I'm the C.O. (in charge of quarters) today and since it's so nice out all the boys took off. I don't blame them.

---

* Late in July of 1945 the Japanese ambassador in Moscow delivered an unaddressed message to the Soviet leadership from Emperor Hirohito, stating that while Japan could not accept "unconditional surrender," it might be willing to reach an agreement short of that. In response the governments of the United States, Great Britain, and China issued an ultimatum calling for unconditional surrender, which was promptly rejected by the Japanese. By then the atomic bomb had been successfully tested at Los Alamos, N.M. American military planning called for an invasion of the home island of Kyushu on 1 November, followed by landings on Honshu in the spring of 1946. The Soviet Union had agreed to declare war on Japan after the defeat of Germany, and was moving troops steadily across Siberia toward the Manchurian border, but had not yet issued a declaration of war. At this juncture, faced with the enormous casualty list that would accompany any invasion of the Japanese home islands, the United States was eager to have Russia enter the war.

Being alone, with the radio playing a Sunday concert and my thoughts of you, I'm as content as it's possible under the circumstances. Today's stubborn communique out of Japan was far from encouraging. And the Army is definitely set against sending older family men home—saying it's unfair to younger men who've seen combat—and prefers sticking to the point system. Even if points were cut to a minimum of 78, I'd still be out of luck—with only 65.

About the transfer you've referred to. I don't stand a chance to "buck" for Z.I. (Zone of Interior, U.S.) assignment. Here's why. I can give them a strong, convincing story as to my family, children and wife who need me, and they say, "Yes, I understand. I'm in the same boat—it's tough, isn't it." Then I say, "I'm older, can't take combat, my feet are bad."—They might say, "Okay, you're now in Class "C" or "D" and we'll see to it that you won't see combat again." So they transfer me to an Occupational Division.

Now here's the rub. (1) Occupational Divisions are the last to go home. (2) The new Division may re-examine me (let's say my present Division takes my word—they like me and want to help) and say, "Your feet are OK. You're good combat material," and transfer me to another Division—a combat Division where I could be an Aid-man—anything. One thing is sure, they'll not give me anything good that always goes to their regulars.

Now let's say my Division could recommend a transfer on the basis of bad general health—yes. But then I must be interviewed by the Corps Surgeon (the Corps is made up of 3 or 4 Divisions), and if I convince him (and he's tough) then I go to the 7th Army Surgeon. Shall I continue? The only way I can get home is to be seriously ill or on an emergency pass because of trouble at home— or at the "convenience" of the Government because of specialized skills. Need I go on?

Sam, the Lt., has been very thoughtful lately.* He says I've been doing everything up until now and it's time others contributed, and says he doesn't want me to do a thing around until further notice. I appreciate his attitude, but I don't do that much.

Here's something that flourishes in France I find amazing. An

---

* Samuel G. Cahoon, who had been given direct promotion to second lieutenant because of outstanding service in combat.

American dollar brings in from 100 to 200 francs—or $2. to $4. In other words, a guy has an American dollar; he gives it to a Frenchman, who in turn gives 1 to 2 hundred francs (usually 200) for which, remember, he has only paid one dollar.

The American dollar is as sought after as rare jewels. What the Frenchman does with the money I don't exactly know. But I believe he is required to have $500.—American dollars, gold or equivalent—in order to get into the U.S., and there must be beaucoup people trying to get in, and willing to pay these "money-changers" fabulous prices—as much as $5. or $10. in French francs for the American dollar. It all seems so astounding in view of our stable monetary system at home.

I'm really keen about a new watch I bought at the PX. Speaking of watches, one of the boys at the Rest Center in Dijon told me that when his outfit (fighting near the Elbe River) met up with the Russians, they wanted his little $3.79 Ingersol watch so badly, one guy paid him $150. for it. Can you imagine that?

This very second—on the radio, I hear—"From the Academy of Music in Philadelphia, we present the Philadelphia Orchestra." Well, Darling, I'm so touched with that I have to wipe my eyes.

30 July

Tomorrow is the last day of July—please note I missed you very few times this month. Of course, writing too often may not be good either. You heard about the guy who wrote his girl friend every day for 3 straight years, and then she goes and marries the mailman! Well, I'll take my chances on that!

The enclosed paper is the *Century Sentinel* and I thought you'd get a kick out of the "Sons of Bitche" society which the 100th Division has formed. Our Bn. takes great pride, as you will note, in the fact that we took the great Maginot fortress.

Tonight I bought a box camera—very good, too, from a civilian for $2.00. American dollars he wanted and American dollars he got.

Kept busy today making up a V.D. file, and if I must say so, it's a honey. I defy any outfit in the Division to outrate it, especially since it's so simple any 5-year-old could follow it.—Such a pleasure up in this quiet little room. It makes writing so easy.—Tonight I plead guilty to a complete turnabout. You know how I dislike for people to go on and on about their kids, and on more than one occasion gave you the "sign" when I thought you had said enough. Well, this same guy couldn't seem to help himself tonight, and I not only talked, but raved and raved about my two kids. It felt so good, even at the expense of beating the other guys' ears.

I have your picture in front of me as I write and it gives me a kind of vicarious pleasure in lieu of you in person.

2 August

Today another rumor—nothing official—but the boy insists it's authentic—that we're to replace the 63rd Division on the return home timetable. According to him we're due home the first week in December. Hope it's true but won't believe it until I'm getting off the boat in New York harbor.

Sam just told me our outfit stands a good chance of getting a 3rd battle star—which will mean 70 points for me. A campaign star for the Vosges campaign is now being considered by the General. That was by far the worst part of our entire action. Sam was told this by a Lt. whose father is a Brig. General with the deployment of troops in the ETO—and he's repeating what his father told him—that as things stand now we'll be on our way to a European P.O.E. the latter part of October or early November, so-o-o let's cross our fingers and hope—but not plan.

Your enjoyment on receiving 5 more crates seems to rub off on me. I had to smile at your reaction to the rickety U.S. mail truck stopping regularly at the house—and the driver's remark, "Another surprise from your soldier today." And your and Neil's excitement as you rush to pry open the cases, like "digging into a grab bag," not knowing exactly what you'll find—and your "squeals" of joy, your "tingling" feeling at the sight of a mail truck, associating it directly with me. You can't imagine how much pleasure this gives me.

I think I'll take another long walk as I did last night—about 4 miles through this awesome, beautiful countryside. The roads are lined with fruit trees—apples, pears, plums and they'll be at their peak of ripeness in about a week.

7 August

What a world we live in. I guess you've heard about Hiroshima's bombing. God, how I hate to hear of innocent people being victims. There must never be another war as the next time the whole world could be destroyed. War is a literal hell, everyone suffers—it's a series of horrors.

That disposition rumor of leaving in late October is gaining weight, which means we'd be hitting the States in Dec. if true. Neil's prayers may be taking effect—since "he isn't saying that for his health." I got a kick out of that remark, and I'm pleased with his progress on the piano. With your violin, my clarinet, and David's pot-lids we could make a quartet!

You ask if I was in the Aid Station when it was bombed. Yes, that incident is only one of 50 narrows—and in the Army Up Front—you learn a miss is as good as a mile.

In one of your letters you say, "I have a feeling in my heart that something will turn up that will bring us together sooner than we now dream." You might have had a psychic feeling that our shipping orders had been set earlier.—Now I hear we leave Waiblingen about Sept. 1 and to the States October 1—the last is pure rumor. By the way, we expect to go to Rheims, and will (in the next 30 odd days) get to Paris once in awhile.—Am being "paged" now, Honey.

8. Victory, Peace

Schorndorf, Waiblingen, Gerstetten, Marseille, and Home

August-December 1945

O n 6 August 1945, the first atomic bomb was dropped on the
city of Hiroshima. Two days later the Soviet Union entered
the war by invading Manchuria. President Truman called upon
Japan to surrender, and when no response came, a second bomb
was exploded at Nagasaki. On 14 August Japan capitulated.

The demand to "Bring the Boys Home" from Germany was
irresistible now. The Pentagon's demobilization plans, which had
called for a steady but regulated flow of troops from Europe, were
discarded, and the point system scrapped. So far as most American
military personnel were concerned, their job was done, and they
wanted to return to civilian life. Those who in later years have
criticized the Truman administration for failure to maintain a
powerful military presence in Europe in 1945–46 in the face of
growing Soviet recalcitrance have taken insufficient account of the
pressure to bring the troops home, as exemplified in the letters that
follow, which are characteristic of the attitude of combat veterans
in Europe after the war.

10 August 1945

Despite the rain today we went on a few quartering parties and
picked up a few things I hope you'll like—which include a white
belt for you which I plan to paint in vivid colors—similar to what
I saw in Dijon for $8.

Our Battalion has a little newspaper and I've been asked to write
in it for the Medics. Don't know why they chose me, except maybe
a few of those over-the-shoulder readers like my "style."

We're planning a little party here next week, and as you know,
we have the setting for it, a large, beautiful house, a piano—and will
hire a small civilian ensemble to play. With civilian help we've
planned a big spread. One of our cooks will bake a huge cake and
provide many of the extras.

Well, Doc Rich has left us and we now have a new Battalion
Surgeon. Doc was transferred out of the Regiment. The new guy
seems to be OK. Sam takes care of everything but medicine in that

area so I'm sure things will continue as they have in the past, but it won't be the same around here.

It looks about over for the Japs. Today they've asked for peace according to the Potsdam terms if Hirohito remains. I hope we accept their offer.

13 August

No mail again. If it weren't for the fact that none of us has gotten mail this week, I'd be seriously concerned. But tomorrow's another day, so here's hoping.

Well, Dearest, it looks good. We plan—officially—to leave between August 24th and 27th and go direct to Le Havre—and GET THIS—leave no later than Sept. 10. Yes, Sept. 10! So it's possible I may be home before Neil's birthday. Isn't that great news! Even with a Jap surrender I believe we'll go through with it—and it sure will be better sweating out a discharge in the States than in Europe—what say!—Now, as far as mail, keep writing, but send no packages. It's pretty likely I'll be going to Dix—the closest separation center to our home. It would be great for you to drive over— about a ¾ hour ride, meet me, and we can go back together. How does that sound? Of course, I'll call you and make all the arrangements—when, where—and if. Things sure do happen fast, don't they. For the next three days we'll be busy giving physicals to the Companies.

Even though it will be a boat-trip—and I dread them because of my susceptibility to "mal de mer," I guess I'll be able to take it 'cause I'll be a-headin' home. Darling, we'll relax plenty when I get back. Boy, that good mattress and linen sheets has me excited. I'm hungry for some news of you. I'd like to see half a dozen letters tomorrow, Dearest.

Did I tell you that I was a member of the Forty-and-Eight Club? That club is composed of soldiers, last war and this, who traveled by French freight car. Each car states specifically in French, 40 Hommes (men) and 8 Chevaux (horses). We traveled from Marseille for 3 days—and now we return to Le Havre in them (2 days,

I hope). It's the furthest thing you could get from a plush comfortable train. And when you get off, it's the closest thing to Heaven!

14 August

Well—the letters came—6 of them! I can see you're sweating it out just as I am.

Things are starting to pop around here. Two of our boys got a chance to visit England. Traveled four days—and no sooner did they get there—received orders to return. The poor guys up and travel four more days—and let me tell you it's no picnic on these European trains.

Sweetheart, quit sitting on "pins and needles"—you should know by this time the Army moves like molasses. The grand old Army motto: Hurry up—and wait. Relax and accept the fact that if the Division moves I'll be home before you know it.

Today I and several others were awarded the Bronze Star in person, by no less a dignitary than General Burress—our Division General—and a better one you couldn't want. We all like and respect him as he's 100% behind the boys, always. It was quite a ceremony—band and parade. Please hang on to the citation I sent you earlier.

It's supposed to be a "holiday" around here today, but really not any different than elsewhere. A few of the boys took a ride to Beerfelden to get Mox who's been there two weeks on Detached Service. Ever since he learned about his parents' fate he's not been the same. He always had a good sense of humor but now he rarely smiles and when he does he looks pathetic. It's pretty sad. I hope he snaps out of it soon.

No mail today but I hope tomorrow is "besser"—pardon the French! When I get home I might have trouble dropping some of my expressions. Over here, among ourselves, we say—"Goot Morgan"—"Nix Fushtay"—"Das is besser," "Warum" (why), "Comsee, comsa" for yes and no in French, and beaucoup similar ones.

Well, Darling, it's late and I think I'll go "shlofin." About expressions again, an amusing one is "I think I'll schnell" (speed) over to the kitchen or "schnell" over to the Motor Pool—schnell here and schnell there. You fushtay?

18 August

Had a good letter from you today and it did help—although I'll admit not too much. Why? Our Division heard that our trip to the States is postponed—one, two or three months. It hurts me to tell you this as I know you're just about at your wit's end, taking all this alone. And now I'm actually no closer to home than I've been in the last eleven months—with very little immediate prospect. And, Sweetheart, please don't anticipate a thing until you hear me calling you up from a telephone in the States. You must remember that. Please try to relax a little. Let the house go, save your energy for the children, for that's the important thing. Oh, I know it's easy for me to talk, with you back home sweating out every hour of every day. But something must give over here, it can't go on indefinitely.

I must admit I'm pretty upset myself. I had banked so heavily on it. And I know just how you'll feel when you get this letter. God bless you, Darling, let's try to make the best of it as we've done in the past—it surely can't be too much longer.

19 August

Another letter from you, and you write of your anticipation of a cable—or that I may not receive your letters as I may be on my way home, etc.—It hurts so to read this with me here completely helpless to do anything. Anyway, by this time you'll have heard from me, and perhaps knowing the situation you'll not be so keyed up with anticipation. It's tough, Sweetheart, it's pretty tough. But again we have to gear ourselves for whatever the Army metes out.

Last night I walked over to our Hdqs. Company clubhouse for

the first time and was surprised to see the elegant set-up they have. It's on a little dirt road in the country a half mile from any civilians. Inside, there's a big dance floor with tables all around. Drinks are served at cost—i.e., one mark for a glass of pink champagne. Then there's a refreshment table with G.I. food, costing nothing.

Some of the things you see points up even more how rotten the Army is especially for young innocent kids. Last night one of our younger boys got stoned. I see so many go off the deep end, drinking and running around with prostitutes, whereas when they entered the Army they were a bunch of clean kids. So many have contracted venereal diseases. I walked him to the jeep and drove him home. The sad part to see—as drunk as he was he was filled with remorse. He said, "I'm so ashamed of myself, Keith, especially in front of you—I look to you as an example."

He threw up all over the jeep, and between gulps, insisted he'd clean it up—and that I shouldn't. But I did, after I put him to bed. This morning he told me he'd never drink again.

Last Saturday night I put another kid to bed who drank himself sick. The young kids are by far in the majority who get drunk or in serious trouble.—I hate to see them drunk. Period. But I burn when they're soused in front of civilians, giving all the fellows a reputation for rowdiness when it just isn't so. The Germans are just looking for isolated cases to blow up way out of proportion, and some of these young kids hand it to them on a silver platter.

There's a new ruling now. You can't send home more than 10% of your salary. Why? The G.I.'s are getting a little too active in the black market. In the Berlin area alone, $1,000,000 was paid to G.I.'s and they sent home $4,000,000. See what I mean?

It seems that cigarettes and coffee go the furthest around here. I obtained the mugs chiefly with coffee. Chocolate and cocoa, too.

22 August

Things continue at a merry chase. The G.I.'s who go out for a "good time" invariably get what they're looking for. The morals in Germany are more than confusing. A woman who appears to be "nice"—good home, family, education—will submit easily to a boy—and openly. In fact, they ask the boys to sleep with them in a kind of business-like, matter-of-fact way. Like trading for cigarettes.

The V.D. we get in the Aid Station, for the most part, is gonorrhea, and not as serious as the average person believes. It usually can be cured in 48 hours with penicillin. However, the catch is that it could develop to serious proportions if not treated soon after infection sets in—not to mention the communicable danger which is serious with actual contact.

We've been running into a lot of persistent minor infections here in Germany—chiefly trench mouth and gingivitis. I think the chief source is the water. Others think it's liquor. For a time my throat was raw, as was the rest of the group. At the time I was drinking spigot water—and with any glass around—and the rawness persisted. Then I tried to treat myself but nothing helped until I started drinking G.I. water, and only from my own canteen cup. It has gradually disappeared and I'm relieved. But throughout the Bn. an awful lot of guys seem to have trouble with their mouths.

Our group is getting a kick out of the fact that some of the boys in the Bn. thought I was a psychiatrist. I don't know why, except, perhaps I try to help them when they come in with their ailments.

26 August

The radio just reported that the point system is now abolished— and that all troops other than occupational will be home by the end of the year. I hardly believe anything I hear anymore, but if this is true, that is good news.

We've been taking little trips that help to shorten the long days. Just returned from Stuttgart where Sam and I saw *Wilson*. Quite a good picture. Tomorrow we're heading for Gunund—a city in these parts. And Wednesday—well, Wednesday is a little different. I'll be taking a trip to Switzerland and look forward to a complete change of scene. God, would I love these trips with you here.

One thing I look forward to especially, Darling, is calling you up on the phone from Switzerland. I can't wait to hear your voice.

Sam went to the Riviera this evening by plane. Lucky guy. That's not the usual mode of travel around here. I'd sure like a plane trip—if it were headed in the direction of home!

Today I've been C.Q. and since I had some time I packed up another box but will hold it until I get back from Switzerland.

1 September   *Thun, Switzerland*

How I miss you. I hadn't heard from you in 3 days before I left— the mail wasn't coming through—so when I return I anticipate beaucoup. I missed writing you, too, as the feeling of utter frustration I've felt lately would not help if my letters did come through. So forgive me, Darling.

I thought I'd seen some of the most beautiful spots in the world, but this land—Switzerland—is a paradise. You can start planning on a trip back here sometime in the next few years. It's simply indescribable.

Yesterday a friend and I visited Berne, the capital. For a city of 160,000—or even a town of 500—I've never seen such cleanliness, modernness, fine architecture, wonderful shops, genuine friendliness—and not one slum district. Everyone is multi-lingual, speaking English, French, German, Italian. Many speak a German dialect called Schwyzertutsch, which even Germans don't understand.

The people on the streets—strangers—smile and shake hands and say "hello."—Yesterday as I was looking in a shop window at some watches, a woman came up to me and said, "Do not buy these watches. They are not good." This in a warm spirit of helpfulness, not busy-bodiness.

After sightseeing in Berne, we are now in a first-rate hotel overlooking a magnificent lake, so blue and clear you can see bottom. Off in the background, and close by are the snow-clad Alps, and the view just about takes your breath away. I've taken a few pictures and hope they turn out OK.

While everything appears old-world, still a modern look prevails. Last night, after eating ice-cream, the proprietor invited us upstairs in his home and it was as modern as tomorrow. And listen to this—

it was built in 1489. Can you imagine that? He took us through the house, showing many old and rare things.

By the warmth and hospitality we've been shown, it appears the American G.I. is very much welcomed.

I want so much to call you. Here's the set-up. We're limited as to spending; only permitted $28. in Switzerland—120 francs in Swiss currency and the call costs 52 francs or $12. Now, I think I'll telegraph you asking you to call me up in Zurich on the 5th or 6th when I'll be there. I'll get the correct dope before I send the telegram. It's a pity we're not allowed to reverse charges.

Things are sky-high here—probably seems more so due to our freeze on spending. I'd like to buy a cheap watch and camera, and you'll have to be content with a phone call as the only souvenir I can afford out of Switzerland!

Today is a rest day on our trip—tomorrow a boat ride and Lucerne. Monday, Tuesday, Zurich; Wednesday, Basel; and Thursday we're on our way back to Waiblingen. We travel everywhere by modern electric trains. It's that way throughout Switzerland.

3 September   *Thun, Switzerland*

Rising at 5:30 A.M. yesterday we started up the tallest mountain in Europe (the tallest reached by railway). Its name is Jungfrau, pronounced "young frau," and it rises two miles above sea level—11,342 feet. On the way up we stopped for lunch. It's surprising what a tremendous tourist business Switzerland has—even among themselves. Of course soldiers swell the tourist trade replacing the losses due to war conditions. Everywhere the souvenir business is heavy. But you know why I didn't buy!

The trip was long, tiresome but extraordinarily beautiful. We returned at 8 P.M. This afternoon we take off for Lucerne—spend tonight and tomorrow night, then on to Zurich where I'm hoping against hope your call comes through. I'll be waiting. But if it doesn't come through I won't be surprised—only disappointed.

Saturday night, after a concert, we went to the "casino" where they drink and dance. It seems I only speak in superlatives but this place is really super. And it's not a rowdy, fast place. All the family comes here—say, a family of 4; a husband, wife, daughter and boy-friend. They all drink in Switzerland but apparently not to excess as no one seems to get drunk. The orchestra played beaucoup American music and the people dance American style. I didn't dance, but had wine—you've got to buy something. They seem to revere Americans—with as many U.S. flags flying as their own—and they do love their country.

6 September   Zurich, Switzerland

I'm still in Zurich and despite not hearing from you last night, cling to the hope your call may yet come in—though we leave this city at 3 P.M. and it's now 11 A.M.

This is the "heart" of Switzerland, and not unlike 5th Avenue or Chestnut Street. It is busy, beautiful and has about everything. Since I last wrote I visited Lucerne on Lake Lucerne. Switzerland—its lakes, mountains, little villages, and large cities, is quaint, ro-mantic and very modern in the midst of medieval architecture. Books or travel agencies can't adequately describe it.

Picked up a little music box which I play all the time. It plays for two minutes after winding. Also a blue linen apron trimmed in embroidery—typically Swiss and most appealing. And a watch. I'm disappointed in the limited funds policy since there are many worthwhile things here—beaucoup needlework, beaucoup watches for little girls like you, and reasonable, too.

We leave for Basel this afternoon, stay overnight, then back to Waiblingen. Darling, I want so much for your call to come through—I'll then know I'm getting the latest about you and the children. But time is moving, and still no call.

Just had lunch and I'll take back what I said about food. In Berne it was mighty sparse, but here in Zurich and Lucerne it was first rate, and ample by any standards. They prepare fish (3 days a week, often twice in the same day) very appetizingly. This hotel is very good. I overhead the manager speaking to one of our boys who was making a request. He said in good English, "Surely, we can arrange it—nothing is too good for the Americans."—In a day or two I'll be back in Waiblingen—and look forward to that order freeing me to go home.

15 September   Waiblingen

After a dry-spell of 7 straight days I finally received 5 letters and my morale is soaring. Tonight we turn the clocks back an hour. You too?

Since my thoughts have been running in the direction of home and a little vacation, I was scanning the show pages of an old *New York Times* issue and sort of got an urge to go to Radio City Music Hall—and just sit in complete comfort viewing a dazzling stage show with all the fancy trimmings and beautiful music—not heavy— but just the way they'd play it, and holding hands with you, eating out, not worrying about hours—. Then to a posh, luxurious hotel and sleep and sleep till 10 A.M. Then after a good American breakfast, a bit of shopping, back to the hotel for a rest and nap. Then a 4 o'clock bite and a nice walk, stopping to look at all the shop windows as we always have, then more relaxation. And finally a leisurely dinner at eight at a plush New York hotel—and then to bed. Maybe 4 or 5 days of that. Just you and me—no friends or relatives to visit—nobody even knowing we're in New York. Does it sound like I'm dreaming? Well, let's make it come true, Dearest.

17 September

Rumors, rumors, rumors. Today's rumor has it that we'll be ready to sail from Le Havre December 1—maybe so. I, too, am inclined to believe the Division will move about then since low pointers are consistently being eliminated. I'll believe anything about early movement because I want so to believe.

We never did receive credit for the Vosges Campaign, nor a Presidential or French citation, and have just about given up all hope of getting these points. The Medics received their Combat

Medics Badge this week—and if only the men who have seen front-line action wore it, it would be worth wearing. But now I hear that Clearing and Collecting companies are wearing them—in fact received them before we did. So *that* medal, along with the others, will never be worn by me unless under a directive.

Dear, I want to get one thing straight right now. I'd never forgive you if you put signs up "welcoming" me home. I don't go in for that stuff—there's absolutely no good reason for it. I want my home-coming to be quiet. This is extremely important to me and please remember it.

I enjoy knowing your reaction to the things I send—it's one of my few pleasures—finding little gifts for you. It's difficult to get things in Germany as she's been at war so long and is only producing pure necessities.

One thing amazes me around here—the individual's desire to rebuild his own kapoot property, whereas in France, the same conditions prevail as when we left. I'm speaking primarily of the dirt and debris all over the kapoot cities and individual homes.

Tomorrow I'm C.Q. again so will stick around the Aid Station for the day.

25 September

Another rumor—not official—we're scheduled to meet a boat leaving Le Havre on the 15th. In the meantime address all your mail to the Medical Detachment 398th Infantry. In two days I'll know the address of my new outfit. I'll have to admit I'm pretty excited about everything.

Today, my last day with the Division and I've been running around getting things set before I leave. You know, it's a funny thing but I have ambivalent feelings about leaving. On the one hand I can't wait to get away, and count every minute—and yet it's going to be hard to leave so many friends who have been through so much with me. But when I realize my leaving means coming home to you, I can't feel badly at all. Along with me come a couple of friends from the Aid Station, and that helps a lot.

Jim called today and I had planned on seeing him this afternoon but got busy and missed out on it. Incidentally, you were wondering why some boys got 21 days traveling through France, England, Scotland while I didn't. Actually, I had the opportunity but turned down both the England and Riviera trips. If you knew how rough the traveling is in these countries, not to mention the overcrowded conditions, you'd understand. We travel on trucks and wooden-seated, filthy trains that travel 15 miles per hour, stopping one hour in every three. Eating delectable K rations and sleeping in a train seat as comfortable as a kitchen chair is not my idea of a fun trip. England means 7 days of this going and 7 days back—do you think it's worth it? Since the Riviera is in France it interested me little. However, Switzerland did intrigue me and I took the trip and it was well worth it.

My letter was interrupted by Doc (our new C.O.) who just stumbled in soused, got everyone out of bed and ordered them into the kitchen, "fighting" with each guy to "drink, drink, drink and drink" his liquor. He kept filling my glass and I kept pouring it down the sink. I hate to waste good old U.S. whiskey but there was no other way—I had to "drink" by "order." Boy, he is loaded—but funny and even gentlemanly—no nastiness or foul talk. The boys say it was the best "order" they've heard since entering the Army, and they're still in there drinking. While Doc was busy "ordering" I made a quick exit, unnoticed.

26 September   Gerstetten, Germany

Well, Darling, I am now a "tank man"—12th Armored Division. Rumor has it we'll leave for the boat in 13 days, and for the States Oct. 15th. Not official—just rumor. We're on the last lap of our separation. We'll be together soon—perhaps this time next month. Not much to do here and I'm planning to visit the old outfit Saturday. Our comfort is nil compared to Waiblingen, but I can stand it for the reason we're here.

We traveled yesterday and it took a little time to get situated and acclimated to the new surroundings. However, this P.M. I'm going over to Heidenheim, a fairly large town where nothing's kapoot, to buy a few things. Will probably write again today from the Red Cross Club there.

Although I won't be getting your mail here for awhile, keep writing until I learn the exact situation. Well, Dearest, every day means one day closer to home.

Gerstetten is a one-horse town with nothing to do. Tomorrow we hope to get over to Waiblingen and spend the night—we won't be missed around here.

3 October   Waiblingen

Here I am—but will be back in Gerstetten in the morning. Found four great letters and boy, you don't know how good that felt. By the numbers on your letters, there's nothing running wild trying to catch up with me. Mail service was pretty dependable after all!

The latest has it that we Medics will receive combat pay, retroactive from January. So-o that will be welcome.—Oh, yes, we're to be stationed at Camp Baltimore in Rheims (that's official). Rheims is about 50 to 80 miles from Paris I believe.

We must be on the right wave-length—your talking about the hotel and all was exactly what I had previously written you. Those snapshots of me make me out better than I am. I am tired and a little older looking, really.

So you're still receiving boxes! It makes me happy to hear of your consistent pleasure in their contents.

4 October   Gerstetten

Here I am back in this joint of a town and going nuts with nothing to do.—And another damn rumor floating around—what it means I don't understand yet. Our trip to Rheims is postponed for 2 weeks. Whether that means a trip directly to the boat, skipping Rheims and the staging area, I don't know. However, we'll be getting the official facts in the morning—conforming with Gen. Eisenhower's order that information pertinent to shipments will not be held back from the troops. As to automatic discharge with 72 points in October—forget it—the big factor isn't discharge, but shipment.

This day-to-day business isn't easy to take, but we'll survive, I hope.

6 October   Waiblingen

Tonight, Saturday, seems to be SOP with beaucoup of the boys getting drunk. With the Captain at the "helm" they're having a hey-day. Right now the boys are putting him to bed. He gets stoned quite often, and though it may be difficult for you to picture him as anything other than a chronic sot, he's nothing like that. In fact, if you saw him during the day, you wouldn't believe he could get so wild in the evening. He's not an alcoholic—merely gets soused for want of something better to do—from sheer boredom—and could stop anytime. He filled up my glass 5 times tonight—and each time I managed to empty it somewhere other than in my stomach.

Drove into Stuttgart with the jeep today. It's a good feeling to be able to use the vehicles here whenever you desire. In Gerstetten there are 2 vehicles for a Company of over 200 men—and they're used for posting guards, getting rations and a dozen other things. Here we have 15 men and 3 vehicles—so you see how pleasant it can be. Compared to the other dump, this is more like home.

10 October   Gerstetten

As I write you, I'm sitting in an open field. It's a lovely clear, sunny day; and I can see miles and miles of open country. This land—away from the Division—is beautiful.

You know what I've been craving for? A thick slice of vanilla layer cake with vanilla icing and gobs of whipped cream. And milk, milk, milk and more milk. We don't get fresh milk and we really need it. Our systems are not up to snuff and I think it might be a lack of calcium foods.

It's so pleasant here in the fields, the weather perfect—and I miss you terribly. Again I repeat, take things easy and don't do any re-decorating or cleaning up for me as I won't appreciate it.

As long as we have a meeting of minds re: our vacation, I'll ask you to make the plans. However, first I want to be home a few days as I gotta see the kids and get to know them—not run out on them. You just don't know how I want to see those children.

11 October   *Gerstetten*

Still cooped up in this hole—nothing new—missing you awfully, and sweating it out. I'll be going to Waiblingen for the weekend again. I hope there's some mail there. I need it.

Tomorrow we have some sort of parade—now isn't that ridiculous at this stage of the game. And we can't get out of it—and what's more we must have our boots shined—rough-finished combat boots not made for shining. Well—it's only a few more weeks (I hope). Today, I and two others were out in the fields (scene of my last letter) taking sun baths. Getting as far away as we can from the Army area helps a little, and since there's nothing else to do we can at least soak up a little sunshine. Darling, your devotion gives me strength to keep going and to take this obnoxious crap.

17 October

Nothing new—haven't seen any mail from you in 4 days—probably some is waiting in Waiblingen.

This hanging out is nothing less than brutal to the men. Why in hell can't they eliminate it all? If there was any kind of decent organization they could say, "Well, you're ready to go home—let's go to the boat"—then take a day to check records and throw new clothes at you—and—GO. But if they're not ready for you, why in hell keep alerting you? Why check records every 2 days—why check clothes every two days—why stick you in a one-horse town 8 miles off the main road so you can't go anywhere—and why kid you every few days that you're going home when you're not?

God knows if I'll be home for Christmas. It's not too far off now and I hope it won't be too much of an effort for you to get the boys a few things. Perhaps a bike for Neil, and a tricycle for David and whatever else you think is right. My thoughts constantly roam homeward, and the everyday routine things we do as a family. That keeps me going.

18 October

Just returned from the beer hall where they're having a dance. There's one every week—orchestra and all. I was remarking to a friend what a strange feeling it gave me—these G.I.'s dancing with frauleins—these same girls whose brothers and fathers we fought against a few short months ago. The brass claims their admission is only permitted because they're "D.P.'s"—but everyone knows better.

But there's a lot to be said for the G.I. side, too, Darling, if you knew the conditions under which they're sweating out a return home. So save your ire till you get both sides. However, they serve pretzels and that is my only concern in getting up there for a few minutes. I stuff my pockets.

The brass are trying to find things for us to do—and their lack of good sense and imagination is something to laugh at—if you could laugh. Imagine a lecture on "Military Discipline" two or three weeks before discharge. This is their idea of a scintillating program and I resent their stupidity to the extent of ducking out of everything I can.

Today I took a 6 mile walk through the countryside, and with autumn in full sway, it is truly magnificent.

21 October

Big event of the day—I took a shower. Since you have to go some distance for one I'm taking few these days. Otherwise, nothing, lying around, taking a walk. I could ride into Heidenheim but the roads are so rutted and bumpy and dusty by the time you make the round trip you're not only worn out—but filthy.

One of the boys I bunk with was in Berlin with the 2nd Armored Division. He was telling me how so many G.I.'s have cleaned up in the black market. He sent $3500. home. For his $28. watch he got $700., sold cigarettes for $150. per carton, soap $5. a bar, candy $10. a bar. This is hard to believe but it's true. He said everyone in his outfit was sending from $500. to $5,000. home until the Army put a halt to it. Some guys even had their families sending them watches and cigarettes to sell!

There's still talk of 70–80-pointers leaving this week to join the Armored, now in a staging area and ready to ship, while 60–70-point men in that outfit are returning here. Poor guys.

How are you, Darling? This sweating-out period is something you can't understand unless you're here. Not a thing to do but sit around, take a walk, talk—waiting every second for the "word."

Please forgive these letters, Dearest. I know they're not too buoying for you, but I know you understand. I hope the time comes when I never have to write under circumstances like these again.

24 October

I know I'm a glutton for punishment and want to believe anything that makes sense—but it really does look like we'll be on our way before the first of the month—that is, to the Port.

The boys, always ready with a joke, started this rumor. One guy was visiting his brother in Bremen yesterday and said he saw the *Europa* enter port—with a sign on the bow reading "Hellcats." (That's the nickname of our outfit.) Of course it was a "funny," but that's the sort of stuff that keeps the guys going or else they'd all go nuts.

1 November

My Darling, after all the Le Havre talk, it appears official that we'll be leaving around the 6th—and due to arrive in—listen to this—Marseille—before the 12th. And last-minute processing to be completed by the 16th. And from there on we board the first ship available. The *Stars & Stripes* have us in the States before the end of the month which means exactly one month behind original plans.

This evening we've been discussing our needs in civilian clothes— it seems that we had all read the same article in this week's *Yank* about civilian clothing. I figured I'd have to spend about $150. to outfit myself. Does that sound about right?

My anxiety gets higher with each day closer to home, and my letters shorter, it seems. But I know you understand what pressure we're under, especially with nothing to do and nothing to say.

2 November

The news really looks "encouraging" and I'm sure this time there won't be any drawbacks. The 56–70-pointers left the outfit today, and more 70's came in, so you see they mean business. Tomorrow the A.P.O. closes—and I was lucky to get under the wire with the last box.

In regard to the furlough, I think the enlisted man takes a dirty deal in not receiving furlough pay, even though discharged upon entering the country.* But I really couldn't care less. As things look now I may be home around December 1, and that's all that matters, Sweetheart.

Thank Rose for her efforts in getting tickets to the Army-Navy game, Dear. But tell her, even if I should be home in time, I have

---

* Commissioned officers in the Army were paid for all accumulated leave-time that had not been taken while in the service. Enlisted men were not paid for their unused furlough time. As an older man who had been an adult civilian for some years before being drafted, Winston very much resented the caste system whereby those receiving commissions in the armed services were considered "officers and gentlemen," while enlisted men, whether drafted or volunteering, were in effect second-class citizens. Winston's response was characteristic of many American soldiers.

no desire to go. Being in the Army as long as I have, I've developed a terrible distaste for these, quotes, "gentlemen." If I'm going to see a game with a Service team, it must have only one participating so I can cheer against them. I resent the way these brass hats operate—not so much for their handling of sheep (that's us) but for all the things they take advantage of. I feel disgust with their constant pulling of rank, especially when there are so many I wouldn't take the time to talk to in civilian life. And I resent their caste system—such as Officers Clubs, special cars on trains (always the best). Twenty officers could be in one car of a train—and 200 boys in another—standing. Oh, why go on, I could write a book.—However, whenever I have the opportunity as a civilian, I'll let my feelings be heard. Fundamentally, the majority are OK, but their rank goes to their head and suddenly they feel a power and authority they never dreamed possible—and many are merciless in their use of it.

15 November   *Marseille*

My Darling, here I am in Marseille—where I landed exactly 13 months ago—but this time I'm a-comin' home—and soon. Thank God I'm actually on the way—we know how many times in these last months I've come close to missing it. But that's all over and done with—I'm *really* coming home!

Dearest, I haven't written you for about two weeks—and this is my first opportunity. I was rattling in a "40 and 8" for a week—which you know is not the ultimate in traveling—and since Sunday I've been freezing in a tent without lighting facilities, in the staging area 15 miles outside of Marseille.

As I write you now, I vividly recall sitting here in the same Red Cross Club—writing you—a little over a year ago. What hell we've both been through since. And it was here I ran into Jim, and the meeting made me terribly happy, and seemed to give me just a little more courage, for instinctively I sensed what would be facing me in the months ahead.

And as I sit here I have a strange feeling in the pit of my stomach, as last year in this same place I was so broken-hearted and dismal and unhappy—so far away from you and the children—wondering if I'd be one of the lucky ones to return. But now I look back at it all as a very bad dream, and I feel differently because I know I'll be seeing you soon—but damn it—not soon enough!

Even now I miss your letters; they were all I lived for, and I must confess I wiped away more than one tear as I read them. You came through 100% in my absence, Dearest, and I shall never forget it.

21 November

My Darling,

Today will probably be the last day I spend on European soil. We expect to sail tomorrow—Thanksgiving Day—and will arrive in New York about December 4th. We'll head straight for Camp Shanks or Kilmer to be processed further, and outfitted with a new, complete set of clothes. Whereupon I'll be sent to Indiantown Gap for discharge.

We are crossing on a Liberty ship (latest says the *Webster*) and if it's anything like the trip over, I'll be anticipating 10 days of sea-sickness—but with one major difference—it will be homeward bound this time.

What can I say now except that I am terribly excited about happenings to come in the next two weeks. I must admit that I can hardly contain my exhiliration at the thought of our joyous re-union.

Until later, my Sweetheart. But this time—*not* by letter.
                    Your always loving husband,
                         Keith

Pfc. Keith Winston left Marseille aboard a troopship on 22 November 1945, landed in New York City on 4 December, received his discharge papers in Philadelphia on Monday, 10 December, and was a civilian once again.

Army of the United States

Honorable Discharge

This is to certify that

KEITH WINSTON   33 927 775   Private First Class

Medical Detachment 398th Infantry Regiment 100th Infantry Division

Army of the United States

is hereby Honorably Discharged from the military service of the United States of America.

This certificate is awarded as a testimonial of Honest and Faithful Service to this country.

Given at   UNIT B SEPARATION CENTER #45
Indiantown Gap Mil Res Penna

Date   10 December 1945

RECORDED in the Office for Recording of Deeds in and for
Del. Co., Pa., in *Soldiers Discharge*
Book   No.   8   Page 380
Witness my hand and seal of office this *twenty-seventh*
day of *December* Anne Domini *19 45*

Sep.

Wm M Howell
Recorder of Deeds

A JONES
Major MAC

Appendix A
A Memory
of Keith Winston

by Samuel G. Cahoon

For those of us in the 2nd Battalion medics of the 398th Infantry
Regiment, Keith Winston was a memorable personality, revered and
loved by all. Never did he shirk a job in the line of duty; to everyone he
came into contact with he was extremely kind and sympathetic. So
much so that we used to call him "Reverend"—the name followed him
everywhere he went.

Winston joined the 100th Infantry Division at Fort Bragg, North
Carolina, in late August of 1945, just as the division was winding up a
training process that had begun in November 1942, and was on the
threshold of departing for service overseas. It was our battalion's good
fortune to have Winston assigned to us, because he immediately fitted
into the routines of the medical team. He served well with the surgeon,
Captain Joseph Rich, and the two tech-sergeants, Douglas Smyth and
Pascal Pironti.

He quickly became a capable adjunct to the battalion aid station—we
thought to keep him there, rather than assign him as a company aid
man or litter-bearer, because of his age. He was not of powerful physique,
but of medium height and slender build. So Keith found his proper
niche, and the aid station was the better for it.

At no time in our seven hazardous months of combat did he complain, or show trepidation. This is not to say that he was without fear;
all of us experienced that. But Winston never showed it on the surface.
He did his job, under conditions that were frequently dangerous and
always demanding.

He was intensely a family man, and his thoughts were always of home.
Almost daily he found time somehow to write to his family, telling of
the war, the bravery of the infantrymen, the wonderful job the medics
were doing, what combat was like, and how his fellow soldiers measured
up to it.

Anyone who has served in the army during wartime knows how important it is to keep accurate records. I was especially grateful to Keith

for his painstaking care, under conditions that were sometimes extremely difficult, at keeping records and seeing that supplies were ordered. I have in my possession the large ledger which he kept, recording everything that happened at the aid station from the first day of combat until the end of the war. Everything from cold sniffles to multiple wounds is on record in his crisp handwriting—a detailed and complete account of the ailments and injuries that beset soldiers in combat. It is all there, a fine documentary for an infantry battalion.

He left us in mid-September of 1945, during our Occupation duty, taking with us all our good wishes. We could see the happiness in his face now that he was going home to his beloved family, and the sadness, too, at saying goodbye to those with whom he had served so closely and so well.

When a few years ago those of us who were left of the 2nd Battalion 398th Infantry medics began to plan get-togethers at the Century Division's annual reunions, we wanted Keith to come, but we learned the sad news that he had passed on. I know he would gladly have joined us. He was that kind of person—a lovely man. God bless him!

Appendix B
Roster of Second Battalion, 398th Infantry Regiment Medics

Aid Station

Armstrong Lewis C., Jr., Pfc, Kittery, Maine
Cahoon, Samuel, Staff Sgt, Newark, N.J.
Chubbuck, Cecil F., Cpl, Prentiss, Maine
Fontaine, Howard, Tec 5, Escanaba, Mich.
Kelley, Alfred H., Tec 5, Seal Cove, Maine
Oakman, William, Lt, Petersburg, Pa.
Pironti, Pascal, Tec 3, Newark, N.J.
Rich, Joseph, Capt, Liverpool, Ohio
Scarpitta, Anthony, Lt, Parkville, Md.
Smyth, Douglas S., Tec 3, New Bedford, Conn.
Van Drasek, Anthony, Cpl, Kaukauna, Wis.
Winston, Keith, Pfc, Westgate Hills, Pa.

Litter Bearers and Aid Men

Annicchiarico, Michael, Pfc, Jersey City, N.J.
Barb, Ralph, Pfc, Pittsburgh, Pa.
Black, Henry, Pfc, Springfield, Mass.
Broker, George, Tec 3, Brooklyn, N.Y.
Brouns, Pierre, Tec 5, Washington, D.C.
Cade, Charles A., Pfc, Parsons, Kansas
Clark, Orville M., Jr., Pfc, Pikeville, Ky.
DeForge, Henry F., Pfc, Hartford, Conn.
Emond, Robert G., Tec 4, Lowell, Mass.
Feldman, Isadore I., Tec 5, New York, N.Y.
Fleming, Edward J., Pfc, Ozone Park, N.Y.
Fontenot, Yves, Pfc, Ville Platte, La.
Fox, Morton, Pfc, Buffalo, N.Y.
France, William P., Pfc, Scotch Plains, N.J.
Friedman, Jack B., Pfc, Brooklyn, N.Y.
Ghingo, Bruno, Pfc, Astoria, L.I., N.Y.

Haas, Max, Pfc, New York, N.Y.
Hart, Fred B., Tec 5, Titusville, N.J.
Horrigan, Harold S., Tec 4, Bronx, N.Y.
Hunger, Irving, Tec 4, New York, N.Y.
Hunter, James H., Pfc, Brooklyn, N.Y.
Kaplan, Abraham H., Tec 5, Brooklyn, N.Y.
Kutzman, Paul J., Tec 5, Brooklyn, N.Y.
Lunt, Samuel G., Pfc, Rockland, Maine
McCoy, Howard C., Pfc, Ardmore, Okla.
Medvin, Ellis, Tec 5, Rochester, N.Y.
Mullens, Willie J., Tec 4, Calcasieu, La.
Murdico, Dominick V., Pfc, Amsterdam, N.Y.
Pavlik, John J., Tec 4, Chicago, Ill.
Peterson, James T., Pfc, Idaho Falls, Ida.
Phillips, Herbert F., Pfc, Fishing Creek, Maine
Powell, Albert F., Pfc, Pleasantville, N.J.
Ranieri, Anthony, Tec 4, Brookline, Mass.
Smith, Harry J., Pfc, Pawhuska, Okla.
Starshak, John J., Pfc, Chicago, Ill.
Sterk, Gerrit, Pfc, Jenison, Mich.
Tasuz, Thomas W., Pfc, Chicago, Ill.
Thomas, Richard L., Pfc, Boonesboro, Md.
Urresti, Alfred, Pfc, East Boston, Mass.
Wheeler, Joseph L., Tec 5, Kansas City, Mo.

Index

Adler, Larry, 273–74
Allen, Fred, 228
Allen, Robert S., 240
American Home, xiii
Annicchiarico, Michael, 243
Antwerp, Belgium, 97, 147, 173
Ardennes, Belgium, German counter-
offensive in, 147, 150, 158–59,
264

Baker, Phil, 228
Baltimore, Maryland, 203
Barb, Ralph L., Jr., 243
Bastogne, Belgium, 147
Beachhead News, 136
Beerfelden, Germany, 202–3
Benny, Jack, 273–74
Bergman, Ingrid, 64, 273–74
Berlin, Germany, 156, 167, 173, 181,
199, 221, 224–25, 237, 285, 297
Bernadotte, Count, 226
Berne, Switzerland, 287 ff.
Bitche, France, 125, 147, 158, 180,
189 ff. 264
Black, Henry, 137, 196–97, 243
Black Forest, Germany, 268
Bowes, Maj. Edward, 16
Boyer, Charles, 64
Bradley, Gen. Omar N., 159, 166
Breen, Bobby, 202
Bremen, Germany, 224, 297
Bricker, John W., 45
Bronze Star Medal, awarded to
Winston, 230, 247, 263, 266
Brussels, Belgium, 193, 232, 250,
260
Buckley, Rev. Michael J., 164
Burns, Bob, 34
Burress, Maj. Gen. Withers, xxi, 71,
74–75, 253, 265, 283

Cahoon, Samuel, 153, 160–61, 225,
245–46, 248–50, 254, 261, 265–
69, 275, 277, 281–82, 286–87,
303–4
Camp Blanding, Florida, 6 ff., 220
Camp Kilmer, New Jersey, 98, 300
Camp Rucker, Alabama, 45
Camp Shanks, New York, 300
Campo, Earl V., 89
Century Sentinel, 208, 227, 276
Champanay, France, 107
Cherbourg, France, 41
Chevalier, Maurice, 194
Churchill, Winston, 166, 168
Clark, Orville M., Jr., 232
Clarke, Bob, cartoons by, 99, 112
Colmar Pocket, 123
Cologne, Germany, 173, 179
Cooper, Gary, 27
Crim, Ed, 100

Davis, Harold G., 261
DeForge, Henry F., 243
de Gaulle, Charles, 123
Devers, Lt. Gen. Jacob L., 151
Dewey, Thomas E., 44, 46, 115,
129
Dietrich, Marlene, 202
Dijon, France, 108, 269 ff., 276
Douglas, Helen Gahagan, 225

Eisenhower, Gen. Dwight D., 123,
130, 159–60, 162, 166, 168, 225–
26, 232, 294
Elbe River, 166, 276
Epinal, France, 259
Ereza, Monty, 165, 171, 181–82,
263–64

Farben, I. G., Co., 222

Fienman, Harry, 103, 120, 126, 131, 133, 183, 193, 218
Fontaine, Harold F., 229, 251
Fort Bragg, North Carolina, 71 ff., 155
Fort Dix, New Jersey, 282
Fort Jackson, South Carolina, 71
Fort Meade, Maryland, 43, 45, 48–49, 52, 58, 71–72, 77, 82, 84
Frankfurt, Germany, 138, 173
Freudenberg, France, 125, 142, 147

Garfield, John, 66
Garland, Judy, 226
Geislingen, Germany, 263
Gerstetten, Germany, 293 ff.
Ghingo, Bruno, 243
Girard College, xi
Goebbels, Joseph, 224
Goetzenbruck, France, 125, 158–59
Grad, Jules, 179
Gunund, Germany, 286

Haas, Max, 202–3, 224–25, 267–68, 283
Halberg, Abraham, 164
Hall, Harold, drawing by, 232
Hamburg, Germany, 226
Hardt Mountains, France, 147 ff., 189
Hart, Fred B., 243
Heatter, Gabriel, 174
Heidelberg, Germany, 205, 222, 268
Heidenheim, Germany, 297
Heilbronn, Germany, 189 ff., 246
Himmler, Heinrich, 226, 248
Hirohito, Emperor, 274, 282
Hiroshima, Japan, 278, 281
Hitler, Adolf, 189–90, 198, 205–7, 216, 224, 229, 233–34, 241, 256, 260
Horner, George, 178
Horrigan, Harold S., 243
Houffalize, France, 158
Huertgen Forest, Belgium, 120
Hugo, Victor, 184
Hunger, Irving, 242–43

Indiantown Gap, Pennsylvania, 300

Jacksonville, Florida, 8, 64
Jodl, Gen. Alfred, xix
Johnston, James N., Jr., 9, 34–35, 49, 65, 75 ff., 85 ff., 94, 100, 109, 123, 141, 153, 180, 194, 205, 292
Jungfrau mountain, Switzerland, 288

Keitel, Gen. Wilhelm, xix
Kocher River, 189 ff.
Koenig, Rose (Mrs. Nathan), 31, 58, 82, 116, 165, 298–99
Kutzman, Paul J., 243

La Plaine River, 107
La Trouche, France, 107
La Vermont, France, 107
Lawrence, David, 163
Le Havre, France, 282, 290, 298
Lemberg, France, 125, 158–59
London, England, 175, 232
Lucerne, Switzerland, 288 ff.
Ludwigshafen, Germany, 187, 202, 204–5, 222

MacArthur, Gen. Douglas, 6
McDonald, Brown, Jr., 122
Maginot Line, 125 ff., 147 ff.
Manila, P. I. 175
Mannheim, Germany, 204–5, 222
Marseille, France, 97, 107 ff., 133, 298 ff.
Marshall, Gen. George C., 166, 237
Mauldin, Bill, 212
Medvin, Ellis, 242–43
Meisenthal, France, 125
Mellenthin, Gen. von, 157
Metropolitan Life Insurance Co., xiii, 15
Meurthe River, 107
Meuse River, 147
"Mr. Anthony" show, 109
Montgomery, Gen. Bernard L., 159, 189
Moscow, Russia, 174
Mullens, Willie J., 243
Munich, Germany, 225, 229, 239, 256
Mussolini, Benito, 224–25

Nagasaki, Japan, 282
Nancy, France, 232
Naples, Italy, 232
Napoleon I, 184
Neckar River, 189 ff., 206, 268
Negro Soldier, The (movie), 49
New York Times, 290
North Carolina, University of, xii
Nurnberg, Germany, 266

Oxford University, England, 267

Paris, France, 123, 130, 156, 171–
    72, 181–85, 224, 256, 260, 269–
    70, 278, 293
Patch, Gen. Alexander M., 108, 139
Patton, Gen. George S., 120, 123,
    212, 217
Pearson, Drew, 58, 121, 240
Petite Pierre, France, 125
Pforzheim, Germany, 268
Philadelphia Bulletin, xiii, 117
Philadelphia Inquirer, xiii
Philadelphia Record, 52, 60, 83, 117,
    147–48, 159, 174
Pine Camp, New York, 40
Pironti, Pascal A., 261, 303
Pius XII, Pope, 207
Pollock, Arthur E., 168
Potsdam, Germany, 282
Purple Heart Medal, Winston re-
    ceives, 131, 252, 266

Radio City, New York, 290
Raleigh, North Carolina, 88–89
Rambersvillers, France, xiv
Ranieri, Anthony, 242
Raon-l'Etape, France, 107, 125
Red Cross, American, 98, 111, 154,
    164–65, 199–201, 218, 262, 271–
    72, 293
Reims (Rheims), France, 237, 278,
    293
Remagen, bridgehead across Rhine
    at, 189
Rhine River, 123, 159, 189, 196,
    211, 222, 248
Rich, Joseph R., 122, 148, 153–54,
    160 ff., 174, 179 ff., 193, 196,

201, 204, 210, 214 ff., 224 ff.,
    241 ff., 258 ff., 282, 303
Ripley, Robert A., 266
Roer River, 97, 120
Romberg, Sigmund, 205
Rome, Italy, 232
Roosevelt, Franklin D., 44, 58–59,
    115, 118, 123, 129, 168, 216–17,
    230–31, 237
Rundstedt, Gen. Gerd von, 180, 233

Saar Valley, France, 97, 120
St. Augustine, Florida, 49
St. Gorgon, France, 108
St. Vith, Belgium, 147
Salm, France, 107
Sarre-Union, France, 189
Sarreinsburg, France, 158–59
Scarpitta, Anthony, 155, 165–66,
    177, 183, 185, 202–4, 253–54
Schiesseck, Fort, 125, 147
Schorndorf, Germany, 255, 281 ff.
Schott, Jacob, 168
Senones, France, 107
Shakespeare, William, 184
Siegfried Line, 97, 120, 179
Smyth, Douglas, 261, 303–4
Sorbonne, 267
Soucht, France, 125
Stalin, Joseph, 159, 168, 173
Stanwyck, Barbara, 272
Starke, Florida, 38–39
Stars and Stripes, 115, 135, 141, 179,
    198, 212, 229, 239, 256, 267, 298,
    299
Stein, Gertrude, 231
Steinheim, Germany, 246
Strasbourg, France, 123, 149, 232,
    265–66
Student Prince, The (Romberg),
    205
Stuttgart, Germany, 214, 242, 246,
    248, 253, 267, 294

Time, 117, 201
Tokyo, Japan, 174–75
Trinque, Marius N., sketches by,
    142, 203, 209

Truman, Harry S, 59, 281

Upper Darby News, 166
U.S. Army: Divisions: 2nd Armored,
    297; 12th Armored, 290; 14th
    Armored, 97; 36th Inf, 262; 44th
    Inf, 147, 151; 45th Inf, 212, 263–
    64, 266; 63rd Inf, 277; 103rd Inf,
    97; 106th Inf, 180, 212
U.S. Business News, 201

Valence, France, 108
Van Gogh, Vincent, 249
Vidmar, Al, cartoons by, 143, 170,
    191
Voltaire, 184

Vosges Mountains, France, 97,
    108 ff., 115 ff., 277, 290

Waiblingen, Germany, 253 ff.,
    281 ff.
Wallace, Henry A., 59
Wasserman, Mutty, 257
Willkie, Wendell, 44, 58–59, 121
Winchell, Walter, 32, 37, 150, 228
Wingen, France, 125
Winston, Mark, 157, 192, 193, 219

Yalta Conference, 168, 226
Yank, 298

Zurich, Switzerland, 288 ff.